# Menu Key Functions

When using the graphical menus supplied by NetWare—such as SYSCON, PCONSOLE, and so forth—a number of key combinations provide shortcuts, and are worth remembering. They are the following:

| Key | Function |
| --- | --- |
| F1 | Activates the help screen |
| F3 | Enables editing of the highlighted option |
| F5 | Marks an item, or unmarks it if it was already marked |
| F7 | Cancels the operation |
| Alt+F10 | Exits the menu utility, regardless of how many layers deep you are |
| Insert | Inserts a new entry |
| Delete | Deletes an existing entry |
| Esc | Goes back to the preceding menu |
| Backspace | Deletes one character to the left of the cursor |
| Enter | Accepts the current entry |
| Home | Moves the cursor to the left-hand side of the entry |
| End | Moves the cursor to the right-hand side of the entry |
| Page Up | Moves up one page |
| Page Down | Moves down one page |
| Ctrl+Page Up | Moves to the beginning |
| Ctrl+Page Down | Moves to the end |

| Key | Function |
| --- | --- |
| Up Arrow | Moves up one line |
| Down Arrow | Moves down one line |
| Right Arrow | Moves right one space |
| Left Arrow | Moves left one space |
| Ctrl+Right Arrow | Moves right one word |
| Ctrl+Left Arrow | Moves left one word |

# Sample NET.CFG File

```
Link Driver NE2000
      INT 5
      PORT 340
      MEM D0000
      FRAME ETHERNET 802.2
NETWARE DOS REQUESTER
      FIRST NETWORK DRIVE=F
```

# Sample STARTNET.BAT File

```
SET NWLANGUAGE=ENGLISH
cd\
LSL
:DRIVER1
3C509.COM
IPXODI
VLM
```

# Managing the NetWare 3.x Server

*William Steen*

New Riders Publishing, Indianapolis, Indiana

# Managing the NetWare 3.x Server

By William Steen

Published by:
New Riders Publishing
201 West 103rd Street
Indianapolis, IN 46290 USA

Copyright © 1995 by New Riders Publishing

Printed in the United States of America 1 2 3 4 5 6 7 8 9 0

**Library of Congress Cataloging-in-Publication Data**

```
Steen, William, 1961-
    Managing the NetWare 3.x Server / William Steen.
        p.    cm.
    Includes index.
    ISBN 1-56205-514-3
    1. NetWare (Computer file)  2. Client/server comput
    ing.  3. Local
area networks (Computer networks)   I. Title.
0A76.76.063S7367   1995
005,7'1369—dc20                          95-36606
                                             CIP
```

## Warning and Disclaimer

| | |
|---|---|
| **Publisher** | DON FOWLEY |
| **Marketing Manager** | RAY ROBINSON |
| **Acquisitions Manager** | JIM LEVALLEY |
| **Managing Editor** | TAD RINGO |
| **Publishing Manager** | EMMETT DULANEY |

**ACQUISITIONS EDITOR**
ALICIA BUCKLEY

**SOFTWARE SPECIALIST**
STEVE WEISS

**LEAD EDITOR**
STACIA MELLINGER

**COPY EDITORS**
PATRICE HARTMANN
MARLENE SEMPLE

**TECHNICAL EDITOR**
LANCE SKOK

**ASSOCIATE MARKETING MANAGER**
TAMARA APPLE

**ACQUISITIONS COORDINATOR**
TRACY TURGESON

**PUBLISHER'S ASSISTANT**
KAREN OPAL

**COVER DESIGNER**
SANDRA SCHROEDER

**COVER ILLUSTRATOR**
BORIS LYUBNER/SIS

**BOOK DESIGNER**
SANDRA SCHROEDER

**MANUFACTURING COORDINATOR**
PAUL GILCHRIST

**PRODUCTION MANAGER**
KELLY D. DOBBS

**PRODUCTION TEAM SUPERVISOR**
LAURIE CASEY

**GRAPHICS IMAGE SPECIALISTS**
JASON HAND
CLINT LAHNEN
LAURA ROBBINS
CRAIG SMALL
TODD WENTE

**PRODUCTION ANALYSTS**
ANGELA D. BANNAN
BOBBI SATTERFIELD

**PRODUCTION TEAM**
ANGELA CALVERT
DAN CAPARO
KEVIN FOLTZ
REGINA REXRODE
ERICH RICHTER
KAREN WALSH

**INDEXER**
CHRISTOPHER CLEVELAND

# About the Author

**William Steen** works as a Senior Customer Support Representative for BI INC. He also owns and operates a consulting firm that specializes in providing networking solutions to small business, and to city and county government offices.

# Trademark Acknowledgments

All terms mentioned in this book that are known to be trademarks or service marks have been appropriately capitalized. New Riders Publishing cannot attest to the accuracy of this information. Use of a term in this book should not be regarded as affecting the validity of any trademark or service mark. NetWare is a registered trademark of Novell, Inc.

# Dedication

I would like to dedicate this book to the following people, for without their patience and encouragement, I never would have been able to complete it:

My family—William R. Steen, Beverly Steen, and Brenda Steen;
My friends—Jeff Pyke and family, Tom Beihold and family, Paul Beihold and family, Tony Shirley, and Jim Beeson and family.

# Acknowledgments

To say that a book is the product of one author is to say that a country consists of only one person—the President. Neither scenario is accurate.

This book simply would not be if it were not for Emmett Dulaney and the direction and guidance he freely offered. He was full of encouragement and advice at every step, and went out of his way to ensure that the book currently in your hands is the very best that I was capable of producing.

I would also like to thank Stacia Mellinger and the editing staff at New Riders Publishing. Were it not for their immense talent, the thoughts that made perfect sense in my head would never have been put in a form that hopefully makes sense in yours.

Lance Skok should be commended for his work as tech editor. He was responsible for making certain the boring information (facts and figures) is portrayed accurately. Having been in his shoes on several previous books, I know how mundane a task it is, and his attention to detail enhanced the final product immensely.

I would also like to thank one other person, although we have never met—Don Fowley, the publisher of New Riders. Were it not for his business sense and commitment, the aforementioned wonderful group of people would never have been assembled in one place. Without them, this would have been a trying endeavor. With them, it was a pleasure, and the man at top is to thank for that.

# Contents at a Glance

# Table of Contents

**xiii**

**1**

**CHAPTER**

# Starting at Ground Zero

Before you can begin to administer a network, you need a thorough understanding of what a network is. That understanding applies not only to the network operating system (NOS), but also to the physical components: wiring, cards, and so forth. This chapter explains how to ascertain what you have from a software and hardware standpoint. If you are already familiar with these concepts, you might want to skip to Chapter 2, "Supervisor Parameters."

# Understanding the Basics of Networking

Many companies today employ a computer network of some kind. As businesses grow, so does the need to share information among employees. When a small business has only three employees, finding out whether a customer's package went out on Thursday is as simple as yelling across the room to Jerry and asking if he sent it. With 30 (or 300) employees—every one of them trying to find Jerry and ask him about a separate package—the lines of communication often break down. That's where networks come in. Networks can help computers—and, subsequently, people—communicate more effectively and efficiently.

## What Is a Network?

A local area network (LAN) is one way you can allow two (or more) computers to communicate with each other. The communication between them can be as simple or as complex as you like. Although some purists would argue the point, a very crude form of networking enables one computer to connect with another through an RS232 cable connected to the serial port (or the parallel port) of each computer.

In so doing, files can be copied from one computer to another through a DOS-based utility. Microsoft offers INTERLNK.EXE and INTERSVR.EXE with DOS 6.x for just this purpose. A bit easier to use is Novell DOS 7.0's FILELINK.EXE. These options are useful when files that won't fit on floppy disks need to be copied from one computer to another. With both utilities, one computer acts as a *slave unit* to the computer that performs the actions.

This capability enables you to perform a listing of the files on one computer from another, and copy files back and forth. Though beneficial, such a process is very limiting.

More often, a network can be defined as the connection of multiple computers for the purpose of sharing software and peripherals—such as printers or CD-ROM drives. In addition to sharing peripherals, the series of cables that make up a network also enables users to communicate with each other.

## Why Use a Network?

As previously mentioned, a network enables computers to share software and peripherals. The reasons for sharing software are many, and best illustrated with the following example.

Suppose your company produces a publication called *300 Ways to Fix Meatballs*. You want to do a series of mass mailings, in hopes that someone receiving one of your flyers will send in $19.95 for a copy of the publication. On your computer, you have a huge database of everyone who has ever subscribed to *Meatball* magazine—the most likely targets for your flyer.

Because this database holds millions of entries, there's no way you alone can perform all the mailings. Your job, therefore, is to make sure everyone who has a last name ending in *a* gets a flier. Bob takes the *b*s, Carl takes the *c*s, and so on. Suddenly, the following scenario occurs: 20 more people subscribe to the magazine, and 50 of those already receiving it send in change-of-address cards.

Now you have to worry about updating the database system. If 26 users are accessing the database—and all 26 have a copy of the database on their own computer—you have to update 26 separate copies. After you update all of them, you can bet that more cards will come in—a list of those who have stopped receiving the magazine—and you'll have to begin making the rounds to every user's computer again.

## Sharing Information

A far better solution is for your company to have one database that all users can access. When changes come in, those changes are made only once, and everyone is working from the same information.

Think of the ramifications if you're doing financial graphing within departments. By having one set of financial data, all departments can pull from that set and all projections will be as accurate as possible. If every department pulls information from its own set of information, the projections can look quite different.

## Sharing Hardware

Networks also help you cut costs by enabling multiple users to share peripherals, such as printers. If every computer in a company is a stand-alone unit, each computer must have a printer connected to it for users to output hard copies of documents.

Dot-matrix printers can be picked up at fairly reasonable prices, but the output they provide is of far lower quality than laser printers. Laser printers provide excellent quality, but are very expensive. Imagine the cost of purchasing one for every computer in a large business.

The solution is to invest the money and buy one good laser printer and put it on the network. In so doing, each user can send output to the printer. Rather than buying 20 lasers at $1,000 apiece, you buy only one, and everyone has the same access.

## What Makes Up a Network?

A network has three components. Every computer connected with it must have a network interface card installed. Each computer must have the software necessary to interface between the internal operating system and the network. The third component is the physical link—usually, a common cable connecting the body of computers together.

There are two types of networks: *peer-to-peer* and *client/server*. The interface cards and wiring are the same between the two types; the only difference is in the server. With a peer-to-peer network, the computer, which contains the database accessed by all workers, is also used by the workers. With a client/server network, the computer containing the shared data is not used by any user; rather, it is *dedicated* to the network.

Suppose Vivian, who works in the Auburn Building Department, has a database on her computer that contains all building permits that have been issued. She uses her computer to access the database, as well as to write letters and documents and update a handful of other databases.

Vivian's boss, Mike, has software on his computer for writing documents and such, but when he wants to check on building permits, he can access the database on Vivian's machine through the peer-to-peer network. Vivian's database, when "called up" on Mike's computer, appears as if it is actually on his PC. Mike has a floppy disk drive (drive A) and a hard drive (drive C) on his computer, and the network creates a mapped drive to the database (drive F). To DOS and all other applications, it looks as if he actually has another physical drive inside his PC containing the Building Permit database.

Both Vivian and Mike can make changes to the database, and each sees the same set of information. The drawback comes when Vivian decides to write a letter complaining about poor service from a vendor. Her computer must split its processing time between the word processor she is using and the database Mike is accessing, causing both operations to be slower than normal.

Imagine if there are multiple shared databases on her computer and multiple users accessing them. Her operations will use approximately half the processor's capabilities; the other half is divided among all the network users. The more operations that take place, the more processing must be shared. Consequently, aggregate operations become increasingly slowed.

The alternative to this setup is to use a file server system. A computer becomes dedicated to the network as a server—serving the requests of users. The *server* contains the databases that are to be shared, and quite often also connects to a printer that all users can access. In so doing, the processor within the server performs the task of responding to requests; no time is taken away for responding to requests from the keyboard.

## Peer-To-Peer Network Software

Although a dedicated server is the preferred option, quite often small companies decide not to use the option initially. A peer-to-peer network is a good first step for a company for many reasons, including the following:

◆ With a small number of users, the delay in processing time is minimal.

◆ The cost of a peer-to-peer network is considerably cheaper. You save the expense of a computer that won't be used by a keyboard operator.

◆ A peer-to-peer network can always be upgraded or converted to a file server network. By using the same cables and cards, the only additional expense (besides the dedicated server) is in software.

Novell, Inc. is the undisputed leader of the networking software world—due to the fact that Novell owns a vast majority of the market share. Their product, Novell NetWare, is still marketed and available under several different versions, including 2.2, 3.11, 3.12, and 4.01. Version 2.2 is the only one that continues to support an undedicated server. It is based on the 16-bit architecture of the 80286 processor and can recognize up to 12 MB of RAM. A major benefit of the package is that if the company decides that processing is too slow and they want to convert to a dedicated server, 2.2 enables them to do so without having to purchasing any additional software. Other peer-to-peer software packages include Windows for Workgroups (Microsoft), Personal NetWare (Novell), and LANtastic (Artisoft).

In very recent developments, Version 2.2 is no longer marketed. Version 3.11 is no longer marketed and is replaced by 3.12. Version 4.01 is no longer marketed and is replaced by 4.1.

**Note** One of the best bargains in software right now is Novell DOS 7.0. This operating system replaces Microsoft DOS on your PC and includes Personal NetWare. If you're interested in dabbling with peer-to-peer networking, DOS 7.0 provides an inexpensive means.

# File Server Software

In the world of DOS PCs, Novell NetWare is the market leader, with software available in variations of 5 up to 1,000 users. Version 3.12 is the one most in use today, featuring a host of utilities that have been perfected in the 15 years or so Novell has been producing NetWare. Its processing is based on the architecture of the 80386 and 80486 chip—32 bit—and it can recognize up to 4 GB of RAM.

Version 4.1, still based on 386 and 486 architecture, has yet to see wide acceptance and is aimed at businesses that have so many users that they must use multiple servers. Rather than requiring users to log in to a different network each time they change servers, 4.1 maintains their identity across all servers—known as the *enterprise*.

# Network Interface Cards

The *network interface cards* (NICs) are installed in a PC (or connected to the back, in the case of laptops) and enable the PC to connect to the network. The NIC slides into an expansion slot on the PC, enabling the network cable to connect to it. Every single message traversing the network cable is received by the interface card. The card must determine whether the message it receives is intended for the PC; and if so, the card sends the message on to the processor. If the message isn't intended for the PC, the card ignores the message and awaits the next.

*Interrupts* (IRQs) represent unique numbers assigned to each component within a PC. One of the most common problems with NICs is that they often have the same interrupt as another hardware component. If this is the case, *lockups* can occur, or unexplained garbled screens. Most NIC manufacturers are aware of this and provide a default address not commonly used by other equipment, and an alternative address in case there's a conflict.

An important concept in networking is that topology, cards, and wiring all remain the same, regardless of whether the network is peer-to-peer or dedicated. The only difference is whether one computer is dedicated specifically to the network, or is shared by a user sitting at its keyboard.

## Using Topologies

Three topologies are used today for creating networks. The Ethernet topology is illustrated in figure 1.1. One common type of Ethernet, know as Thinnet or 10BASE2, utilizes the bus topology. With Thinnet, each NIC card is connected to a T-Connector. The cable connected to the right side of the T-Connector comes from one computer; the one connected to the left goes to another. The two computers at the end of the chain have 50 *ohm terminators* connected to the one side of the T-Connector, rather than another cable.

**Figure 1.1**

The bus topology, in which computers are connected in a linear line, with a terminator at each end of the chain.

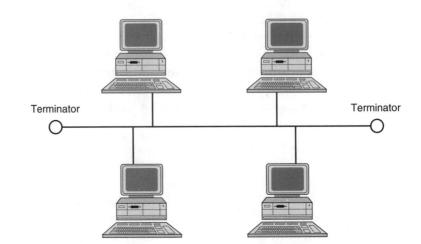

8

As mentioned previously, every NIC hears each message sent on the cable and decides whether to respond to it. The terminator's job, however, is to kill all messages that come to it (because it's at the end of the cable). Without a terminator, every message sent echoes back down the cable again and again, causing an exponential growth in messages that each NIC has to check. Eventually the number of messages—the amount of traffic on the wire, so to speak—becomes so great that the entire network system crashes due to message collisions.

The second common topology, shown in figure 1.2, is the *ring*. With a ring—of which the most common is IBM's Token-Ring—shielded wires connect each workstation in a loop.

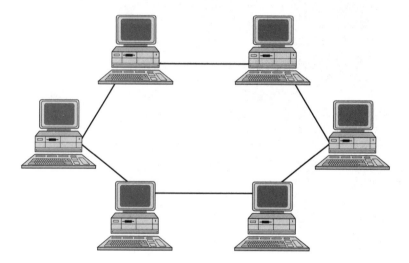

**Figure 1.2**

The ring topology, in which computers are connected to each other without the necessity of terminators.

The third topology is the *star*. A *concentrator*, or *hub*, is centrally located, and each computer is connected to it. The hub is then connected to the server. Star topology is used with great frequency these days, for dedicated servers and peer-to-peer networks alike. One advantage of the star topology is that if there is a break in the cabling going to a workstation, the other workstations are still able to communicate with the file server.

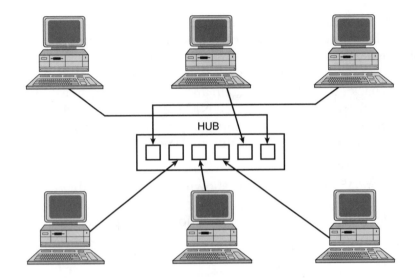

Each topology and cable type has a maximum length which each piece of cable can be. If all computers are located in close proximity, then the ring topology is acceptable—because the distance between any two computers is minimal. If, however, the computers are spread out, even in different rooms, it might become difficult to stay within the distance restrictions and the ring topology must by waylaid for a daisy chain.

## Cable

The type of cabling used in a network is dependent on several things—mainly the topology and type of network interface cards used. The most common cabling choices are *coaxial cable*, *twisted pair* (or telephone wire), *shielded twisted pair*, and *fiber optic*. Wireless networks, which use radio signals in place of cable, are seeing a surge in notoriety.

When discussing cable, you should be aware of three key terms:

◆ **Attenuation**. Indicates how much of the signal is lost over a distance. Unshielded twisted pair has the greatest loss; fiber-optic cable maintains the majority of its signal.

- ◆ **Bandwidth.** The number of simultaneous transmissions a cable can carry. The higher the bandwidth the more capacity, and also the higher the cost.

- ◆ **Impedance.** Gives the amount of resistance the cable itself gives to the messages it is carrying. The higher the impedance, the more force working against the signal you are trying to send.

The cheapest cable scenario to use is *Ethernet twisted pair*. For a bit more, however, you can upgrade to *Ethernet coaxial cable*, which provides an excellent backbone by which to build a network. (Fiber-optic cabling, not surprisingly, is the most expensive way to go.)

## Putting the Pieces Together

A network consists of computers with network interface cards installed, a cable connecting them together, and software. These three components work together to form the total picture. The type of cards used is dependent on the type of cable and software; the cable and software is dependent on the cards, and so on.

# Understanding Dedicated Server Networking with NetWare

NetWare 3.1x uses a dedicated server. The physical components remain the same whether the network is using a dedicated or nondedicated server—each workstation must have a network interface card (NIC) installed, and there must be a cable connecting the computers together. The difference comes in two places. First, different software is used. Second, one computer is not accessed by any user; its sole purpose is to sit alone and respond to all information requests made by users. It is *dedicated* to this task, and thus termed a dedicated server. Figure 1.4 illustrates this concept.

All workstations are connected to a network cable, which is terminated at both ends. One end of this particular cable leads to the server. Every request for shared files is processed by the server (where the files are stored). In a peer-to-peer network, shared files can be located on multiple workstations; in a dedicated server network, those files must be on the server. With a dedicated server, no workstation has the capability of accessing any other workstation.

**Figure 1.4**

An example of a dedicated server, with all workstation requests routing to and from the server.

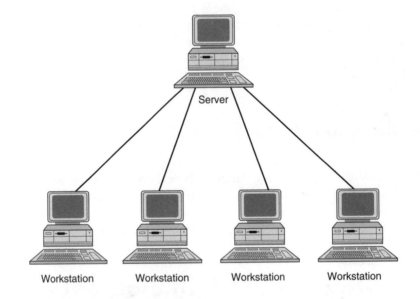

Server

Workstation    Workstation    Workstation    Workstation

# History of Networking

Novell, Inc. released one of the first PC networking systems in 1983. It quickly became popular with businesses that were straining under the inability to share information between PCs. The earliest versions could share printers and files—and little else. Over time, modifications have evolved the product into what it is today: NetWare.

Version 2.2 was written for the 286 processor, and served as a workhorse in the business community for years. In 1994, Novell announced that they were finally stopping the marketing of 2.2, and would begin phasing out the support function as well.

Version 2.2 is the last of the products that enable NetWare to run on dedicated or nondedicated servers. Although it was never encouraged, a user could start DOS on the server and function as if at a workstation. In so doing, the network operating system (NOS) had to fire up DOS, and then the application—all the time sharing the user's processing with the networks. This practice was acceptable for businesses consisting of two or three users, but little more because the server ran so slow.

Bear in mind, as well, that any crash of the DOS application also crashed the NetWare all other users were using. Versions 3.11 and 3.12 were written to take advantage of the 386 processor (and above) and represent the most popular versions in use today. Novell upgraded 3.11 to 3.12, by fixing a number of bugs and adding a few features. A surprising note, however, is that most businesses that invested heavily in 3.11 never encountered the bugs, and have never bothered to upgrade—making 3.11 still heavily used.

Version 4.0 was released to reach a completely different market— not businesses, but enterprises. In other words, businesses with more than one hundred users and multiple servers. Version 4.01 quickly replaced it—fixing bugs that inherently appear in a new product aiming so high. In November of 1994, version 4.1 came out and replaced 4.02.

This book focuses on the 3.1x version because it is used by over 50 percent of the desktop networks in existence.

## Running NetWare

After the software is installed and all connections are made to each workstation, operations are very simple. The server should be up and running before any of the workstations. After it is up, the workstations can be brought up and attached to the server.

When a user makes a request, the Network Requester, or Network Shell, reads the request and decides whether it is a remote or local request. If it's local, it passes it through without further processing to the local operating system. If it's a remote request, the Requester sends it across the server and the response comes back. All this transpires without the necessity of the user knowing that any of it has taken place.

NetWare usually maps the first remote drive as drive F, and can map additional drives all the way to drive Z. In addition to creating mapped drives, NetWare also creates search drives where it looks for common executables.

Capture statements can reroute the local printer ports to the server, enabling one laser printer to serve dozens of users. When the user prints from an application, NetWare *spools* the request in a temporary file, enabling the user to return to work immediately—without the delay of waiting for the printer to begin or end. Multiple requests can be made to print at the same time, and all spool up as files. As the printer becomes available, each file is fed to it from the queue in the order in which it was submitted.

## Communications

Messages can be sent to users in a variety of ways. The BROAD-CAST command enables the supervisor or another user of the server to send a message to all, or selected, users. Intended to warn users when maintenance is imminent, BROADCAST can transmit messages up to 55 characters in length. SEND is a command that can be used by all users to send messages back and forth. It, too, is limited to 55 characters in length, and can be sent to one, multiple, or all users.

SEND and BROADCAST both pose a potential problem, in that when a message comes in to a user's workstation, a message appears on-screen and all processing is suspended until the user presses Ctrl+Enter to clear the message. Imagine, for example, that you're compiling a large spreadsheet during lunch, only to return to find that no processing has taken place because someone sent a message asking whether you wanted to join the bowling team.

Fortunately, CASTOFF is a command that can be issued by each user to prevent messages from coming in to him or her. Countered with CASTON, the two can be used prior to processing big jobs in order to stop incoming messages, and after completion, to enable their arrival again. The server and the system administrator are always allowed to send messages to users, even if CASTOFF has been used.

 **Note** NetWare doesn't ship with a mail program. It does contain all the ingredients for one, however, because it's based upon mail-handling service (MHS) technology. Several good mail packages are available that run on NetWare (my favorite is ExpressIT from Infinite Technologies).

There are also several shareware programs available that offer Chat or Talk features, enabling users to open screens in which they can communicate directly with each other. One of NetWare's primary benefits is that there are so many programs written to run on it, and shareware is no different. A quick perusal of any major bulletin board uncovers dozens of utilities aimed at simplifying operations.

## NetWare Summary

NetWare is the network software of choice for most corporations. In a recent poll of Fortune 500 companies, more companies said they would consider using NetWare than any other product in their establishment. As prices have reduced over the years, NetWare has become a viable choice not just for Fortune 500 companies, but for anyone needing to network computers together.

NetWare offers excellent features for sharing peripherals and devices, as well as files and data. By becoming a standard throughout the industry, it is also a safe bet for future growth and potential.

# Identifying the Software

Because several versions of NetWare are on the market, it's important to understand which version you are running—for a number of reasons. First, so that you'll know what options are available, and second, because this book concentrates only on NetWare 3.11 and 3.12.

Several utilities provide you with information about the network and NetWare, including the following:

◆ SYSCON

◆ NVER

◆ VOLUMES

◆ NAME

◆ CONFIG

These utilities are discussed in the following sections. The first two are available for use from any workstation connected to the network, while the latter three can be run only from the file server console.

## SYSCON

The SYSCON utility can be run from any workstation connected to the network—by any user. Many of the options in the utility are available only to the supervisor, but there are several others that regular users can access as well (such as changing their own passwords).

When you first start SYSCON, a menu similar to that shown in figure 1.5 appears. This is the main screen. From this menu, select File Server Information to learn more about the file server.

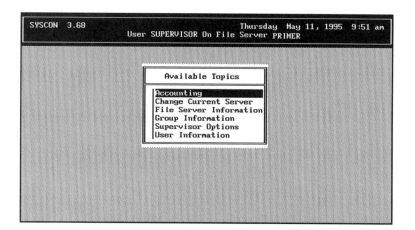

**Figure 1.5**

The SYSCON main menu. Use the down arrow to highlight File Server Information, then press Enter.

After you've selected File Server Information, a second menu appears showing the known servers. If you have only one server, that's the only one listed. If your network is connected to a number of servers, all are shown. Use the down arrow to highlight your server in the list (if it isn't already highlighted) and press Enter. Figure 1.6 shows an example of the information given.

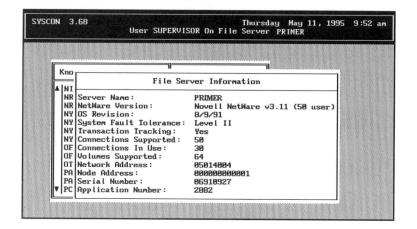

**Figure 1.6**

The information available from the File Server Information screen.

# NVER

NVER is a simple, easy-to-use, command-line utility that tells you the version of NetBIOS, IPX/SPX, LAN driver, workstation shell, workstation DOS, and file server operating system. In other words, it offers a great deal of good information, all in one convenient location.

When executed, the output resembles the following:

```
NETWARE VERSION UTILITY, VERSION 3.12
IPX Version: 3.30
SPX Version: 3.30
LAN Driver: 3Com 3C509 EtherLink III Adapter V1.00
            IRQ A, Port 0300
Shell:    V4.10 Rev. A
DOS:      MSDOS V6.20 on IBM_PC
FileServer: PRIMER
Novell NetWare v3.11 (50 user) (8/9/91)
```

Note that the utility version—in this case 3.12—is not indicative of NetWare version (3.11) as shown in the last line.

# VOLUMES

VOLUMES is a file server command that can only be run from the console. It lists the drive volumes that are available (that is, mounted). It won't list volumes that are not mounted. Figure 1.7 shows a sample listing.

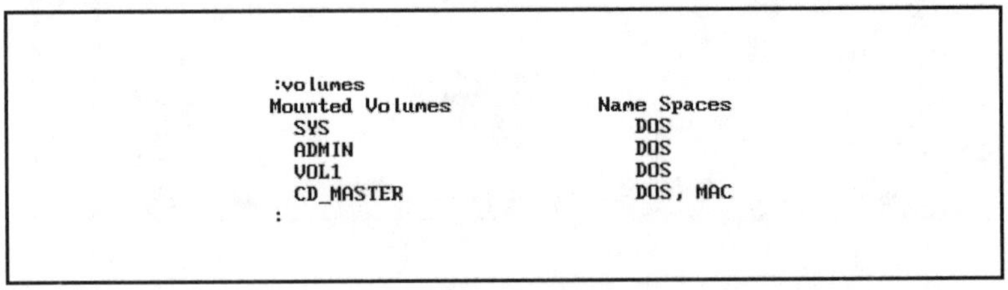

**Figure 1.7**

Available drive volumes are shown by the VOLUMES command.

```
:volumes
Mounted Volumes          Name Spaces
    SYS                  DOS
    ADMIN                DOS
    VOL1                 DOS
    CD_MASTER            DOS, MAC
:
```

# NAME

The NAME utility, which can only be invoked from the file server, gives you the name of that file server. The following is an example of the output:

```
This is server PRIMER
```

# CONFIG

The CONFIG utility, executed from the file server console, offers a number of essential data pieces, as shown in figure 1.8. Among the items shown are the name of the file server, the IPX internal network number, and information on all the installed cards and where they are linked to.

```
File server name: PRIMER
IPX internal network number: 05014004

3Com EtherLink III 3C509 Family
     Hardware setting: Slot 8, I/O Port 8000h to 800Fh, Interrupt Ah
     Node address: 00608C85C72B
     Frame type: ETHERNET_802.2
     Board name: ETHERNET_802.2
     LAN protocol: IPX network 000B0FF0

3Com EtherLink III 3C509 Family
     Hardware setting: Slot 8, I/O Port 8000h to 800Fh, Interrupt Ah
     Node address: 00608C85C72B
     Frame type: ETHERNET_802.3
     Board name: ETHERNET_802.3
     LAN protocol: IPX network 00501429

3Com EtherLink III 3C509 Family
     Hardware setting: Slot 8, I/O Port 8000h to 800Fh, Interrupt Ah
     Node address: 00608C85C72B
     Frame type: ETHERNET_SNAP
     Board name: ETHERTALK2
     LAN protocol: AARP
     LAN protocol: APPLETLK
:
```

**Figure 1.8**

Information available from the CONFIG utility.

---

**PRACTICE EXERCISE**

Using the software that came with this book, you can emulate a running network—without needing access to such. Because the executable file is called PRIMER, you can execute any command by preceding it with that call. For example, if a command is called XYZ, the command would be PRIMER XYZ.

Using this software, obtain the file server information using the following steps:

1. Type **PRIMER SYSCON**

2. Select File Server Information by moving the highlight to that entry, and press Enter.

3. Select the server (there is only one present) and press Enter.

4. View the information.

5. Press the Esc key several times to exit (or press Alt+F10 to do so with only one keystroke).

Using the software, obtain the NVER information:

1. Type **PRIMER NVER**

2. View the information.

# Real World

Use the utilities described in this chapter to document your network. Using the those utilities, you should be able to fill in the following fields, which will be invaluable in the event of a system crash:

File server name:

NetWare version:

Number of concurrent user version:

IPX version:

SPX version:

IPX internal network number:

Number of volumes:

Names of volumes:

Number of network cards in server:

Type of cards:

Hardware settings:

Node address:

Frame type:

Board name:

LAN protocol:

System Fault Tolerance level:

Serial number:

# Summary

This chapter introduces the basics of networking and describes the five essential utilities used to ascertain what type of NetWare network you are currently running.

Chapter 2 delves into supervisor parameters and shows how to establish defaults that are carried throughout the system and assigned to every newly created user.

# Supervisor Parameters

As the *supervisor* (or *administrator*) of a system, you are responsible for a number of duties. One of those duties is defining the *variables*, or *parameters*, that affect the operation of the entire network. This task includes defining default values for user accounts and restrictions, as well as establishing file server console operators and routinely checking the file server error log.

This chapter examines these topics and explores the best way to set them for your site.

## Understanding SYSCON Options

Default account balances and restrictions can be applied to all new users who are added to the system through the SYSCON utility. To access this utility, type **SYSCON** at any DOS prompt; the menu shown in figure 2.1 appears.

**Figure 2.1**

The initial SYSCON menu screen.

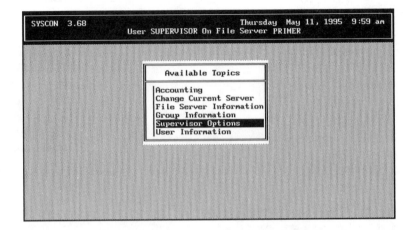

Using the arrow keys, select Supervisor Options and press Enter. Eight additional options appear (see fig. 2.2).

**Figure 2.2**

The Supervisor Options menu of SYSCON.

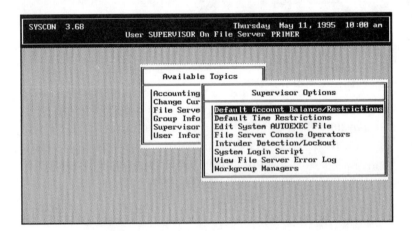

The eight choices presented are discussed in this and other chapters. Briefly, they include the following:

◆ **Default Account Balance/Restrictions.** Discussed in the following section.

◆ **Default Time Restrictions.** Set when a user can log in to the file server. It's often used to keep users from logging in during times other than when they should be working. Occasionally, this option is used for security reasons, although it can also be used to perform backups, or other maintenance operations. The default, shown by a screen full of asterisks, enables a user to log in at any time. Removing the asterisks keeps the user from logging in at the times when they're absent.

The default established here is effective for all newly created users. Those users who already existed before you made any changes have the permissible login times that existed when they were created.

The default login time is without restriction—24 hours. Upon installing the NetWare operating system, two users—guest and supervisor—are added by the installation routine. That means that they have 24-hour logins regardless of any changes that might be made here immediately after installation. To change the default, you must go into their individual user login restrictions and change the times manually.

◆ **Edit System AUTOEXEC File.** Enables the server startup file to be modified.

◆ **File Server Console Operators.** Defined later in this chapter.

◆ **Intruder Detection/Lockout.** Enables you to specify how many incorrect attempts (of logging in to the system) you want to allow before considering that user an intruder. After an intruder is declared, you also define what actions are to take place (that is, how long their account is disabled and how long they remain locked out).

◆ **System Login Script.** Enables you to view and change the system login script. This is the script that contains mappings and other commands you want to pertain to all users. Stored as an ASCII file, it lives in the PUBLIC directory as NET$LOG.DAT.

◆ **View File Server Error Log.** Not only can you view the log from here, but you also can clear it and monitor the system for activities that should not be transpiring.

◆ **Workgroup Managers.** Enables you to create user accounts that have supervisory privileges to manage other users and groups. A means by which a supervisor can offload some of the workload; workgroup managers can only delete accounts assigned to, or created by, them.

## Account Balances and Restrictions

Figure 2.3 shows a sample screen of account balances and restrictions. The very first field indicates a Yes or No (as to whether the account has an expiration date). If the answer is No, the second field does not apply.

**Figure 2.3**

The Default Account Balance/Restrictions screen from Supervisor Options.

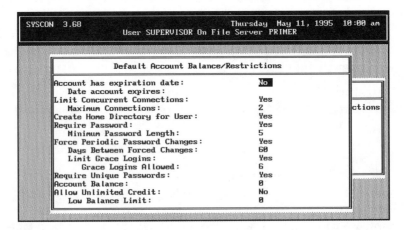

```
SYSCON  3.68                          Thursday  May 11, 1995  10:00 am
                      User SUPERVISOR On File Server PRIMER


                  ┌────────────────────────────────────────┐
                  │      Default Account Balance/Restrictions │
                  │ Account has expiration date:        No   │
                  │   Date account expires:                  │
                  │ Limit Concurrent Connections:       Yes  │
                  │   Maximum Connections:              2     │      ctions
                  │ Create Home Directory for User:     Yes  │
                  │ Require Password:                   Yes  │
                  │   Minimum Password Length:          5    │
                  │ Force Periodic Password Changes:    Yes  │
                  │   Days Between Forced Changes:      60   │
                  │   Limit Grace Logins:               Yes  │
                  │       Grace Logins Allowed:         6    │
                  │ Require Unique Passwords:           Yes  │
                  │ Account Balance:                    0    │
                  │ Allow Unlimited Credit:             No   │
                  │   Low Balance Limit:                0    │
                  └────────────────────────────────────────┘
```

The third field enables you to limit the number of concurrent connections that can exist. There is little valid reason why any user (other than the supervisor) needs to be logged in to the network more than once. Allowing a user to do so on an unlimited basis opens you up to potential security breaches. Two is a good limit on this number, and should not pose a problem to many users.

A Yes or No field specifies whether you're creating a home directory for each newly added user, and whether a password is required. Common sense dictates that in today's world, where the most valuable thing your company owns is the data stored on its network, everyone should be required to have a password. That password should also have limitations, as the next fields illustrate.

The minimum password character length should never be less than five. It's far too easy to guess passwords with lengths less than that. Periodic password changes should be forced somewhere between 30 and 90 days, and unique passwords should be required.

NetWare keeps track of the passwords that have been used for eight renditions. Should a user attempt to use one that was used before (providing it was not nine or more iterations ago), that user is told that the password is not unique, and the user must specify something else.

*Grace logins* should be limited, and that shown in figure 2.3 is very liberal—six times. That means a user is allowed to make six more logins after his or her password has expired. (Three times is more than generous on most systems.)

The final three fields relate to accounting and credit—a topic not discussed in this book.

## File Server Console Operators

File server console operators are those who can access key functions of the file server while sitting at their workstations. Figure 2.4 shows the highlight on that selection from the SYSCON Supervisor Options menu. Figure 2.5 shows the listing of those defined as such on this system.

**Figure 2.4**

Selecting File Server
Console Operators
from the menu.

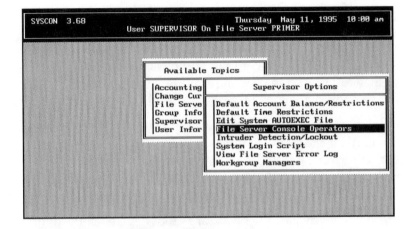

**Figure 2.5**

A table of those
defined as console
operators.

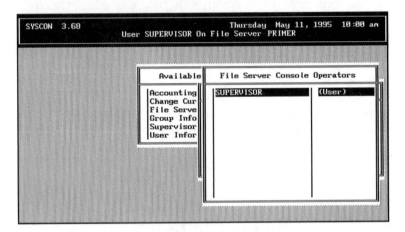

To be a console operator is to be able to invoke the FCONSOLE
utility. Unless you've been specifically defined as a file server
console operator, you cannot run FCONSOLE. The importance of
this cannot be overstated. Figure 2.6 shows the main FCONSOLE
menu.

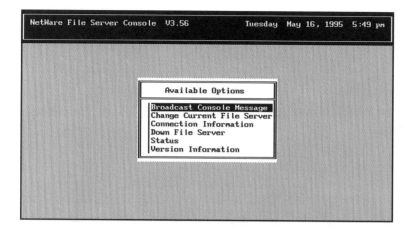

```
NetWare File Server Console  V3.56          Tuesday  May 16, 1995  5:49 pm


                        ┌─────────────────────────┐
                        │    Available Options     │
                        ├─────────────────────────┤
                        │ Broadcast Console Message │
                        │ Change Current File Server │
                        │ Connection Information    │
                        │ Down File Server          │
                        │ Status                    │
                        │ Version Information        │
                        └─────────────────────────┘
```

**Figure 2.6**

The main
FCONSOLE menu.

Notice some of the choices available from this menu and you'll know why this utility must be so highly guarded. Being able to run FCONSOLE means that you can, among other things, do the following:

◆ Send messages to all users.

◆ Check on the connection information of any user, and even kill that connection.

◆ Down the file server.

It's the last option that brings about the most fear, as it makes it possible for any user with FCONSOLE rights to sit at his or her workstation and bring down the entire network.

**Note**  One interesting note about FCONSOLE that fits into Chapter 1, "Starting at Ground Zero" (but was not mentioned there because you must specifically be defined as a file server console operator to access it), is the bottom choice on the menu. Version Information tells you additional information about the file server and the software it's running. Figure 2.7 shows an example of the information found there.

**Figure 2.7**

Version information is available through FCONSOLE.

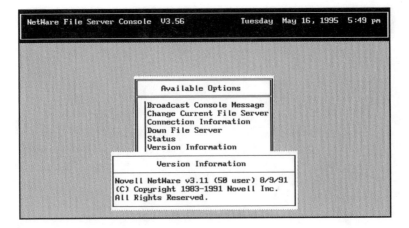

No one other than the supervisor should be defined as a file server console operator. Allowing any other user such wide-ranging abilities is asking for trouble.

## File Server Error Log

The file server error log keeps track of everything on the server that doesn't function as it should. A classic example is a *backup routine*. If the backup routine begins to run and finds that all users have not logged out, it then—most of the time—kills the connections and proceeds. Somewhere, the fact that it had to kill those connections must be documented, and that's where the error log comes into play. It also can show errors that occur with the backup routine itself.

Figure 2.8 shows the option highlighted on the SYSCON Supervisor Options menu; figure 2.9 shows errors that were generated when ARCserve Scheduler was unloaded.

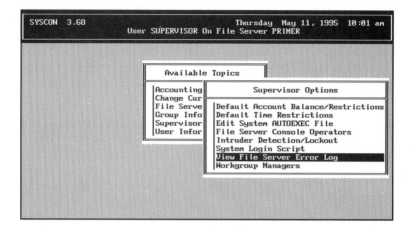

**Figure 2.8**

Selecting View File
Server Error Log
from the Supervisor
Options of SYSCON.

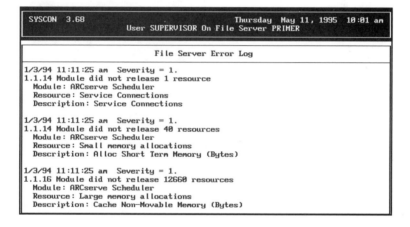

**Figure 2.9**

An example of
an error log.

You can use the Page Up and Page Down keys to view the log and
see what errors have occurred. This screen can often be your first
indication of something that warrants further investigation.

Pressing the Esc key exits you from the error log, but not before
you are asked if you would like to clear the log. If you do not clear
it, it continues to grow in size, with the most recent information
appearing at the end of the file. If you do clear the log, all past
information is deleted and the file begins anew.

*PRACTICE EXERCISE*

Using the software that comes with this book, you can emulate a running network—without needing access to such. Because the executable file is called PRIMER, you can execute any command by preceding it with that call. If a command is called XYZ, for example, the command would be PRIMER XYZ.

Using this software, examine the default account balance and restrictions, as well as the File Server Console Operators List and the File Server Error Log.

1. Type **PRIMER SYSCON**

2. Select Supervisor Options by using the down arrow to go to that selection and then pressing Enter.

3. Select Default Account Balance/Restrictions by pressing Enter.

4. View the information.

5. Press the Esc to go back one menu.

6. Select File Server Console Operators by using the down arrow to go to that selection; then press Enter.

7. View the information.

8. Press the Esc key to go back one menu to Supervisor Options.

9. Use the down arrow to move to View File Server Error Log and press Enter.

10. Note the information presented.

11. Press Alt+F10 to exit the utility.

# Real World

Use the SYSCON utility to add to your network documentation. A wonderful tool for any administrator's toolkit is a screen capture utility. A number of them are commercially available, such as Collage and HiJack. Using any of them, you can capture what's on your screen into a text file, PCX, BMP, or other type of graphics file.

These come in handy with such things as the Default Account Balance/Restrictions menu. Rather than having to write out all that information, a screen capture utility enables you to snap the screen and send the output to your printer. Take that printed page and keep it in a place where your other documentation is, and where you can find it easily when it's needed for a recovery operation.

Assuming you have no such tool at your disposal, however, fill in the following blanks, and keep this book where you can find it:

Limit concurrent connections:

Maximum connections:

Create home directory for user:

Require password:

Minimum password length:

Force periodic password changes:

Days between forced changes:

Limit grace logins:

Grace logins allowed:

Require unique passwords:

File server console operators:

# Summary

This chapter explores the most rudimentary of supervisor parameters available from the SYSCON menu and explains their purposes. The following chapters expand on those principles.

Chapter 3 looks at ways of adding and deleting users, and the three key utilities used to do so.

**3**

**CHAPTER**

# Adding and Deleting Users

Wouldn't it be wonderful if, after creating a network and adding all your coworkers to it, you could just walk away and forget about it? Unfortunately, there's no such perfect world, and there are very few networks from which you can just walk away. New employees are constantly being hired, and some employees leave. For these reasons, you need to know how to add and delete users, and you will most likely find it to be one of the tasks you do on a regular basis.

Three utilities enable you add new users (the first two also enable you to delete users):

- ◆ SYSCON
- ◆ USERDEF
- ◆ MAKEUSER

This chapter focuses on these three utilities. Because the first two are graphical in nature, much of this chapter consists of screen shots. This chapter walks you through each of the steps necessary to add users.

# Understanding SYSCON

Only three chapters into this book, it should by now become evident that SYSCON is one of the most important utilities available in the NetWare 3.x arsenal. One of the choices available from the main menu, as shown in figure 3.1, is that of User Information. This option enables you to choose to add or delete users.

**Figure 3.1**

Select User Information from the main SYSCON menu.

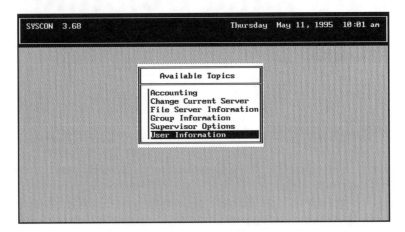

A list of users known to the system appears (see fig. 3.2). You can use the up and down arrows to scroll through the list, or use the Page Up and Page Down keys to scroll more rapidly through the list. List scrolling and user selection are important when you want to see or change information on already defined users. To create a new user, however, you need only press the Insert key, and a box similar to that shown in figure 3.3 appears.

**Note** The list of defined users always appears in alphabetical order. When adding a new user, it doesn't matter where you are in the list—press Insert and add that user. The user is automatically placed alphabetically in the listing.

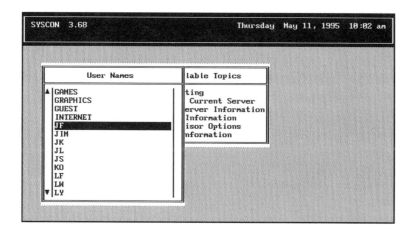

**Figure 3.2**

A list of currently defined users appears.

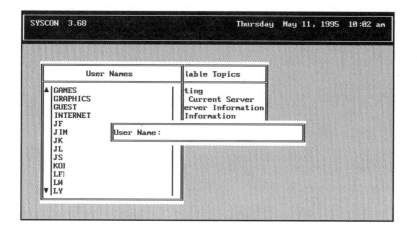

**Figure 3.3**

Pressing Insert prompts for a new user name.

**37**

Enter the name of the user you want to create. You should keep user names uniform. Most of the time, this practice translates into using the initial of the user's first name and up to seven digits of his or her last name. In small organizations, this rule works quite well, because there is rarely a replication in names. In very large organizations, however, it's not unusual to have two Bill Smiths or Jack Joneses.

If your organization is small to moderate in size, use the BSMITH, JJONES approach to user names. If your organization is large, however, you should consider options that make the most sense for your company. The important thing is to make user names as easy to think of as possible.

 Let's say, for example, I want to send a message to Bill Smith. If my user name is WSTEEN, then his is obviously BSMITH. I shouldn't have to think that it could be BILLS, B_SMITH, or any other derivative thereof. The user name needs to be easily ascertained not only by that user, but also by everyone else on the system who might interact with that user (for example, by sending e-mail).

In a large corporation (in which two users have the same name), I'd make one user BSMITH, and the other WSMITH, for William. Likewise, one user would become JJONES, and the other JACKJONES. User names must contain at least two characters, but can be up to fifteen in length, which offers you a great deal of flexibility. You can even add department names if necessary: JJONES_ACCT, and so forth.

Figure 3.4 shows a standard user name being entered; figure 3.5 shows the prompt that determines whether to create a *home directory* for the new user.

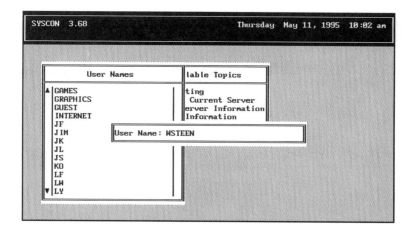

**Figure 3.4**

Adding a user named WSTEEN.

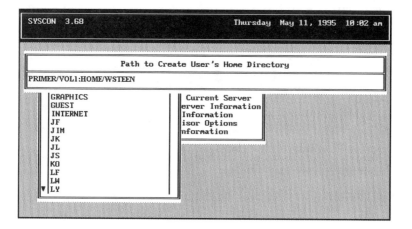

**Figure 3.5**

Prompting for the creation of a home directory.

Figure 3.6 completes the process by asking whether you want verification of the home directory creation. The home directory can be a kicker when going with long user names. By default, the home directory attempts to create itself with the user name. The limitation on the directory file-name length is eight characters, as opposed to the fifteen on the user name, another reason why it makes sense to go with the standard user-naming convention (the first initial and up to seven characters of the last name).

**Figure 3.6**

Verification of the home directory is an option.

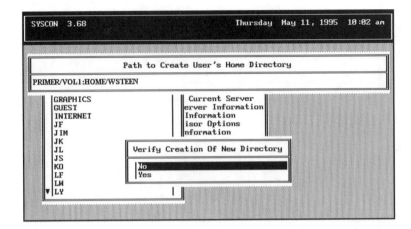

Technically, that's all there is to it; the new user has been added to the system, as shown in figure 3.7. Realistically, however, there are a few additional steps that need to be done in most instances.

**Figure 3.7**

The new user has now been added to the system.

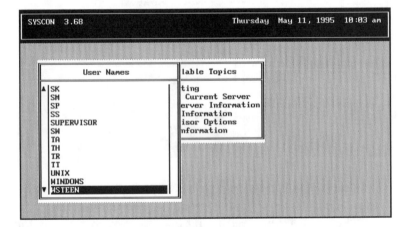

Move the cursor to the user name and press Enter. Another menu of options appears, as shown in figure 3.8. These are all the operations you can use with the one user you've selected. The first option is that of defining the account restrictions. Select the option by pressing Enter; a screen similar to that shown in figure 3.9 appears.

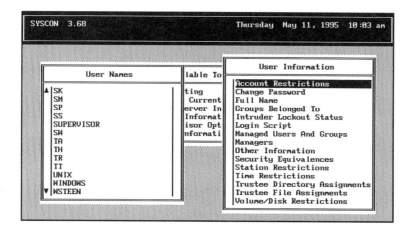

**Figure 3.8**

Additional menu choices available for the selected user.

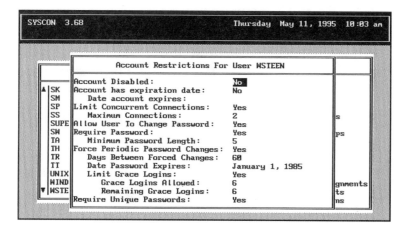

**Figure 3.9**

The account restrictions for the newly created user.

The very first field is simply a Yes or No field, indicating whether the account has been disabled. If it has, the other fields have no meaning. The second field indicates whether the account has an expiration date. If the answer is No, the third field does not apply.

The fourth field enables you to limit the number of concurrent connections that can exist. There is very little valid reason why any user other than the supervisor needs to be logged in to the network more than once. Allowing a user to do so on an unlimited basis opens you up to potential security breaches. Two is a good limit on this number—one that should not pose a problem to many users.

**41**

Whether users are allowed to change a password—and whether users are required to have a password—comprise the next fields. The minimum password length should never be less than five characters. It is far too easy to guess passwords with lengths less than that. Periodic password changes should be forced somewhere between 30 and 90 days, and unique passwords should be required. Requiring unique passwords means that NetWare keeps track of the passwords that have been used for eight renditions. Should users attempt to use one that they used before (providing it was not nine or more iterations ago), they are told that the password is not unique, and that another one must be specified.

Grace logins should be limited, and that shown in figure 3.9 is very liberal—six times. This is six logins that a person is allowed to make after his or her password has expired. Three times should be more than generous on most systems.

Where do these values, which are arbitrarily plunked in as account restrictions, come from? Simple: they come from the system default account balance and restrictions that were set up by the supervisor and defined in Chapter 2, "Supervisor Parameters." For comparison, figure 3.10 shows that screen and the data that was entered there.

**Figure 3.10**

The system defaults for newly created user accounts.

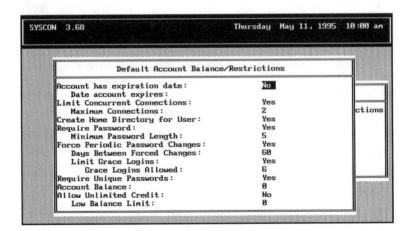

The next task you need to perform after checking the account restrictions is to enter the user's full name. This is a free-text field used for identification purposes only. Figure 3.11 shows the third field of the menu highlighted; figure 3.12 shows the appropriate entry being entered.

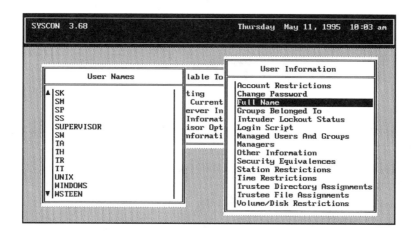

**Figure 3.11**

Choosing Full Name from the menu.

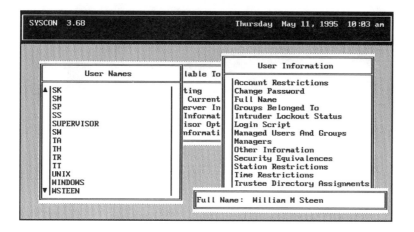

**Figure 3.12**

Entering the full name of this account.

One last thing to check is the Other Information choice, which appears halfway down the User Information menu. Figure 3.13 shows this selection, and figure 3.14 shows the information that it presents. Because this is a newly created account, there has never been a login; thus, the last login is unknown. By default: the user is not enabled to use FCONSOLE; there is zero byte space in use from the user on the server; and the last field shows the user ID.

**Figure 3.13**

Selecting Other Information from the menu.

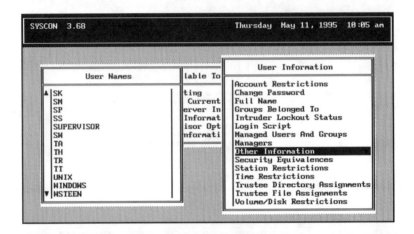

**Figure 3.14**

The other information available on a user.

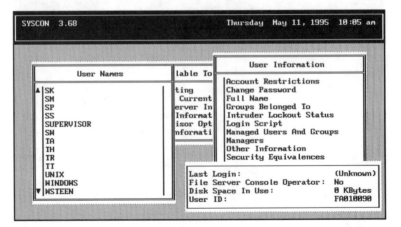

The User ID field is one of the more important ones. This field indicates how the user is known to the system—in this case, FA010090. This field also represents the name of a directory created beneath MAIL (where the user's mail entries go).

## Deleting a User

To delete a user with SYSCON, go into the User Information option in the main screen. Highlight the user name in question and press the Delete key. You are then prompted as to whether you want to complete the transaction. Answer Yes, and the transaction is completed.

# Understanding USERDEF

USERDEF is the second of the three utilities that enable you to add users, and is graphically menu-based, like SYSCON. With USERDEF, you also can create templates for automating the creation of network user accounts.

Those templates contain specific parameters and define login scripts, which will then be applied to all newly created user accounts. In other words, when you use SYSCON, all newly created users default to whatever is set up as the default user settings and restrictions. If you want different user settings, you must go into their options, one by one, and make the changes. It may be that you need to have more than one default. If that is the case, USERDEF is the utility to use—the defaults here are known as templates.

Figure 3.15 shows the opening menu of the utility.

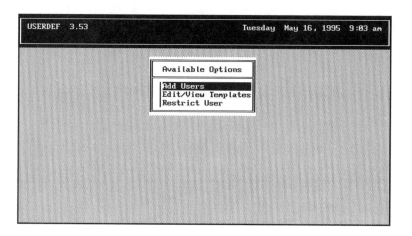

**Figure 3.15**

The opening menu of USERDEF.

Notice that only three options exist:

◆ Add Users

◆ Edit/View Templates

◆ Restrict User

Skipping over Add Users (which is self-explanatory), the other two options are described briefly in the following sections.

## Edit/View Templates

This option enables you to create new templates or edit existing ones. Figure 3.16 shows the screen that appears when you select this option.

**Figure 3.16**

The list of existing templates.

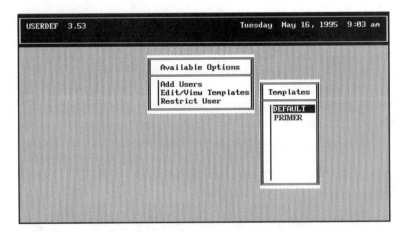

When you choose this option, a list of templates is displayed. From the list of templates, you can choose an existing template and edit its parameters, or select Insert and provide a template name to create a new one. Figure 3.17 shows the menu that appears when one of the templates is selected; there are now two definition sets to choose from: the login script or the parameters.

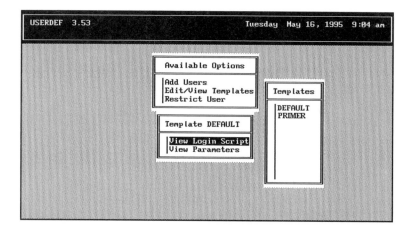

**Figure 3.17**
The two templates
that exist under
DEFAULT.

The login script is the default for most systems, and is shown in figure 3.18. This merely maps a search drive to PUBLIC and one to the OS version under PUBLIC, and sets the default directory to the login name directory.

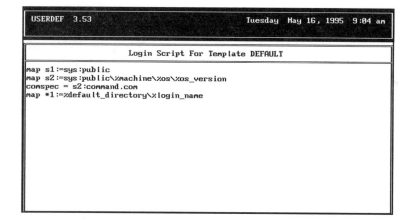

**Figure 3.18**
The DEFAULT user login script.

Figure 3.19 shows that parameters are being chosen from the previous menu, and figure 3.20 shows those parameters that exist.

**Figure 3.19**

Choosing View
Parameters for the
DEFAULT template.

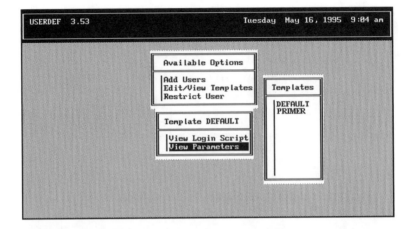

**Figure 3.20**

The parameters inside
the DEFAULT
template.

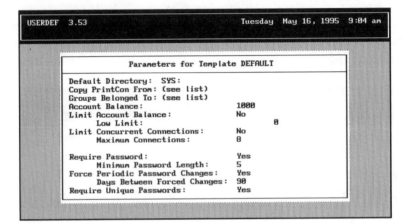

Note the similarities between fields here and in the SYSCON
menu choices. Both accomplish the same thing, so there is much
overlap. Figure 3.21 shows the same thing as figure 3.20, only now
it is for the PRIMER template. Here, Maximum Connections is no
longer defined as eight, and there is a change in the Groups
Belonged To. Under DEFAULT, there are no groups that the new
user was automatically a member of. Under PRIMER, the new
user automatically joins EVERYONE, as shown in figure 3.22.

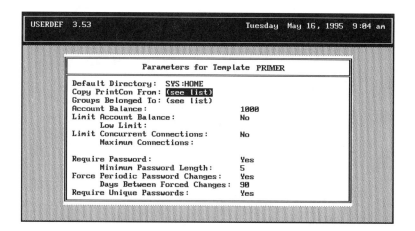

**Figure 3.21**

The parameters for the PRIMER template.

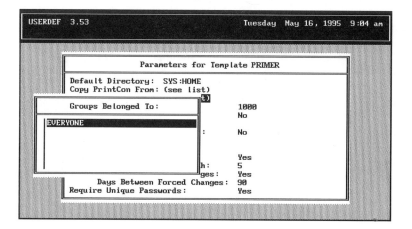

**Figure 3.22**

The groups newly created members join when the PRIMER template is used.

# Restrict User

Choose the Restrict User option to set restrictions for user accounts.

# Add User

Finally, here's how to add a user after the templates have been created. Figure 3.23 shows the menu that appears when Add Users is selected; this is a list of the known templates. Select one and press Enter. A list of the currently existing users appears, as shown in figure 3.24.

**49**

**Figure 3.23**

A template listing appears once Add Users has been chosen.

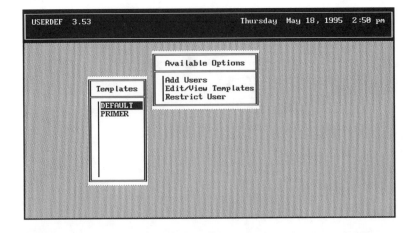

**Figure 3.24**

The list of current users.

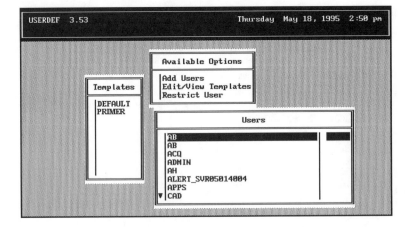

Notice that the list is in alphabetical order, as was also the case in SYSCON. NetWare automatically alphabetizes lists for you. You don't need to move anywhere in the list to add a user; simply press Insert.

**Note** If you want to delete a user, follow all the steps up to this point. Then, using the arrow keys or Page Up and Page Down, highlight the user in question. Press Delete. You are prompted as to whether you want to carry out the action. If you answer Yes, the user is deleted.

After Insert has been pressed, a box similar to that shown in figure 3.25 appears.

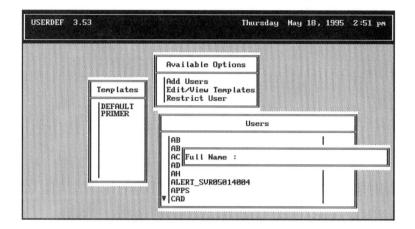

**Figure 3.25**

A box appears prompting for the name of the new user.

Enter the name of the new user, as illustrated in figure 3.26, and you are prompted to complete the transaction (see fig. 3.27). After answering Yes, the user is created.

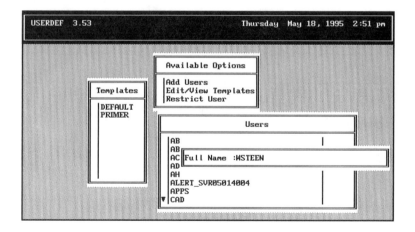

**Figure 3.26**

The name of the new user is entered.

**51**

**Figure 3.27**

Select Yes to complete the process.

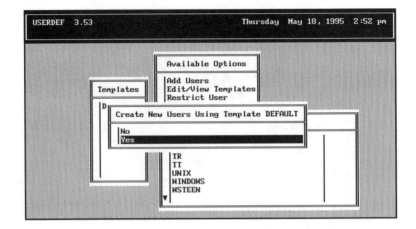

An interesting thing happens if any errors occur during the USERDEF process: the error messages refer to MAKEUSER.EXE, as illustrated in figure 3.28. This is because USERDEF is really little more than a graphical means of accessing the final utility of this chapter: MAKEUSER.

**Figure 3.28**

USERDEF error messages refer to MAKEUSER.

```
Please wait...Unable to find makeuser.exe.
Makeuser.exe must be in your path or in sys:public or sys:public\os2.
Type a return to continue. . .
```

# Understanding MAKEUSER

MAKEUSER is a command-line utility used to create and delete user accounts on a regular basis. To create and delete users, first create a USR script file containing the keywords necessary to create the user(s), assign rights, assign trustee restrictions, assign a home directory to new users, or delete existing users from the system.

You can use any ASCII text editor with USR files, but the file must be saved in ASCII format and have a USR extension. You also must process the USR file with MAKEUSER before the accounts are created or deleted.

The keywords used in a USR file to create and delete users in MAKEUSER are as follows:

```
#ACCOUNT EXPIRATION month, day, year
#ACCOUNTING balance, lowlimit
#CLEAR or #RESET
#CONNECTIONS number
#CREATE user name [option ...]
#DELETE user name
#GROUPS group
#HOME_DIRECTORY path
#LOGIN_SCRIPT path
#MAX_DISK_SPACE vol, number
#PASSWORD_LENGTH length
#PASSWORD_PERIOD days
#PASSWORD_REQUIRED
#PURGE_USER_DIRECTORY
#REM or REM
#RESTRICTED_TIME day, start, end
#STATIONS network, station
#UNIQUE_PASSWORD
```

# Real World

Practice using each of the three utilities available to add users to your system. Make minor changes to the defaults and add other users. Notice that the defaults apply to the new users only and not to those already created.

Use SYSCON to then delete all the users at one time, using the F5 key to mark them before pressing Delete.

# Summary

This chapter explores the three utilities included with NetWare that enable you to add users. Two of those utilities also enable you to delete users.

Chapter 4, "Restricting Hard Drive Space," follows in this train of thought and shows how to restrict the storage space allotted to each user. Further, Chapter 5, "All about Groups and Trustees," looks at adding and deleting groups.

# Restricting Hard Drive Space

A NetWare file system must include at least one volume (named SYS), but there can be many more. Likewise, there must be one hard drive, but there can be many more. In fact, one volume can span multiple hard drives, and one hard drive can hold multiple volumes. Regardless of which way your data is structured, you need to allocate space in the most efficient manner possible.

If you don't allocate space properly, users can potentially fill their hard drives with every GIF file they can download from an online service. If this is done, it increases your backup time, fills the storage space with unnecessary clutter, and prevents legitimate files from being stored—or forces you to purchase more hard drives.

Fortunately, storage space can be limited in a number of ways: by user, volume, or directory. Three primary utilities enable you to perform this task:

◆ SYSCON

◆ DSPACE

◆ USERDEF

This chapter explores each of these and shows methods by which storage space can be limited.

# SYSCON

The SYSCON utility enables you to limit space on a user-by-user basis per volume. You cannot use SYSCON to broaden the restriction set (say to a group) beyond that of user. You also cannot use SYSCON to limit anything (such as a directory or subdirectory) beneath the volume level.

Figure 4.1 begins the progression of steps showing how this is done. Select User Information from the menu, and then select the user in question. Next, choose the last option, Volume/Disk Restrictions, as shown in figure 4.2.

**Figure 4.1**

Selecting User Information from the main SYSCON menu.

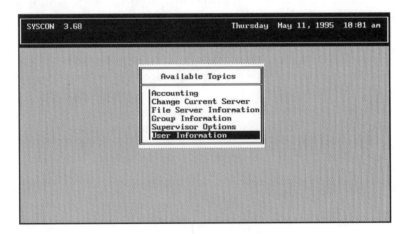

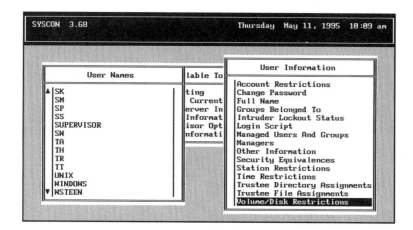

**Figure 4.2**

After choosing a user, select Volume/Disk Restrictions.

The next step in the progression is to choose a volume, as shown in figure 4.3. The default restriction, as depicted in figure 4.4, is for space to not be limited; thus, the Volume Space Limit field is blank.

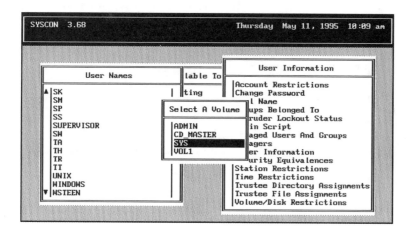

**Figure 4.3**

Select a volume to restrict.

Toggling the Limit Volume Space field to Yes enables you to establish a maximum volume space limit for the user. In figure 4.5, the user WSTEEN has been limited to 100 KB on the SYS volume. Should the user attempt to save any files beyond that limit, that user is notified that there is not enough space to do so.

**Figure 4.4**

By default, there are no restrictions.

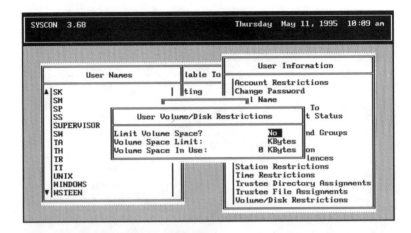

**Figure 4.5**

Setting the limitations on disk space for WSTEEN.

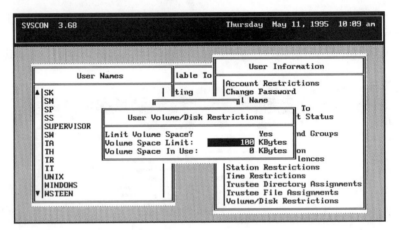

The most important thing to know about SYSCON is a fact pointed out earlier in this chapter: you cannot broaden the restriction to anything other than a user. Thus, you must go into each user's account separately and do the restriction if you want it to apply to multiple users. You cannot change the restriction to a directory, or subdirectory, as the next utility enables you to do.

# Understanding DSPACE

DSPACE has an advantage over SYSCON that becomes apparent the moment you first bring up the utility. Figure 4.6 shows the main menu, and you'll notice that a Directory Restrictions choice is on the main menu. DSPACE can go beneath the volume level offered by SYSCON and enables you to make more precise restrictions.

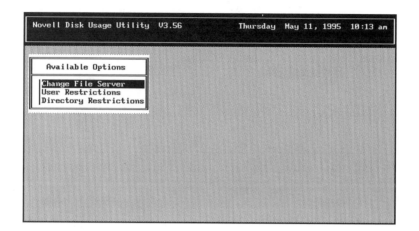

**Figure 4.6**

The main DSPACE menu.

The bad news is that you are limiting the amount of space the entire directory consumes, and not the amount of directory space used by any individual user. On a user level, the volume is the lowest common denominator that can be restricted.

Figure 4.7 illustrates the user progression, showing User Restrictions being selected from the main menu; figure 4.8 selects a user.

The next order of business is to select a volume, as shown in figures 4.9 and 4.10.

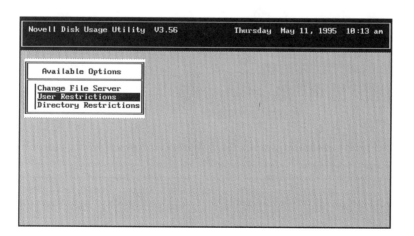

**Figure 4.7**

Choosing User Restrictions from the main DSPACE menu.

**Figure 4.8**

Select the user in question.

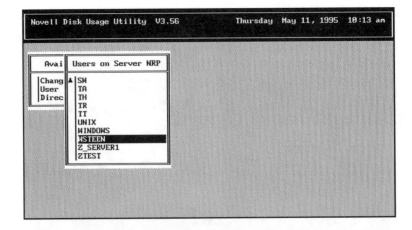

**Figure 4.9**

The list of available volumes.

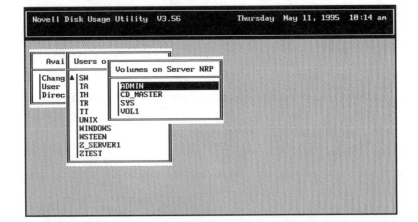

**Figure 4.10**

Selecting the VOL1 volume.

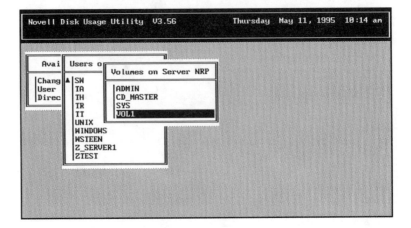

The following screen enables you to set limitations (see fig. 4.11).

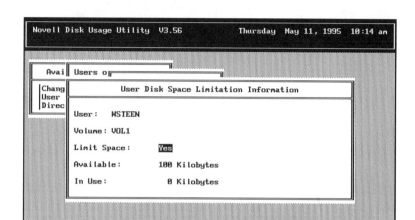

```
Novell Disk Usage Utility  V3.56          Thursday  May 11, 1995  10:14 am

    Avai  Users o
    Chang
    User        User Disk Space Limitation Information
    Direc
            User:    WSTEEN

            Volume:  VOL1

            Limit Space:        Yes

            Available:          100 Kilobytes

            In Use:               0 Kilobytes
```

**Figure 4.11**

The disk limitation options.

# Directory Restrictions

As mentioned previously, DSPACE can be used to limit the amount of space that any individual directory consumes on the volume. The default is that there are no restrictions and a directory\subdirectory (they are used interchangeably here) can span the entire volume without restriction. A set size can be set to limit this.

Figure 4.12 shows the selection of Directory Restrictions from the main DSPACE menu; figure 4.13 shows the prompt that appears next. Any directory name can be provided here, or the prompt can be left as-is to limit the volume as opposed to a directory.

Figure 4.14 shows a familiar screen in which the Limit Space field can be toggled to Yes; then, a restriction can be placed on the size the directory can expand to. After that size is met, any user attempting to save an additional file receives a message that the directory is full and that no more files can be saved until additional free space is created.

One of the most useful directories to limit is each individual's home directory. Users have a tendency to stick all files, which they want to include in the server backup, in their home directory—then forget that those files are there.

**Figure 4.12**

Selecting Directory Restrictions from the DSPACE menu.

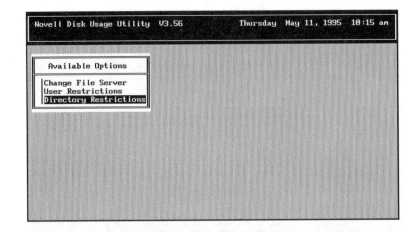

**Figure 4.13**

Enter the volume or directory\subdirectory path.

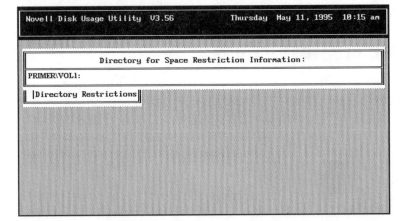

**Figure 4.14**

The restrictions available for a directory.

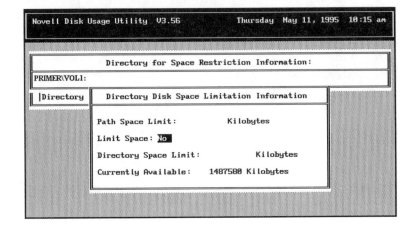

# Understanding USERDEF

The USERDEF utility works in much the same way as SYSCON, enabling you to limit the volume space available to any individual user. Figure 4.15 shows the Restrict User choice being selected from the main USERDEF menu; figure 4.16 depicts the selection of an individual user.

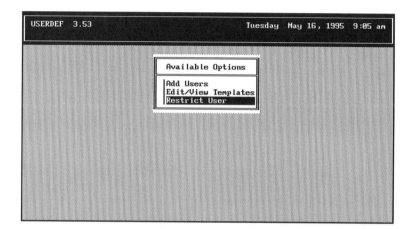

**Figure 4.15**

Choose Restrict User from the main USERDEF menu.

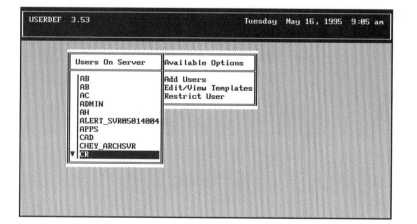

**Figure 4.16**

Choose a user.

After selecting a user, the next order of business is to choose a volume, as shown in figure 4.17, and then set the limitations (see fig. 4.18).

**Figure 4.17**

Choose a volume to limit.

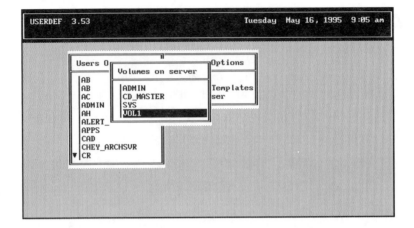

The operations, menus, and screens for USERDEF parallel those in use by SYSCON, and it shows when comparing figure 4.18 with figure 4.5.

**Figure 4.18**

Setting the volume limitations for user CR.

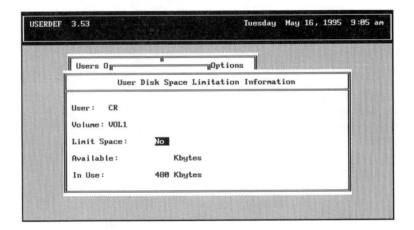

## PRACTICE EXERCISE

Using the software that came with this book, you can emulate a running network without needing access to such. Because the executable file is called PRIMER, you can execute any command by preceding it with that call. For example, if there were a command called XYZ, the command would be PRIMER XYZ.

Using this software, examine the volume restrictions for user GUEST through SYSCON.

1. Type **PRIMER SYSCON**

2. Select User Information from the main menu.

3. Select GUEST from the list of users.

4. Select Volume\Disk Restrictions from the menu.

5. View the information.

6. Press Alt+F10 to exit the utility altogether.

# Real World

Use the SYSCON utility and select yourself from the user list. Go into the volume disk restrictions and select a volume. Notice the amount of space that you presently have in use. Change your limitations to equal that of the amount of space you are currently using, then exit SYSCON.

Go into any word processor and create a document, then try to save it to the volume you have restricted. Notice the error message you get.

Exit the word processor and go back into SYSCON. Go to Volume\Disk Restrictions and remove the limit you earlier placed upon yourself.

**Note** If you restrict volume SYS and run out of space, you will not be able to print because volume SYS is where print jobs are temporarily stored.

# Summary

This chapter looks at the methods by which users and directories can be limited to the amount of storage space they consume on a volume. Three utilities enable the restrictions to be placed: SYSCON, DSPACE, and USERDEF.

Chapter 5, "All about Groups and Trustees," looks at ways of adding and deleting groups. It also talks about trustees and the concepts behind them.

# All about Groups and Trustees

Two closely related concepts within NetWare enable users to be assigned special groupings and permissions. These two concepts—groups and trustees—are the subject of this chapter. Utilizing the SYSCON utility, the chapter discusses and illustrates the various aspects of these topics.

## Adding Members to Groups

A *group* is an object containing individuals who share something in common. You can create a group of SALES, for example, and place the user ID of every salesperson within that group. You can then assign the SALES group ownership of a directory containing sales projections and estimates. Only members of the SALES group can access that directory, and it saves you the trouble of allowing each individual user access to the directory, and subdirectories, beneath it.

Figure 5.1 shows the Group Information selection from the main menu of SYSCON. Selecting this topic presents a listing of the existing groups, as shown in figure 5.2.

**Figure 5.1**

The Group Information menu choice on the SYSCON menu.

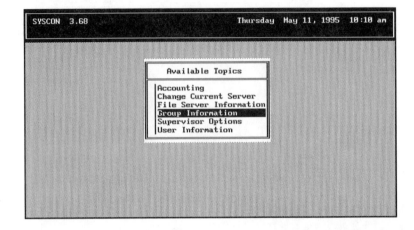

**Figure 5.2**

A listing of existing groups.

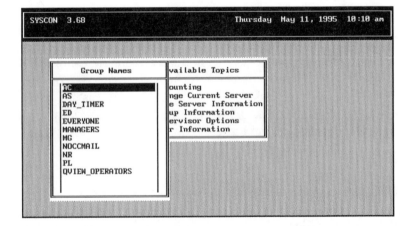

Select a group and another menu appears, as shown in figure 5.3. The Full Name field is free text, enabling you to more easily identify the group. The most important selection on the menu, for purposes of this discussion, is Member List (see figure 5.4).

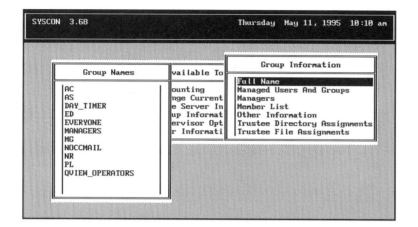

**Figure 5.3**

The main Group Information menu.

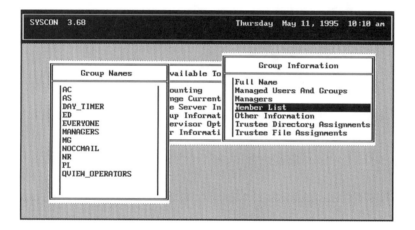

**Figure 5.4**

The Member List option.

Selecting Member List brings up an alphabetical listing of all users who are members of that group (see fig. 5.5). To make an additional user a member of that group, press Insert. A listing of those users who do not belong to the group then appears (see fig. 5.6).

**Figure 5.5**

An alphabetical listing of the current group members.

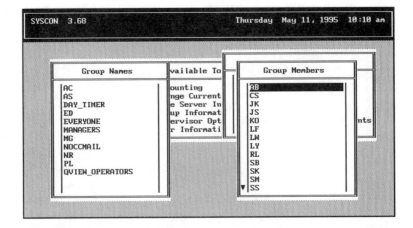

**Figure 5.6**

Users who are not in the group, as well as those who are.

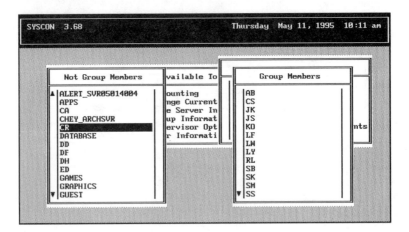

To move a user into the group, select the user's name from the list on the left and press Enter. To move multiple users at the same time, use the F5 key to mark them (F7 unmarks, should you make a mistake), then move them over.

Figure 5.7 shows that user CR has now been made a member of the group.

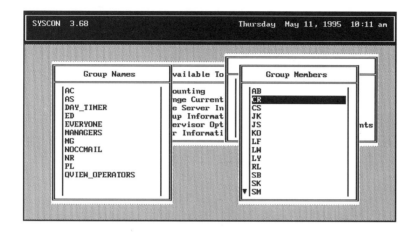

**Figure 5.7**

User CR is now a member of the group.

Using the method described here, select a group from the group list, then add one or multiple users to that group.

# Adding Members to Groups— Part II

Another means by which you can add users to groups is on an individual basis. In the scenario described in the previous section, you select the group, then choose who you want to be members of that group. In this section, you choose a user, then select what groups you want him to be a member of. Thus, the first method described can be said to be group-centric; this method is member-centric.

To perform this operation, select User Information from the main SYSCON menu, then select a user from the alphabetical user list that appears. A menu similar to that shown in figure 5.8 appears. Select Groups Belonged To.

**Figure 5.8**

Choose Groups
Belonged To from the
User Information
menu.

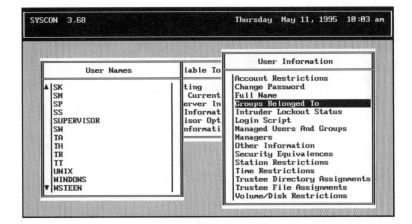

In the case of figure 5.9, the user is currently only a member of the
EVERYONE group. The next order of business is to press Insert;
those existing groups that the user is not a member of appear on
the left (see fig. 5.10).

**Figure 5.9**

The user is currently
only a member of the
EVERYONE group.

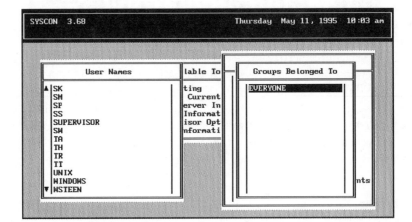

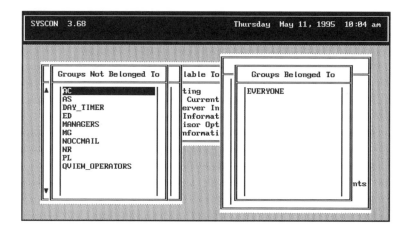

**Figure 5.10**

A list of the groups the user is not a member of appears on the left.

You can now add the user to additional groups by pressing Enter when the chosen group is highlighted; or press the F5 key to mark several groups (F7 unmarks in the event of an error) and move them over at once. Figure 5.11 shows the new groups to which this particular user was added.

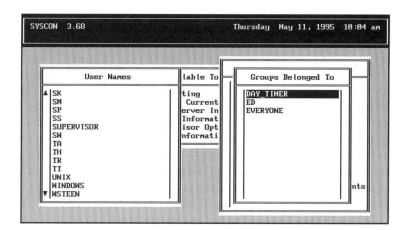

**Figure 5.11**

The user has now been added to the DAY_TIMER and ED groups.

Using the method described in this section, one individual user at a time may be added to one or more groups.

# Understanding Group Trustees

By making a group a trustee of a directory, you are granting specific rights to the members of that group. Those rights are the only rights those members have in that directory; thus, the directory can be used to reduce what rights they would have had, or to increase the rights they would have had. Those rights granted apply to that given directory, as well as to any subdirectories further buried beneath the existing one.

 **Note**  Rights are discussed in greater detail in Chapter 16, "Rights and Attributes."

Figure 5.12 shows the selection from the Group Information menu that enables you to make trustee assignments. Figure 5.13 shows the rights that are currently specified for the given group.

**Figure 5.12**

The Trustee Directory Assignments choice on the group menu.

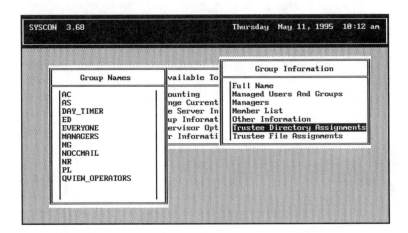

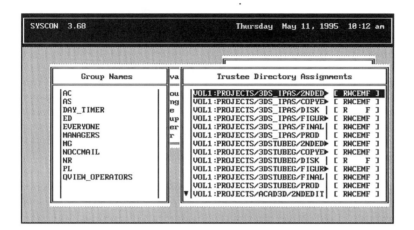

**Figure 5.13**
Current directory assignments.

To add another directory, press Insert and type in the path. The default rights given to that directory will then be R (read) and F (File Scan). These are the same rights that all newly created users are given to system directories.

To add additional rights, press Enter when the highlight is on that directory; a list of the current rights appears. Pressing Insert brings up a list of those rights that are not granted, and you can move them over one at a time by highlighting them and pressing Enter, or by marking them in mass by pressing F5.

To delete a directory from the trustee list, highlight that directory, then press Delete. After you confirm that it is indeed what you want to do, the directory is removed from the list.

# Understanding User Trustees

*User Trustees*, as the name implies, are individual users who are granted specific rights to a directory—as opposed to a conglomeration of users (group). Figure 5.14 begins the sequence of events. From the main SYSCON menu, select User Information. Then select an individual user (in this case WSTEEN), and select Trustee Directory Assignments.

**Figure 5.14**

Select Trustee
Directory
Assignments after
selecting a user.

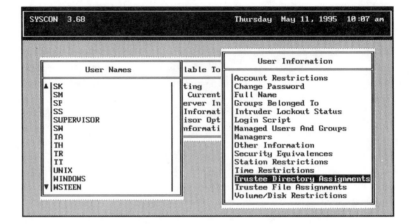

The existing trustee rights appear for that user. There should
always be a listing for the user's mail directory, and home directories appear there if you're using such a convention (see fig. 5.15).
To remove a user from trustee status of a directory, highlight that
directory and press Delete, as illustrated in figure 5.16.

**Figure 5.15**

The directories for
which the user is
presently a trustee.

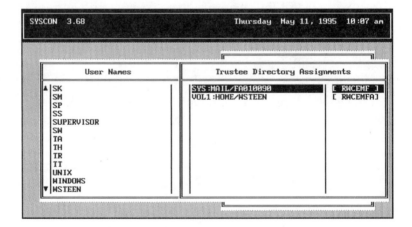

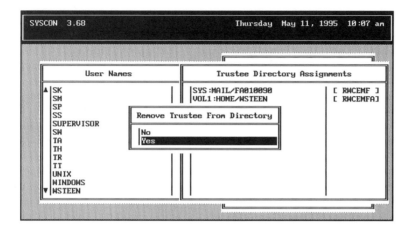

**Figure 5.16**

Removing trustee permissions for a specific directory.

To make the user a trustee of another directory, press Insert; a box similar to that shown in figure 5.17 appears. Type in the appropriate directory name and press Enter. The new directory is added to the existing list, as shown in figure 5.18.

**Note**  Remember that you are not only making the user a trustee of this directory, but also of every subdirectory beneath that directory.

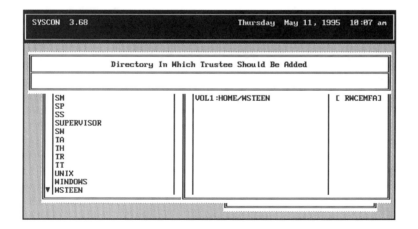

**Figure 5.17**

The prompt to enter a directory path and the specification for that path.

**Figure 5.18**

The new directory appears in the trustee list.

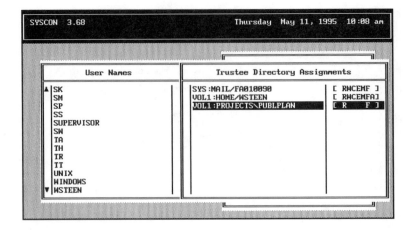

Notice that the rights assigned to the user in the new directory are R (Read) and F (File Scan). These rights are always the default right set given to any new directory—and the ones all users have to the PUBLIC and LOGIN directories, by default.

Pressing Enter when that directory is highlighted allows you to change those rights. The existing rights appear in a box on the left of the screen, as shown in figure 5.19. Pressing Insert causes a box to appear on the right, containing the rights not presently granted to the user (see fig. 5.20).

**Figure 5.19**

The rights presently granted to the user.

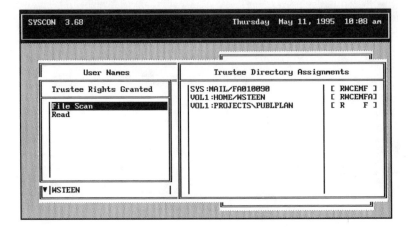

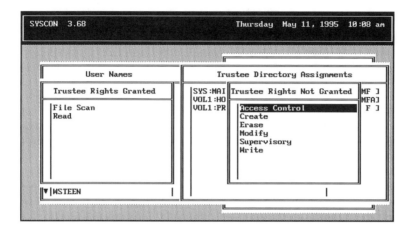

**Figure 5.20**

Rights the user does
not presently have.

Rights can be moved over one at a time by highlighting them and
pressing Enter; or you can mark them collectively by pressing F5
and then moving them over. If you accidentally grant rights you
did not mean to, highlight them from the box on the left and press
Delete.

Figure 5.21 shows the rights moving from Not Granted to
Granted, and figure 5.22 shows the resulting assignments when
Esc is pressed.

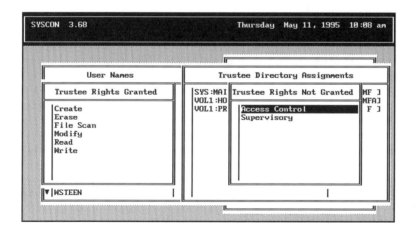

**Figure 5.21**

Rights are transferred
from Not Granted
to Granted.

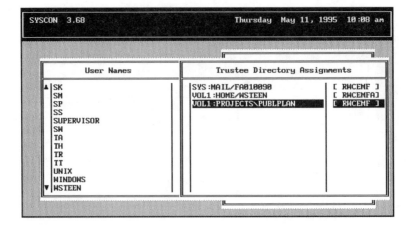

**Figure 5.22**

The right assignments
now include the
new values.

Keep in mind that trustees can be users or groups. If you want to grant a specific set of rights to hundreds of users, you can use the methodology described in this section to add the directory to their rights set, and then grant the corresponding permissions. A much easier method in such a case is to look for (or make) a group that they all are members of, and grant trustee rights to that group.

## Trustee File Assignments

Trustee File Assignments, whether on a user level or group level, work in the exact same manner as described for directories. You are assigning specific rights to that file and that file only.

# Adding and Deleting Groups

To create a new group, go into the Group Information selection from the main SYSCON menu. A listing of the existing groups appears in alphabetical order. Press Insert; the prompt shown in figure 5.23 appears. Enter the name of the new group and press Enter. You can now begin adding users to the new group.

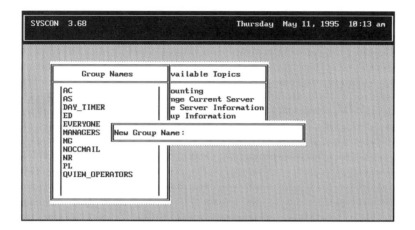

**Figure 5.23**

Pressing Insert brings
a prompt for the new
group name.

To delete a group, go into the Group Information selection from
the main SYSCON menu. Move the highlight within the alphabetical listing of existing groups to the one you want to remove and
press Delete. The confirmation box shown in figure 5.24 appears.

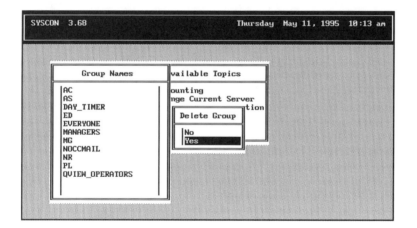

**Figure 5.24**

The confirmation box
for deleting a group.

# Other Information

Other information is available on groups from the Group Information screen. This selection, as highlighted in figure 5.25, shows the
information shown in figure 5.26. The main field of interest is
whether the group is defined as a file server console operator. If it

is, you must be very careful who you add to the group, for the group members then have unlimited access to FCONSOLE—which directly accesses key file server functions.

**Figure 5.25**

Selecting the Other Information option.

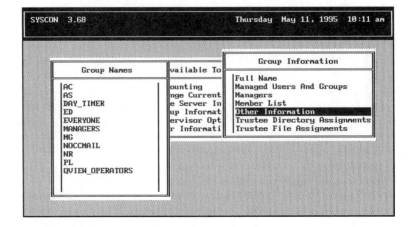

**Figure 5.26**

The other information available.

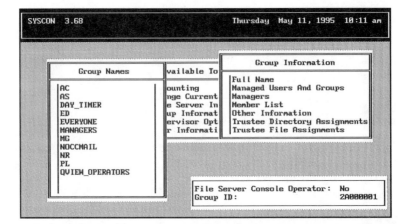

## PRACTICE EXERCISE

Using the software that comes with this book, you can emulate a running network, without needing access to one. Because the executable file is called PRIMER, you can execute any command by preceding it with that call. If there were a command called XYZ, for example, the command would be PRIMER XYZ.

Using this software, examine the volume restrictions for user trustee information and group information through SYSCON.

1. Type **PRIMER SYSCON**

2. From the main menu, select Group Information.

3. Pick the group EVERYONE.

4. Check the full name by pressing Enter at the first menu choice.

5. Press Esc.

6. Select Member List.

7. Write down members of this group. The EVERYONE group is created upon software installation and, as the name implies, all users should be members of it.

8. Check the Other Information data.

9. Is EVERYONE a file server console operator?

10. Press Esc.

11. Check the Trustee Directory Assignments.

12. Press Esc.

13. Are there any Trustee File Assignments?

14. Press Esc three times to get back to the main SYSCON menu.

15. Select User Information.

16. Select the GUEST user.

17. Select Groups Belonged To and note what they are.

18. Press Esc.

19. Check the Trustee Directory Assignments.

20. Press Esc.

21. Are there any Trustee File Assignments?

22. Press Alt+F10 to exit SYSCON altogether.

# Real World

Select a server directory at random and use it to conduct some tests of an indestructive nature. Go into the Group Information choice from the main SYSCON menu and press Insert. Create a group called TEST. Add yourself and several other users to that group. Next, go into Trustee Directory Assignments and assign TEST as a trustee of the arbitrarily selected directory. Exit SYSCON and go into that directory; type **RIGHTS**. You should have R (Read) and F (File Scan) only. Move back one directory (to the parent) of the current directory and type **RIGHTS**.

You probably have more rights here than you do in the child directory. The child directory would have inherited the rights for you of the parent, had you not restricted yourself by making TEST a trustee. Now, go back into SYSCON and Trustee Directory Assignments and grant all but S (Supervisor) and A (Access Control) rights to that arbitrary directory. Exit SYSCON and go to that directory. Type **RIGHTS**. You should now have all the specified rights to that directory.

In other words, you first limited yourself from what you would have had, then expanded your rights beyond what you would have had. Trustee assignments work both ways.

# Summary

This chapter examines two concepts crucial to effective NetWare administration: groups and trustees. Using these concepts effectively can save you a tremendous amount of time and energy in the administrative process, plus they can enable you to effectively secure your system, and govern rights granted to sets of users.

Chapter 6, "Security and Passwords," follows the train of thought created here and specifically details security. The chapter discusses methods of changing passwords, as well as detecting intruders. Further discussions center on one utility that every supervisor needs to know about—the wonderful SECURITY utility.

**6**

**CHAPTER**

# Security and Passwords

The most valuable single piece of information your business owns is its data. A conundrum occurs because that data must be available to everyone who needs access to it, yet it must be secured and hidden from everyone who should not have access to it.

Companies routinely place deadbolts on their front doors, install card scanners at interior doors, and run wiring for after-hour security systems and silent alarms. Yet those same companies (or rather, the managers of those companies) become upset when they have to enter complex passwords to gain entry into their network. Managers don't mind locking their front doors, but they do mind guarding their most valuable possession. That's because they can see and touch a metal door, but can't see and touch their data—and that can generate a false sense of security if they feel the data is inaccessible.

You guard a physical entry with a lock. The way you guard data entry is with a *password*. Passwords and security have gone hand in hand since the beginning of electronic data. This chapter examines the utilities used to govern such, and focuses primarily on the following three:

◆ SYSCON

◆ SECURITY

◆ SETPASS

# Understanding Intruder Detection

To NetWare, an *intruder* is a person who attempts to log in using an invalid login id and password combination. A valid user might be mistaken for an intruder for several reasons, including the following:

◆ Forgotten password

◆ Mistyped password

◆ Mistyped login ID

For the most part, however, legitimate users should not be mistaken for intruders.

When an outsider attempts to break in to a network, that individual usually tries to ascertain the user ID of a person known to the network. They then set about attempting to guess (or *crack*) that password. Within NetWare, there's no method of catching an invalid ID, because the intruder could easily be a legitimate user who mistyped it. You can, however catch invalid passwords.

Figure 6.1 shows the Supervisor Options available from the SYSCON menu. Figure 6.2 shows the options available after Intruder Detection/Lockout has been chosen from that menu.

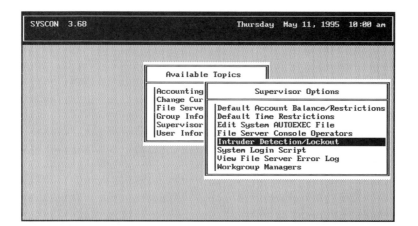

**Figure 6.1**

Select Intruder
Detection/Lockout
from the Supervisor
Options menu.

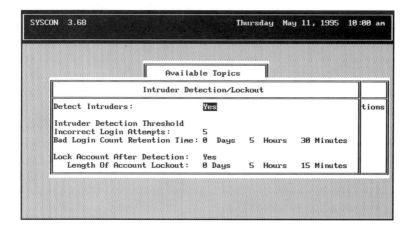

**Figure 6.2**

The variables that can
be applied to the
system.

The first field includes a Yes or No toggle, determining whether
you want to catch intruders. There should never be a system that
does not have this field turned on.

The second field is the number of incorrect passwords a user is
allowed to provide before that user is considered an intruder. The
third field is the amount of time in which to keep track of the
number of attempts. According to figure 6.2, the user can provide
five incorrect passwords within five-and-a-half hours before he or
she is considered an intruder.

The next fields determine what should be done after the user has been classified as an intruder. Here, the account is locked (not allowing login) for a time period of five hours and fifteen minutes.

After the account has been locked, the user has two options:

◆ Wait for the lock time to expire.

◆ Inform the supervisor.

The supervisor can override the lock by going into the User Information options of SYSCON (see fig. 6.3). From there, select the user from the alphabetic list, and select Intruder Lockout Status, as shown in figure 6.4.

A status box, such as that shown in figure 6.5, appears.

**Figure 6.3**

Select User Information from the SYSCON menu.

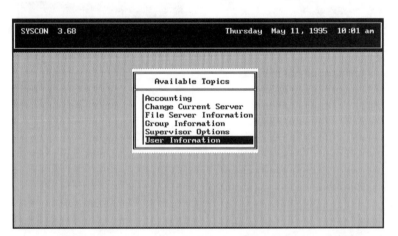

**Figure 6.4**

After selecting the user, select Intruder Lockout Status.

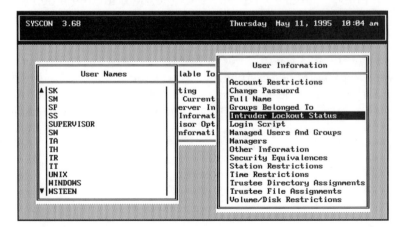

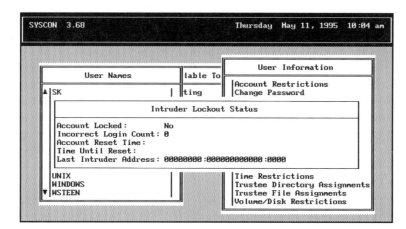

**Figure 6.5**

The Intruder Lockout Status box.

If the account is locked, the first field indicates that information. By pressing Y, the supervisor can enable the account for login once more. The supervisor also can see the number of failed attempts and when the account would have been reset. Most important, however, is the last field, which shows the physical address from where the login attempts were coming. If someone is attempting to break in to your system, it pays to know where he or she is attempting to do so.

## Grace Logins

*Grace logins* are the number of times a user is allowed to log in after a password has expired. This number is defined on a system level under the Supervisor Options—Default Account Balances. Figure 6.6 shows an example of the message that comes up during the login process.

**Figure 6.6**

The password has expired, and the user has five grace logins.

```
C:\>f:

F:\LOGIN>login wsteen
Enter your password:


You are attached to server PRIMER


Now executing your personal login script.

Password for user WSTEEN has expired.
    You have 5 grace login(s) left to change your password.
Would you like to change your password? (Y/N) Y
```

Setting this number too high is risky, because it offers no incentive for a user to immediately change passwords if a high number of grace logins remain. Setting the number too low causes a problem if the user waits too long to change it.

 **Note**

A number of NetWare tools, which are available from third-party vendors, wrap around the shell and run additional checks. One of these checks is during the login process.

Tools available from Saber, for example, are notorious for using multiple logins (two) during one login. If you use the Saber login routine and set the number of grace periods to two, it automatically uses them both on the first expired login.

A good rule of thumb is to keep the number of grace logins to between 3 and 6.

# Understanding the File Server Console Operators

One topic that is addressed in Chapter 2, "Supervisor Parameters," merits another discussion when it comes to security.

Figure 6.7 shows the File Server Console Operators option from the Supervisor Options menu of SYSCON.

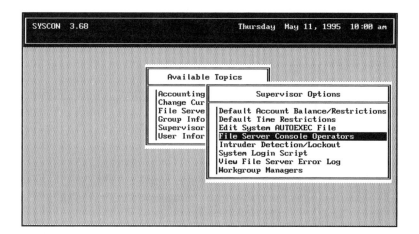

**Figure 6.7**

File Server Console Operators are defined from the SYSCON menu.

Anyone defined as an operator has the ability to sit at a workstation terminal and run FCONSOLE. FCONSOLE is the most dangerous utility that can be executed from a workstation because it contains such menu choices as downing the file server. For that reason, the number of operators should be kept to a bare minimum, as depicted in figure 6.8.

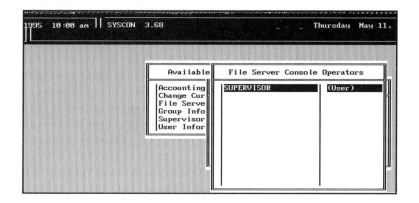

**Figure 6.8**

The only File Server Console Operator should be the supervisor.

# Changing Passwords

An individual user can change a password in one of two ways:

◆ With the SETPASS command-line utility

◆ With SYSCON

The supervisor, or a supervisor-equivalent user, can change a password with SYSCON. Figure 6.9 shows the Change Password option on the User Information menu that appears after a user has been selected from the list.

**Figure 6.9**

The Change Password option from the User Information menu.

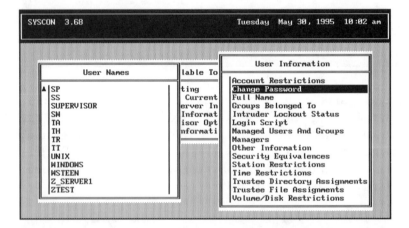

```
SYSCON  3.68                          Tuesday  May 30, 1995  10:02 am


           ┌──────────────────┐  ┌─────────────────────────────────┐
           │    User Names     │lable To│        User Information    │
           │                   │     ├─────────────────────────────────┤
           │▲│SP               │ting   │ Account Restrictions        │
           │ │SS               │  Current│Change Password            │
           │ │SUPERVISOR       │erver In│ Full Name                  │
           │ │SW               │Informat│ Groups Belonged To         │
           │ │TA               │isor Opt│ Intruder Lockout Status    │
           │ │TH               │nformati│ Login Script               │
           │ │TR               │        │ Managed Users And Groups   │
           │ │TT               │        │ Managers                   │
           │ │UNIX             │        │ Other Information          │
           │ │WINDOWS          │        │ Security Equivalences      │
           │ │WSTEEN           │        │ Station Restrictions       │
           │ │Z_SERVER1        │        │ Time Restrictions          │
           │ │ZTEST            │        │ Trustee Directory Assignments│
           └──────────────────┘        │ Trustee File Assignments   │
                                        │ Volume/Disk Restrictions   │
                                        └─────────────────────────────────┘
```

After you select this option, a prompt appears for a new password, as shown in figure 6.10. After entering the new password, another prompt appears, as shown in figure 6.11. The user, or supervisor, must enter the same password the same way both times. If the two entries don't match, the password is not changed, and the old value remains.

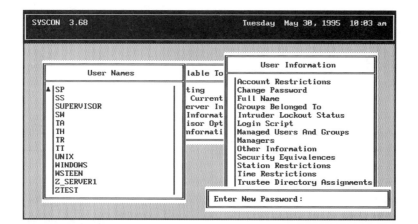

**Figure 6.10**

The new password must be entered.

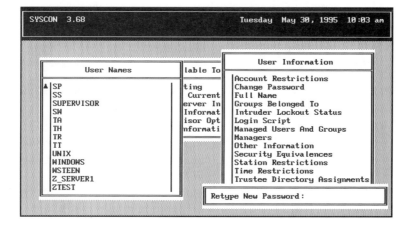

**Figure 6.11**

The password must be entered accurately a second time.

NetWare is not case-sensitive. You, therefore, have only 26 alphabetic characters from which to choose. (Numeric and punctuation characters also can be used.) This is different from many operating systems, such as Unix, where upper- and lowercase characters are distinct. In NetWare, GOOFBALL and Goofball count as the same entry; in Unix, they don't.

If a user changes a password in this fashion, the new password is in effect until it expires again. If a supervisor changes a user's password, the system allows the user to log in, but tells the user that he or she is now using up grace periods and should change the password immediately. Passwords should not be known by anyone other than the user who establishes them—not even the supervisor.

Within NetWare, passwords reside in the *bindery*—an encrypted database available only to the system. You can further choose whether passwords should be *encrypted* before being sent down the wire for login purposes. If they're encrypted, they're much harder to catch using a *sniffer*—a device used by hackers to catch passwords. Encryption delays the login process by a few micro-seconds because the password must be decrypted before being checked for validity.

To use encryption on the wire, include the following code:

```
SET ALLOW UNENCRYPTED PASSWORDS=OFF
```

in the AUTOEXEC.NCF file on the server.

Conversely, to not use encryption, use the following code:

```
SET ALLOW UNENCRYPTED PASSWORDS=ON
```

## SETPASS

SETPASS is a command-line utility that enables an individual user to change a password. The syntax of this capability follows:

```
SETPASS {servername} {options}
```

*Servername* is the name of the file server that stores the password, and *options* can be one of the following:

◆ **/?.** To view online help.

◆ **/VER.** To display version and related-files information.

**Note** If you're attached to multiple servers when you change your password, and the user names and the passwords are the same, SETPASS asks if you'd like to synchronize your passwords. Responding Yes updates all the attached servers with your new password.

# Understanding Security Equivalences

Security equivalences enable one user to have the same *rights* (to certain information) as another user; meaning, there are multiple ways for a user to have access to an option or data, as follows:

1. As the user

2. As a member of a group

3. As an equivalent to another user who has specific rights

Figure 6.12 shows where equivalences are defined in the SYSCON menu. They are granted on a user-by-user basis; thus, you first select User Information from the main menu, then select a user, and finally, select Security Equivalences.

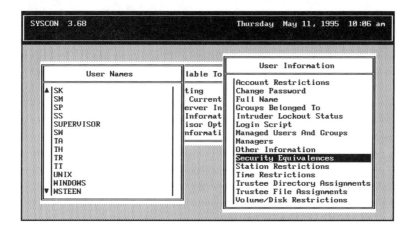

**Figure 6.12**

The Security Equivalences option of the User Information menu.

95

In figure 6.13, the chosen user is *equivalent* to (has the same rights as) the groups to which the user belongs. In this case, the user is a member of three groups and has the same rights as those three groups.

**Figure 6.13**

The user is equivalent to the groups to which that user belongs.

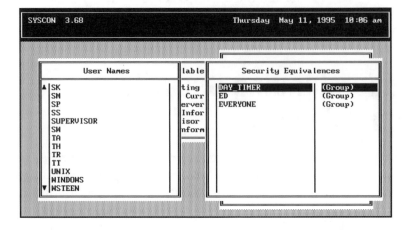

Figure 6.14 is another story. According to this figure, the user is equivalent to the groups to which he or she belongs and equivalent to the supervisor user. Thus, a user can be equivalent to anything—a group or another user. The apparent danger in figure 6.14 should be obvious, and such equivalency should only be applied to the user who backs up the regular supervisor.

**Figure 6.14**

The user is also equivalent to the supervisor.

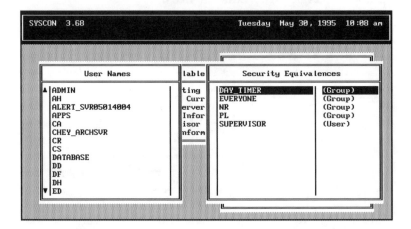

# Managing Security

The command-line utility SECURITY displays a list of possible
security problems. This list can include users, passwords, login
scripts, and access privileges. The syntax for it follows:

`SECURITY {/C}`

/C causes the generated list to continuously display without
prompting for a key press at the end of every screen page.

 To use the SECURITY program, you must log in as
the supervisor or as a supervisor equivalent. The
SECURITY program is run from the SYS:SYSTEM
directory.

Figure 6.15 shows an example of the output generated by
SECURITY. The first listing, of which the top line was chopped
off to fit on the screen, shows a blatant violation of every security practice imaginable. A user is equivalent to the supervisor,
yet that user isn't required to have a password.

```
     Is security equivalent to user SUPERVISOR
     Has incorrect access security on the SECURITY_EQUALS property
     Does not require a password

User GAMES
   Has no login script
   Account has not been used for more than 3 weeks
     Last Login: Thursday  August 5, 1993  1:55 pm
   Does not require a password
   No Full Name specified


Group EVERYONE
   No Full Name specified


User SUPERVISOR (Full Name: .System Supervisor)
   Is not required to change passwords periodically


C:\>
```

**Figure 6.15**

Sample output from
the SECURITY
command.

---

**PRACTICE EXERCISE**

Using the software that comes with this book, you can emulate a running network without needing access to one. Because the .EXE file is called PRIMER.EXE, you can execute any command by preceding it with that call. For the command XYZ, for example, the command you type is **PRIMER XYZ**.

Using this software, examine the security components of the system available through SYSCON:

1. Type **PRIMER SYSCON**

2. Select Supervisor Options.

3. Select Intruder Detection/Lockout.

4. Write down the values you see.

5. Press Esc.

6. From the main SYSCON menu, select User Information.

7. Select the guest user.

8. Select Intruder Lockout Status.

9. Note the information presented.

10. Press Alt+F10 to exit SYSCON.

11. Type **PRIMER SECURITY**

12. Are there any holes here?

# Real World

Run the SECURITY utility on your system. Look for loopholes and leaks that could be easily exploited by someone attempting to break in to your system.

Remember that the way a hacker works is by using a known user ID and attempting to crack the user's password. Every copy of NetWare 3.x installed on a server automatically creates two users: GUEST and SUPERVISOR. If a hacker attempts to break in to a system, the hacker would automatically know two login IDs.

Make *very* certain those two are safely guarded.

Sniffers enable hackers to see packets that are sent down the wire. During the login procedure, they can see a workstation attempting to log in and gather information. If the command the user provides is LOGIN, then LOGIN shows up on the sniffer. The user is then asked for a login ID, which is transmitted across the wire encrypted (under most cases) and is somewhat difficult to interpret. If the user, however, adds the line LOGIN WSTEEN to the AUTOEXEC.BAT file, then LOGIN WSTEEN is what gets transmitted across the wire and the login ID is easily picked up by the sniffer. Encourage your users to include a LOGIN line in their AUTOEXEC.BAT files, but not to include their ID. (By the same token, just sitting at a user's terminal and viewing AUTOEXEC.BAT triggers a security violation if I'm a hacker.)

Encourage your users to also use some degree of intellect when choosing passwords. Passwords shouldn't be easily guessed entities. Further, they should not be so difficult that they're written on a note and attached to the underside of the keyboard.

Use SYSCON and view your intruder-detection variables. Determine whether they're as stringent as they should be, and make any changes deemed necessary.

# Summary

This chapter examines security and passwords and the way they interact with each other. The following chapter examines this concept in greater detail, looking at time restrictions and station restrictions.

**7**

**CHAPTER**

# Restricting Login Times and Stations

When it comes to NetWare and security, one of the most simple topics of all is that of restricting the times when users are allowed in to the system—and the workstations from which they're allowed to log in. In fact, the concept is so simple that it's quite often the most misunderstood and overlooked component of all.

This chapter explores those topics, and you are highly encouraged to review the material—regardless of how well you think you might know it.

## Using Default Login Times

The default login times is a template assigned to all newly created users. To access it, go into the SYSCON utility and select Supervisor Options. From there, select Default Time Restrictions, as shown in figure 7.1.

Figure 7.2 shows an example of what appears. Asterisks all the way across indicate that users are allowed to log in around the clock. Removing asterisks keeps them from logging in during that time period. Each asterisk equals 30 minutes.

**Figure 7.1**

From the Supervisor Options of SYSCON, select Default Time Restrictions.

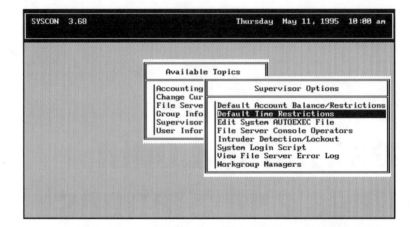

**Figure 7.2**

Each asterisk represents 30 minutes of granted login time.

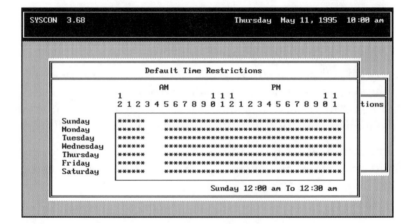

 **Note** Many beginning administrators mistakenly think that Default Time Restrictions limits the server to availability during the specified times. It does not. The server is available 24 hours a day. Default Time Restrictions limits specific (newly created) users to the time they are allowed to log in.

Use the spacebar to remove asterisks and keep the user from logging in at specified times. The template shown in figure 7.2 is very poor. Although it's better than the default of 24-hour access, no new user should be given that much access (22 1/2 hours) to the network.

# Understanding User Time Restrictions

After a user is created, that user inherits the default time restrictions described in the preceding section. To access a user's individual restrictions, select User Information from the main SYSCON menu, then Time Restrictions, as shown in figure 7.3.

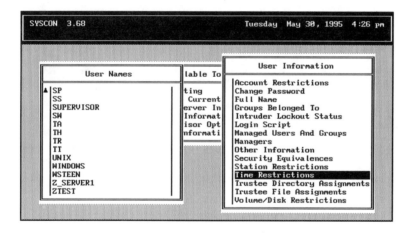

**Figure 7.3**

Select Time Restrictions from the User Information menu of SYSCON.

Figure 7.4 shows that a newly created user inherited the restrictions assigned as the system template. Any user who was created before the template was changed, however, has that old template as his restriction (see fig. 7.5). Remember that GUEST and SUPERVISOR were automatically created by the installation process; thus, they inherited the system default restriction of none. This is a security concern, particularly with GUEST, that you should never let go unchanged.

**Figure 7.4**

The allowed login times for a newly created user.

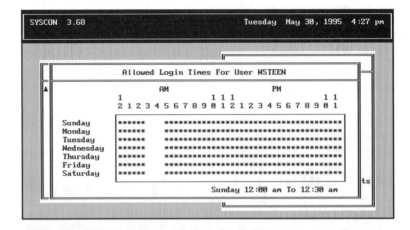

**Figure 7.5**

The allowed login times for user GUEST.

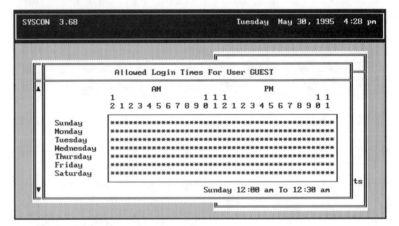

The restrictions prevent users from logging in during the times when they shouldn't. If they're already logged in, however, they first receive a warning message at the expiration time. This enables them to close files and exit in an orderly manner. If they don't log out, a watchdog process gives them an additional five minutes to exit.

Should that five-minute grace period expire without their logging out, the connection is closed, and an entry is made in the server error log:

```
6/1/95 3:08:10 am  Severity = 4.
1.1.120 User WSTEEN at station 16 connection terminated
User did not logout within 5 minutes after security watchdog notice
```

Quite often, this error log entry indicates a user who walks away from the machine without bothering—or forgetting—to log out. From an administrative standpoint, however, it pays to monitor the error log and see who's accessing the system beyond the times designated for them to do so.

 **Note** Time restrictions apply only on a user-to-user basis. You can't make a restriction apply to a group of users, or to the system itself. If you want to restrict the system, you must clear the connections, then disable logins.

# Understanding Station Restrictions

Station restrictions, like time restrictions, are applied on a user-by-user basis. You can't broaden the restriction to any level other than user (group, for example).

To access this function, select Station Restrictions from the User Information menu of SYSCON, as shown in figure 7.6. The allowed physical login addresses appears, as shown in figure 7.7.

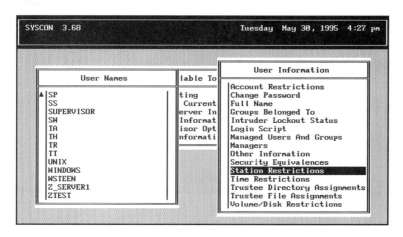

**Figure 7.6**

After selecting a user, select Station Restrictions.

**Figure 7.7**

The Allowed Login Addresses list box.

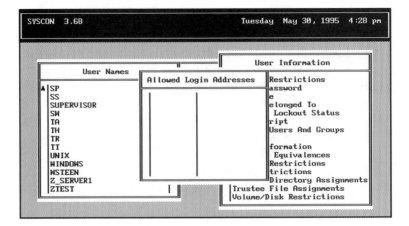

If nothing is shown in the box—contrary to what the name implies—the user is allowed to log in anywhere. If an entry appears in the box, the user is only allowed to log in from that particular address.

Traditionally, user SUPERVISOR must be able to go anywhere and troubleshoot the system, so that user is not a good candidate for confining login addresses. User GUEST, however, should be someone visiting the site for a short time—not meriting his or her own login. In this case, there's usually one machine set aside for the individual to use, and that should be the only location the user can log in from.

To create an address restriction, press Insert. A Network Address box appears, as shown in figure 7.8. Enter the physical address then press Enter. The restriction now applies, as shown in figure 7.9.

**Figure 7.8**

The prompt for an address appears when Insert is pressed.

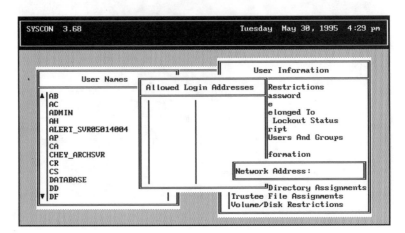

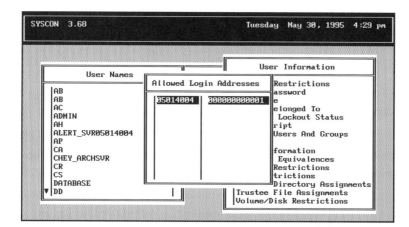

**Figure 7.9**

The given restriction now applies.

## PRACTICE EXERCISE

Using the software that comes with this book, you can emulate a running network without needing access to one. Because the .EXE file is called PRIMER.EXE, you can execute any command by preceding it with that call. For the command XYZ, for example, the command you type is **PRIMER XYZ**.

Using this software, examine the security components of the system available through SYSCON:

1. Type **PRIMER SYSCON**

2. Select Supervisor Options.

3. Select Default Time Restrictions.

4. Make a mental note of the values you see.

5. Press Esc twice to get back to the main menu.

6. From the main SYSCON menu, select User Information.

7. Select the GUEST user.

8. Select Time Restrictions. Notice how the time differs from the default because the GUEST and SUPERVISOR users are created before defaults become active.

9. Press Esc, then choose the GUEST user again and Station Restrictions. There are none. The user can log in from any workstation on the network.

10. Press Alt+F10 to exit SYSCON.

# Real World

Look at the default time restrictions applicable for newly created users. Are they as stringent as they should be? Is there value in allowing new users to log in at three o'clock in the morning, or does it represent a security risk?

Look at the station restrictions for individual users and see if there are any. In not restricting them to the physical network, you're allowing them to log in from virtually everywhere in the world.

# Summary

This chapter examines the restrictions on login times and stations. Chapter 8 examines mapping.

**8**

**CHAPTER**

# Mapping

Maps are to NetWare what paths are to DOS. Maps are pointers to drives where executable programs are found. If a drive has no map, the only way to execute programs within that drive is to actually be in that drive, or to give the full path, pointing to the executable (directories, subdirectories, and so on).

There are a maximum of 26 drive mappings available to any user, 16 of which can be search mappings. Search maps are created from the end of the alphabet in a descending order. The drive letter assigned to the search map is also added to the DOS environment variable PATH; regular map drive letters are not.

Mapped drives can be created, changed, and deleted in one of two ways:

◆ With the MAP command

◆ With the SESSION utility

This chapter looks at both methods.

# Using the MAP Command

The MAP command can list, change, or create drive mappings. When issued without parameters, MAP displays the current drive mappings. When attempting to map a drive to a specified path, the path named, naturally, must exist.

 **Note** You must be attached to at least one file server before you can map drives to it.

Options that can be used with MAP include the following:

♦ **INSert.** Enables you to change the order maps are searched by inserting a new search map between two existing search mappings.

♦ **DELete.** Deletes a drive mapping.

♦ **REMove.** Deletes a drive mapping.

♦ **Next.** Maps next available drive letter to the specified path.

♦ **ROOT.** Maps the drive as fake root (useful for Windows applications).

♦ **drive.** Represents the drive letter mapped to the directory you want to work with.

♦ **path.** Represents the directory path you intend to work with.

♦ **Change.** Represents a toggle that enables you to change a drive mapping from search to a regular map or vice versa.

♦ **Physical.** Maps to physical volume; must be used as the first or second option.

♦ **No Prompt.** MAP will not prompt when overwriting search or local drives; must be placed first or second on the command line.

♦ **/Ver.** Displays version information for this utility, and lists the files it needs in order to run.

To see a list of your current maps, enter the MAP command without parameters. A display similar to the following appears:

```
Drive   A:   maps to a local disk.
Drive   B:   maps to a local disk.
Drive   C:   maps to a local disk.
Drive   D:   maps to a local disk.
Drive   E:   maps to a local disk.
Drive   F: = PRIMER\SYS:  \LOGIN
Drive   H: = PRIMER\VOL1:HOME\WSTEEN   \
Drive   I: = PRIMER\VOL1:APPS\DTORG   \
Drive   P: = PRIMER\VOL1:PROJECTS   \
Drive   S: = PRIMER\VOL1:SCHEDULE   \
Drive   V: = MP-MAIL2\SYS:  \CCMAIL
          - - - - - - - - - -
SEARCH1:  = Z:. [PRIMER\SYS:   \PUBLIC]
SEARCH2:  = Y:. [PRIMER\SYS:   \MHS\EXE]
SEARCH3:  = X:. [PRIMER\VOL1:   \APPS\EXCEL]
SEARCH4:  = C:\NWCLIENT
SEARCH5:  = C:\NETWORK\WINSOCK
SEARCH6:  = C:\PB3
SEARCH7:  = C:\WINDOWS
SEARCH8:  = C:\DOS
SEARCH9:  = C:\PROGRAMS\WIN
```

To map a fake root for applications (such as Windows applications) that write files to—or create directories from—the root directory, type the following:

**MAP ROOT H:=SYS:WSTEEN**

A space that appears between the end of the path and the last slash of a MAP listing indicates that it is a fake root drive.

From a fake root, you cannot use the DOS CD (change directory) command to return to the original root directory. To change to the original root, you must remap the drive. Or you can type the CD command and reference the volume level.

To map an additional search drive, type the following:

**MAP S16:=SYS:APPS\JUNK**

Only 16 drive letters are available for search drives. Thus, by typing **S16:**, regardless of how many already exist, you automatically assign it to the next available search-drive position.

The MAP command accepts forward slashes (/) or backslashes (\) as part of the path. To maintain consistency with DOS, however, you should use only backslashes (\) in the path designation.

 If a valid DOS drive is used in the MAP command, the user is asked to verify overwriting the drive assignment. To regain access to the local drive, use MAP DEL *driveletter*, where *driveletter* is the local disk's identifier.

# Understanding SESSION

SESSION can be thought of as a graphical representation of MAP. It enables users to do a number of tasks, including all of the following:

- ◆ Perform file server selection- and drive mapping-related tasks.

- ◆ Change file servers.

- ◆ View groups.

- ◆ Send messages to groups or users.

- ◆ Choose a default drive.

- ◆ Change (temporarily) your drive mappings and search mappings.

- ◆ List user information.

# Understanding Drive Mappings

The second menu choice on the SESSION menu—shown in figure 8.1—is that of Drive Mappings. Selecting this option lists your existing maps, as shown in figure 8.2.

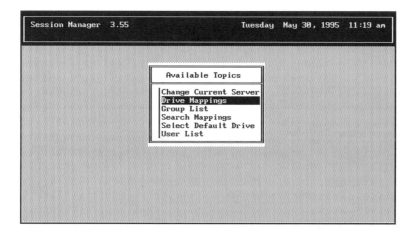

**Figure 8.1**

The main SESSION menu.

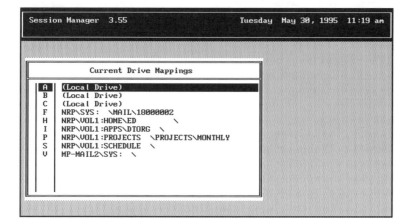

**Figure 8.2**

The current drive mappings.

## Deleting Existing Drives

To delete an existing drive, highlight it within the list and press Delete. A confirmation box, as illustrated in figure 8.3, appears. From here, you can delete any NetWare mapping, although you cannot delete local drives (see fig. 8.4).

**Figure 8.3**

Selecting Yes allows you to remove an existing map.

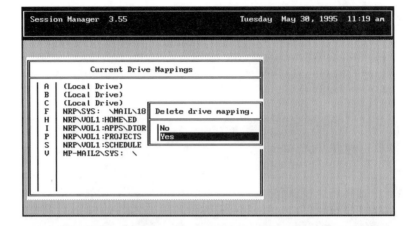

**Figure 8.4**

You cannot delete local drives.

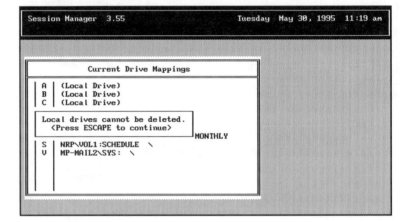

## Creating New Drives

To add an additional mapping to this list, press the Insert key. A box indicating the next available logical drive mapping appears (see fig. 8.5). You can change the drive designation letter, or accept it by pressing Enter. A prompt box, as shown in figure 8.6, appears. You can type the location of the directory for the drive mapping, or press Enter to see a list of available servers (if you have multiple servers). If the correct server is not in the list, press the Insert key; otherwise, select the server.

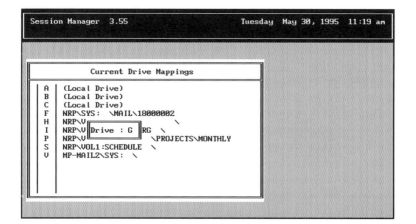

**Figure 8.5**

Pressing Insert creates a new mapping.

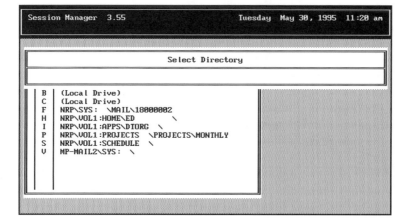

**Figure 8.6**

A prompt for the path appears.

Select the server, volume, and directory by highlighting the appropriate option and pressing Enter. Or, type in your entry, as shown in figure 8.7. Next, you can choose whether this should be a root drive, as shown in figure 8.8. (MAP ROOT enables you to simulate a root directory anywhere in the path, rather than just at the volume level.) If you select Yes, the drive mapping is added to your list of current drive mappings.

**Figure 8.7**

Enter the path the new drive will be.

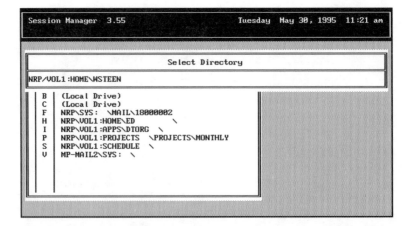

**Figure 8.8**

Choose whether the mapped drive should be a root drive.

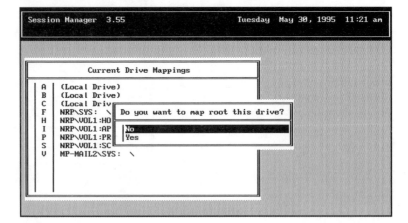

# Using Search Drives

Search drives are shown separately from regular mapped drives in SESSION, and are displayed from the fourth menu choice, as shown in figure 8.9.

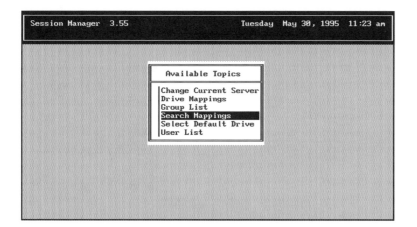

**Figure 8.9**

The Search Mappings option.

Choosing this option displays a list of your current search-drive mappings (see fig. 8.10). To add an additional search mapping to this list, press Insert. A box indicating the next available search drive appears, as shown in figure 8.11. You can change the drive designation number to the number of your choice, or accept it by pressing Enter. A box then appears asking you to type the location of the directory for the search-drive mapping.

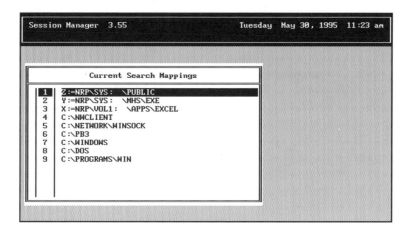

**Figure 8.10**

The existing search drives.

**Figure 8.11**

Pressing Insert
enables you to create
another search drive.

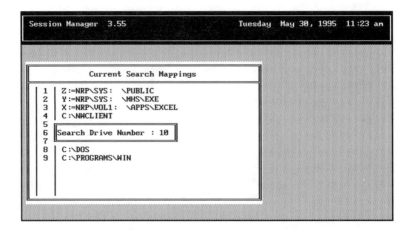

After selecting a server, you can designate the volume and directory by highlighting the correct option and pressing Enter. Optionally, you can enter the full path, as shown in figure 8.12, which then adds it to the list, as shown in Figure 8.13.

**Figure 8.12**

Enter the path for the
new search drive.

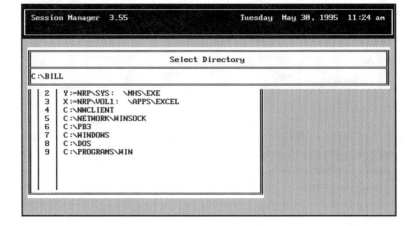

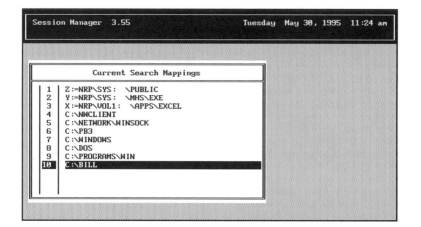

**Figure 8.13**

The newly created drive is added to the list.

To see the effective rights for a directory, press Enter and the rights are displayed (see fig. 8.14). You cannot view effective rights for anything other than NetWare drives, however, even though they appear in the list (see fig. 8.15).

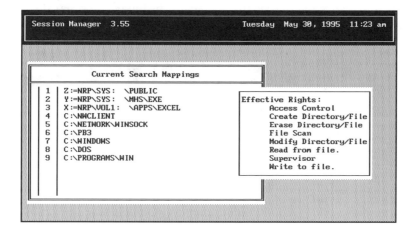

**Figure 8.14**

The effective rights for the directory

**Figure 8.15**

Effective rights exist only for NetWare drives.

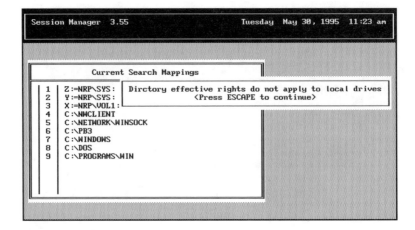

## Deleting a Search Drive

To delete a search-drive mapping, highlight the appropriate search-drive designation number and press Delete. A confirmation box appears (see fig. 8.16). You cannot delete the default drive or drives that are local, as shown in figure 8.17.

**Figure 8.16**

A confirmation box appears on all deletions.

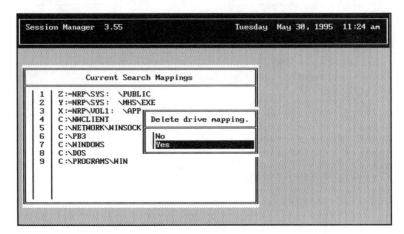

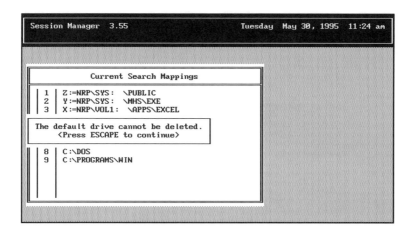

**Figure 8.17**

You cannot delete local drives.

# Select Default Drive

Choosing Select Default Drive from SESSION's main menu (see fig. 8.18) activates a window that has all the current drive mappings, including the local drives (see fig. 8.19). Highlighting the NetWare drive designations and pressing Enter makes that drive your default drive.

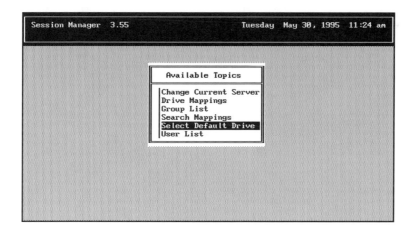

**Figure 8.18**

The Select Default Drive option from SESSION.

**Figure 8.19**

The drives available to be defaults.

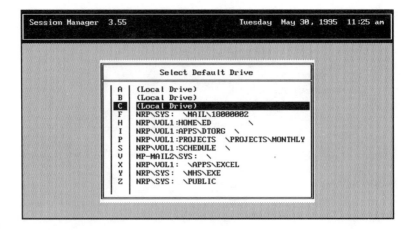

## User List

Selecting User List from SESSION's main menu (see fig. 8.20) provides you with a list of users who are currently logged in to the file server, as shown in figure 8.21. If a user is listed more than once, that user has logged in to the server from two different workstations.

**Figure 8.20**

The User List option from SESSION.

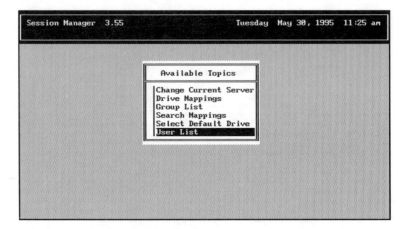

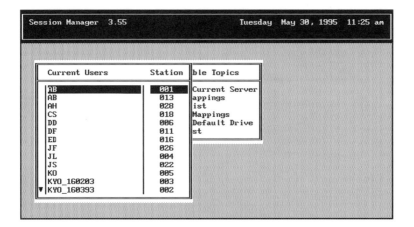

**Figure 8.21**

A list of currently logged-in users.

Selecting a user gives you two options (see fig. 8.22): Display user information and Send Message. If multiple users are marked with the F5 key, you will not get these options; you will only be allowed to send a message.

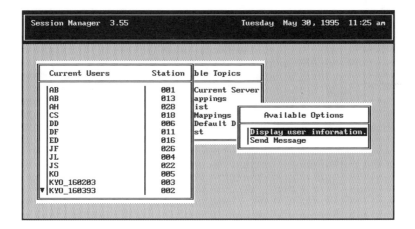

**Figure 8.22**

The two options available for every logged-in user.

To display a user's information, select User List from SESSION's main menu, highlight a user, press Enter, then select Display user information. Figure 8.23 shows the information available for a typical user; figure 8.24 shows the information available for a print server.

---

**Figure 8.23**

User information available.

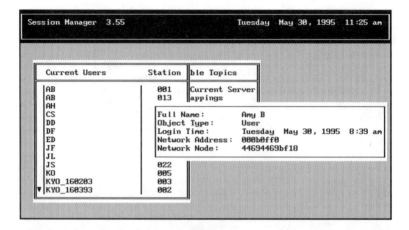

**Figure 8.24**

Print Server information available.

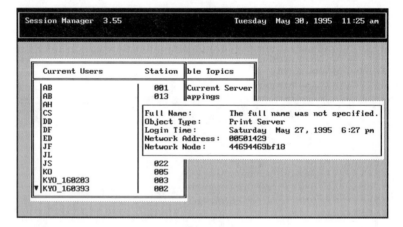

To send a message to a particular user, select User List from SESSION's main menu; a list of users appears. Select a user, or mark several users with the F5 key, then press Enter. If one user is selected, select Send Message. If multiple users are selected, a message dialog box appears. Enter the message that you want to send, then press Enter.

## Group List

To view a list of groups, select Group List from SESSION's main menu (see fig. 8.25), and a box with a list of groups appears on your screen (see fig. 8.26).

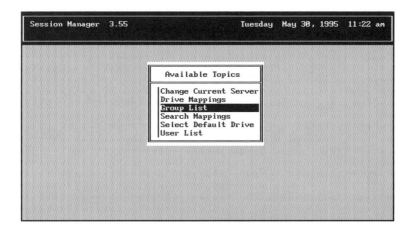

**Figure 8.25**

The Group List option
of SESSION.

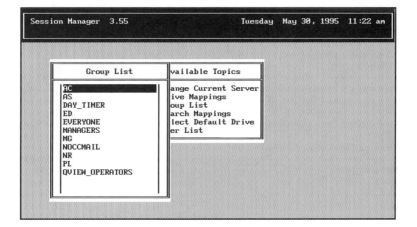

**Figure 8.26**

A list of existing
groups appears.

To send a message to each of the members contained in one of
these groups, select the appropriate group and press Enter. A
message dialog box appears in which you can type your message.
To send the message, press Enter; a prompt allowing 55 characters
to be entered is presented (see fig. 8.27).

**Figure 8.27**

All members of the group can now be sent a message.

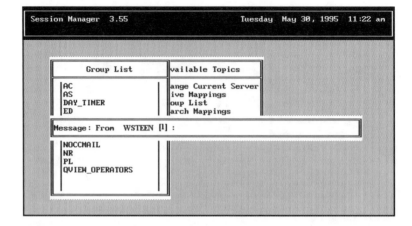

```
Session Manager  3.55                    Tuesday  May 30, 1995  11:22 am

        Group List        vailable Topics
      AC                ange Current Server
      AS                ive Mappings
      DAY_TIMER         oup List
      ED                arch Mappings

     Message: From   WSTEEN [1] :

      NOCCMAIL
      NR
      PL
      QVIEW_OPERATORS
```

## PRACTICE EXERCISE

Using the software that comes with this book, you can emulate a running network without needing access to one. Because the .EXE file is called PRIMER.EXE, you can execute any command by preceding it with that call. For the command XYZ, for example, the command you type is **PRIMER XYZ**.

Using this software, examine the components of SESSION:

1. Type **PRIMER SESSION**

2. Select Change Current Server and see what servers are available.

3. Press Esc to get back to the main menu.

4. Select Drive Mappings.

5. Note that local and mapped drives are shown.

6. Press Esc to get back to the main menu.

7. Select Group List and see what is shown.

8. Press Esc to get back to the main menu.

9. Select Search Mappings.

10. Note that the local drives from your PATH statement are at the bottom of the search and the new network drives are at the beginning.

11. Press Esc to get back to the main menu.

12. Select Default Drive and see the choices available.

13. Press Esc to get back to the main menu.

14. Choose User List and see which connections are active and which are not now, but have been recently.

15. Press Alt+F10 to exit the utility.

# Real World

1. View your current drive mappings with the command MAP.

2. View your current drive mappings with SESSION, being certain to look at both the search drives and regular drives.

3. Create a fake direcotry that you will use only for test purposes on your hard drive with the following command:

   `MKDIR JUNK`

4. Use SESSION to map to this directory as the available drive.

5. Use MAP DEL to remove the drive.

6. Check to make certain it is gone with MAP.

7. Map to that drive once more with MAP INS.

8. Delete the mapping once more, but now with SESSION.

9. Map to it once again with SESSION—this time making it a fake root drive.

10. Type **MAP** and notice the space that appears after the listing and the last slash; this space indicates that it is a root drive.

11. Delete the map once more.

12. Remove the directory completely with RD JUNK.

# Summary

Mapping enables you to find executable programs in directories other than the one you're currently in. Maps can be created, deleted, and modified using two programs—MAP, which is command-line based; and SESSION, which is a graphical menu utility.

Changes made from SESSION and MAP are temporary; they're lost when the user logs out. To make the changes permanent, they should be added to the user's login script.

**9**
**CHAPTER**

# Login Scripts

Login scripts can be thought of as batch file routines that run each time a user logs in. Because they are kept in ASCII format, you can readily locate and modify them with almost any editor. Additionally, you can create and modify login scripts with the SYSCON utility. The network supervisor can change any and all scripts, but individual users can change only their own.

There are three types of login scripts: System, User, and Default. The Default Login Script is part of the LOGIN.EXE file. It runs if no other login script is defined to execute.

The two specific rules governing login scripts are the following:

1. Each line can contain only one executable command.

2. No line can be longer than 150 characters.

# Executable Commands

Every scripting routine has its own language. This is true of DOS batch files, which enable you to use such commands as CALL, SET, and PROMPT, to name just a few. It is true of the BASIC language, which includes GOTO, GOSUB, and PRINT. It is equally true of login scripts.

The commands that you can use within a script include the following:

- ◆ **# (the pound sign).** Executes a command outside the login script—an external .COM or .EXE file. You cannot run programs that terminate and stay resident in memory.

- ◆ **BREAK ON.** Provides a method to terminate the login process by enabling the Ctrl+C key combination. This command is useful in the event that something goes awry and you do not want to complete the login. An example is if you have the login routine map to a number of devices that are normally up, but for some reason are down for maintenance. Rather than continuing on through the mapping process only to get a screenful of errors, use Ctrl+C to stop the login script processing so you do not execute all of it. **BREAK OFF** does the opposite. It disables the ability to break from the routine.

- ◆ **DOS SET.** Appoints local PC variables in the same way the DOS command SET does. Using this command, it is possible to pass variables from the network to an individual PC. One word of caution: the amount of space that you have available for local variables is controlled by the COMMAND.COM file. If you find that you cannot load all variables into memory, then you must increase the local PC environment size.

- ◆ **FDISPLAY.** Works in the same manner as the TYPE command in DOS in that it displays the contents of an ASCII file on the screen. One major difference, however, is that if a file is specified that does not exist, no error message is generated.

- ◆ **EXIT "specifications."** Ceases the processing and executes whatever commands are within the quotation marks.

Specifications can be for DOS internal commands, .BAT, .COM, or .EXE files. The only restrictions are that the specifications cannot be more than 14 characters long and cannot load programs that terminate and stay resident in memory.

◆ **INCLUDE.** Enables you to include commands in locations other than the login script. One of the major benefits of this command is that you can shorten restrictions in the login script by placing them in subscripts. You can change the subscripts as frequently as necessary to meet specifications present at the moment.

◆ **PAUSE.** Causes the implementation to hesitate and wait for the user to strike a key before continuing. This command is predominantly used when displaying the contents of a file that must be read before proceeding to the next command.

◆ **WRITE.** Works in the same manner as the ECHO command for DOS. Novell variables can be used, as long as they are preceded by a percent sign (%) and typed in capital letters. GREETING_TIME, for example, becomes morning, afternoon, or evening, depending on the actual time. You also can include commands such as \n for a new line, or \7 for the computer to emit a beep.

# Variables

Following is a listing of variables that NetWare uses. These variables can be used for conditional execution in login scripts, or echoed to the screen with the WRITE command. Traditionally, variables are preceded by a percent sign (%), and written in capital letters.

| Variable | Function |
| --- | --- |
| DAY | Shows the day of the month, from 1 to 31. |
| DAY_OF_WEEK | Spells out Sunday, Monday, Tuesday, and so on. |

*continues*

**131**

| Variable | Function |
| --- | --- |
| NDAY_OF_WEEK | Represents Sunday as 1, Monday as 2, Tuesday as 3, and so on. |
| MONTH | Shows the month of the year, from 01 to 12. |
| MONTH_NAME | Spells out January, February, March, and so on. |
| YEAR | Shows all four digits of the year—1994, 1995, and so on. |
| SHORT_YEAR | Shows the last two digits of the year—94, 95, and so on. |
| HOUR | Shows the hour, from 01 to 12. |
| HOUR24 | Shows the hour, from 00 to 23. |
| MINUTE | Shows the minute, from 00 to 59. |
| SECOND | Shows the second, from 00 to 59. |
| GREETING_TIME | Returns either morning, afternoon, or evening. |
| AM_PM | Returns one or the other, depending upon which is appropriate. |
| FULL_NAME | Gives the user's full name. |
| LOGIN_NAME | Shows the login name used. |
| USER_ID | Shows the user's id. |
| PASSWORD_EXPIRES | Shows how many days remain before the password expires. |
| FILE_SERVER | Shows the name of the current server. |
| NETWORK_ADDRESS | Shows an 8-digit hexadecimal number. |

| Variable | Function |
|----------|----------|
| DOS_REQUESTER | Returns the version of DOS in use. |
| NETWARE_REQUESTER | Returns the version of NetWare in use. |
| MACHINE | Returns the machine hardware in use. |
| OS | Returns the operating system in use. |
| OS_VERSION | Shows 3.3, 5.0, 6.2, and so on, for the operating system running. |
| P_STATION | Shows the node address in 12-digit hexadecimal form. |
| SHELL_TYPE | Returns the type of shell calling the login script. |
| SMACHINE | Shows the machine name in short form. |
| STATION | Returns the workstation connection number. |
| ACCESS_SERVER | Returns a value of true if the server is functional. |
| ERROR_LEVEL | If any error level is existing, its value is returned. |

# The System Login Script

The System Login Script is what executes for each user who logs in to the system. If the user has no User Login Script, then the Default Login Script also executes. If the user does have a user script of his or her own, the system script executes first, then gives way to the user script.

**133**

The system script is created, modified, and saved by accessing that option from the Supervisor Options of the main SYSCON menu. Figure 9.1 shows this option.

**Figure 9.1**

SYSCON enables the creation and modification of the System Login Script.

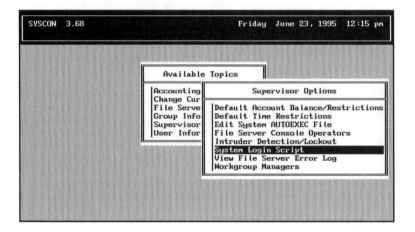

The sole purpose of the System Login Script is to run a series of routines common to every user. Classic examples of these routines include mappings to shared directories, capturing to common printers, and mappings to home directories, such as the following:

```
MAP root h:=primer/vol1:home/%LOGIN_NAME
```

Capitalization is not important at the command line, or within the login script. The example:

```
MAP root h:=primer/vol1:home/%LOGIN_NAME
```

works the exact same as:

```
MAP ROOT H:=PRIMER/VOL1:HOME/%LOGIN_NAME
```

or:

```
map root h:=primer/vol1:home/%login_name
```

# User Login Scripts

Individual users can have their own login scripts of commands to execute each time they log in. To create a User Login Script, go into SYSCON and select User Information. Select the appropriate user name, as shown in figure 9.2, and then select Login Script (see fig. 9.3).

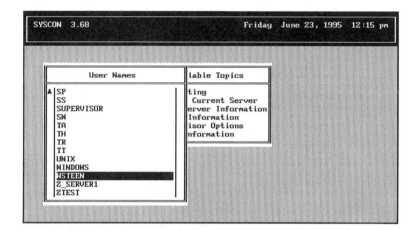

**Figure 9.2**

Select a defined user.

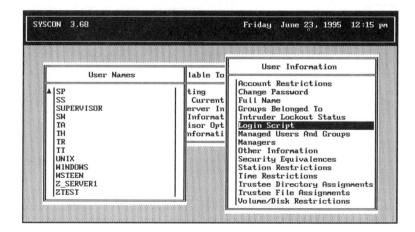

**Figure 9.3**

Select the Login Script option.

If the user currently has a login script, you can edit or modify it in any way. Save the changes; those changes will be effective the next time the user logs in.

If the user does not have a login script yet, a message to that effect appears. You can type in the name of another user and copy the other user's login script to this user, or you can press Enter without making any changes and start a script from scratch.

# Detailed Information

Two ASCII text files are created for every user added to the system—the login scripts. As soon as you create the user, an arbitrary mail directory is created for that user as well. In that mail directory, there is a LOGIN file and a LOGIN.OS2 file. To find where these files are stored, select Other Information from the SYSCON User Information menu. This option shows the User ID, as in figure 9.4.

**Figure 9.4**

Other Information identifies the User ID.

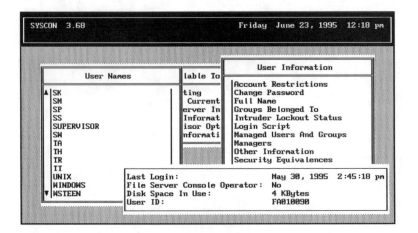

The User ID is the same as the name of the mail directory created for the user. From the command line, you can move into that directory and see the existing script. If there is no script (meaning that only the system default will run), the size of the file is zero bytes, as illustrated in figure 9.5.

```
FA010090      <DIR>          05-11-95  10:02a
         1 file(s)                 0 bytes
                     123,580,416 bytes free

F:\MAIL>cd fa010090

F:\MAIL\FA010090>dir

 Volume in drive F is SYS
 Directory of F:\MAIL\FA010090

.               <DIR>
..              <DIR>
LOGINBAK                   0 05-11-95   10:02a
LOGIN    OS2               0 05-11-95   10:02a
LOGIN                     55 05-11-95   10:05a
         5 file(s)              55 bytes
                     123,580,416 bytes free

F:\MAIL\FA010090>type login
write "Now executing your personal login script."


F:\MAIL\FA010090>
```

**Figure 9.5**

Viewing the login
script from the
command line.

A major benefit of command-line access is that you can use any editor you choose to edit the files and save them back in ASCII format. You are not confined to using only SYSCON.

Figure 9.6 reiterates the fact that each user has two login entries in his or her mail directory, whether or not he or she has a login script. User 9C000097 has a login script, as does 2403000C, and 3D00009B. The other users do not.

```
F:\MAIL\3D00009B
         login.os2          0 bytes    7:49 am   Tue Nov   1 94
         login             66 bytes    7:51 am   Tue Nov   1 94
F:\MAIL\9C000097
         login.os2          0 bytes   11:20 am   Wed Nov 30 94
         login            119 bytes    9:07 am   Wed Feb   1 95
F:\MAIL\A100004F
         login              0 bytes    8:21 am   Mon Dec 12 94
         login.os2          0 bytes    8:21 am   Mon Dec 12 94
F:\MAIL\240000F9
         login              0 bytes    3:54 pm   Wed Feb 15 95
         login.os2          0 bytes    3:54 pm   Wed Feb 15 95
F:\MAIL\2403000C
         login.os2          0 bytes    3:11 pm   Tue Feb 28 95
         login             89 bytes    3:12 pm   Tue Feb 28 95
F:\MAIL\3A0200B7
         login              0 bytes   11:53 am   Thu Mar 16 95
         login.os2          0 bytes   11:53 am   Thu Mar 16 95
-- More --
```

**Figure 9.6**

A listing of the login
scripts for each user.

Figure 9.7 gives an example of one user's login script, which first inserts a search map to a CCMAIL drive. Next it sets a DOS variable, then sets another search map to the SYS volume.

**Figure 9.7**

A sample login script.

```
F:\MAIL\6000001>type login
*map insert s4:=v:\ccmail
map del i:

dos set exdefdir="c:\docs"
map s16:=nrp/sys:system
map del v:
map ins s4:=mp-mail2\sys:ccmail

#capture /l=2 q=express nb nff nt ti=5

if P_STATION <> "00608C85C72F" then begin
#castoff all
end
F:\MAIL\6000001>
```

Another benefit of command-line access, in addition to using the editor of your choice, is that quite often there will not be enough memory on your workstation machine to bring up the scripts in SYSCON and edit them. If this is the case, an error similar to that shown in figure 9.8 appears. The only solution is to close out the TSRs that you have running, free up some more memory, and try the process again.

**Figure 9.8**

The SYSCON out-of-memory message.

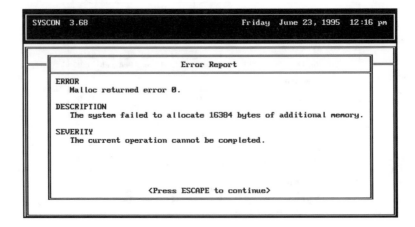

```
SYSCON  3.68                          Friday  June 23, 1995  12:16 pm


                              Error Report

    ERROR
        Malloc returned error 0.

    DESCRIPTION
        The system failed to allocate 16384 bytes of additional memory.

    SEVERITY
        The current operation cannot be completed.




                    <Press ESCAPE to continue>
```

---

**PRACTICE EXERCISE**

Using the software that comes with this book, you can emulate a running network, without needing access to it. Because the executable file is called PRIMER, you can execute any command by preceding it with that call. If there were a command called XYZ, for example, the EXECUTE command would be PRIMER XYZ.

Using this software, examine the login scripts by performing the following steps:

1. Type **PRIMER SYSCON**

2. Select Supervisor Options.

3. Select System Login Script.

4. Examine the routines that will execute for every user who logs in.

5. Press ESC.

6. Select User Information.

7. Select user GUEST.

8. Select Login Script.

9. Examine what will execute when this user logs in.

10. Press Alt+F10 to exit the program completely.

# Real World

Examine your own System Login Script and the User Login Script for yourself and a handful of users. Next, add a dummy user to the system. Then select Login Script. Because none exists for the dummy user, you are asked from where the script you want to edit is to come. Type in your User ID.

This action copies your login script into the SYSCON memory for the new user. If you exit at this point without saving, you still have not given the new user a login script. Instead, press ESC, and choose to save it as the new user's script.

Next, go to the Other Information option of SYSCON for that user and see what the User ID is. Go to the command line and change to the mail directory of that User ID. Note that the login script now exists. You can view it with the TYPE command.

# Summary

This chapter discusses login scripts and examines the three types: System, User, and Default. If there are no other login scripts, then the default is executed. It is a component of LOGIN.EXE. If a user script exists, then the default script is not executed.

The second type of script is a System Login Script, which executes for all users when they log in to the system. Following its execution, if there is a User Login Script, then it executes as well.

The following chapter examines the topic of menus and how to create them for your users. They can simplify tasks and save a great deal of command-line work for you and your users alike.

**10**
CHAPTER

# Creating Menus with the MENU and NMENU Commands

The ability to create graphical menu interfaces for networking functions is one of the most overlooked features of NetWare. An administrator can put together a menu that enables an inexperienced user to accomplish complex tasks with little or no time involved—and make modifications almost on the fly.

By creating custom menus, you can organize tasks that normally run together and save the time of entering each one manually. Additionally, you can combine several utilities into one and speed up the operation. Users need not remember cryptic commands when a menu choice will suffice. DOS and NetWare commands can be grouped together in the same menu.

Of the four versions of NetWare currently in use, 2.2 and 3.11 have a utility appropriately titled MENU that enables these operations. Versions 3.12 and 4.x use NMENU instead. NMENU (as in New MENU) is a modified version of MENU that utilizes less memory and offers additional features. Because these two entities are so different, this chapter treats the two separately, focusing first on MENU, then NMENU.

# Creating a Simple Menu with MENU

NetWare Version 2.2 and 3.11 menus can be created using any ASCII text editor. The name of the created file should have the extension .MNU, although this is not necessary. If it does have that extension, you can later run it without specifying the extension—as in:

`MENU CHOICES`

Otherwise, you must give the extension as well:

`MENU CHOICES.WMS`

The format of the file must follow that which is shown in the following example:

```
%MenuTitle,#,#,#
Option1
     commands
Option2
     commands
Option3
     %SubMenu
%SubMenuTitle ,#,#,#
Option1
     commands
Option2
     commands
```

A percent sign (%) at the beginning of the line indicates a menu title. To create a menu with the title "Choices," for example, it must appear in the text as %Choices. Three numeric values can follow, indicating:

◆ The vertical location of the menu on the screen

◆ The horizontal location of the menu on the screen

◆ The color to use

Default values can be specified with zeroes, or blank spaces between the commas.

The following is an example of a simple menu program:

```
%William's Choices,0,0,1
Q&A Version 4
      P:
      QA
      F:
Lotus 1-2-3
      S:
      123
      F:
Additional Choices
      %Choices
%Choices,10,50,1
Print Shop
      MAP G:=SYS:APPS\PS
      G:
      PS
      F:
Quit
      !logout
```

There are three choices on the first menu. Choosing the last option brings up another menu with two more choices. All menus, whether they are main menus or submenus, must be preceded by the percent sign. The percent sign is what tells the parser to begin a separate menu. It is also always a good idea to include Quit or Logout as menu options.

## Important Note

Regardless of the order in which you list the menu options, when the parser moves through the list and prepares it for display, it puts them in sorted order. Most of the time this does not present a problem. If, however, you do not want the list alphabetically displayed, there are ways around it, both entailing additions to the beginning of each choice.

The following entry shows the numeric entries added to each choice:

```
%William's Choices,0,0,1
1. Q&A Version 4
     P:
     QA
     F:
3. Lotus 1-2-3
     S:
     123
     F:
2. Additional Choices
     %Choices
%Choices,10,50,1
1. Print Shop
     MAP G:=SYS:APPS\PS
     G:
     PS
     F:
2. Quit
     !logout
```

## Screen Placement

The first two sets of numbers following a menu title depict where it will be displayed on the screen. The first number gives vertical positioning; the second, horizontal. There are several key points to note when determining where your menus will appear.

As mentioned previously, using a blank value or the value of zero puts the menu in its default position. Vertical placement is determined by the number of lines from the top of the screen to the middle of the menu. The number of lines you specify, therefore (when not using the default), must be equal to the number of lines from the top of the screen to the beginning of the menu *and* the number of lines from the beginning of the menu to the middle.

If a menu is 10 lines long and you want it to begin five lines from the top of the screen then the equation is

$$5 + (10/2) = 10$$

When placing a menu vertically, the best procedure is to guess at a number and run it once. If you want it lower, just edit the file and increase the number as needed.

Horizontal placement is measured in columns from the left side of the screen to the middle of the menu. The horizontal value, therefore, has to be equal to the number of characters you want before getting to the left edge of the menu, plus half the number of characters in the menu.

If a menu is 30 characters wide and you want it to begin 35 characters from the left side of the screen, then the equation is

$$35 + (30/2) = 50$$

As with vertical placement, a lot of guesswork is incorporated when first writing the horizontal placement of the menu. Values can always be increased or decreased in the ASCII file as necessary.

## Menu Colors

The third number defined on each menu title is the color scheme to use. The palette defines the colors that are to be used for the foreground and background. The palette can be changed with the COLORPAL utility, but is usually kept standard.

**Note**  Every menu, whether it is one that you create, or one that came with NetWare, pulls its color information from COLORPAL. Any changes you make to improve the appearance of a menu will also affect all other menus.

**145**

There are five existing color palettes numbered from 0 to 4. In the absence of a number, the default color palette of 0 is used. NetWare uses each of its five palettes for a specific purpose. They are the following:

- ◆ **0.** Lists, menus, and text.
- ◆ **1.** Main headers and screen background.
- ◆ **2.** Help screens.
- ◆ **3.** Error messages.
- ◆ **4.** Exit messages.

## Special Characters

Just as the percent sign (%) informs the menu parser that a menu or submenu definition follows, there are other characters that NetWare interprets to have special meaning. The most important among these is the *at* symbol (@). It enables the user to enter a variable to replace a prompt. The prompt must follow the character and be enclosed in quotation marks.

For example, the command:

```
Dir @"Which Drive?"
```

does a directory listing on the drive specified after the user answers the prompt. More than one variable can be read in by the same routine if a number is used in conjunction with the ampersand—@1, @2, @3, and so on. This feature can prove invaluable when a command requires a source and target, as in:

```
DISKCOPY @1"What is the source drive?"
@2"What is the target drive?"
```

Once a variable has been assigned in this fashion, it retains its value until the menu is exited. In this manner, more than one operation can take place on the variable. For example:

```
DISKCOPY @1"What is the source drive?"
@2"What is the target drive?"
FC @1:\appl\kristin @2:\appl\kristin
CHKDSK @2
```

The second character of note is the backslash (\). If, for some reason, you need to include the ampersand or percent sign in a menu and *not* have them take on their assigned meaning, but print instead, then they must be preceded by this character. Assume you want a menu choice of "Compute % Revenue." This choice must appear as `Compute \% Revenue` to keep the % sign from signaling the start of a new menu.

The question then comes up, What if you need the backslash to appear in the menu and not have it interpreted as giving the next character literal value? The answer is that two backslashes must be used in succession; `\\` displays only one.

## Cool MENU Tricks

Knowing a bit more about the operation of MENU, there are two circumstances you can plan for, and even incorporate into your operations. The first is that if you run MENU without giving it the name of a file to run, it uses a default file of SYS:PUBLIC\MAIN.MNU. It is a good idea to create this file, just in case someone does accidentally type **menu**—a common enough command.

Secondly, users can be given individualized menus by creating files named with their login name. When MENU is called, follow it by the login name variable and a different menu will appear for each user. An individualized menu can be incorporated into the login script with an exit command, as in:

```
EXIT "MENU %LOGIN_NAME"
```

When this technique is used, individual users are presented with a menu of the applications they are most likely to work with, and the menu can be different for every user. Similarly, any variable can be substituted for the login name. When group IDs are used, for example, the accounting department can see a different menu from the sales department.

# Using NMENU

Although MENU is an adequate utility useful for simplifying multiple operations into automated steps, it is really nothing more than a batch language. The tasks that can be done are limited by the commands, a handful at best. This left a market wherein third-party vendors have developed and are selling menu application programs for NetWare that far exceed MENU's abilities.

One of these third-party vendors, Saber, did quite well in the market. Novell noticed the missing features in their product and licensed a copy of the SABER utility for inclusion in NetWare. It became NMENU (as in New MENU). Offering more capabilities than most administrators will ever need, it is still a scaled down version of the SABER utilities, which can still be purchased.

In addition to offering a more complete language, NMENU is a compiled program, capable of running programs faster and in less memory than its earlier counterpart. Whereas MENU was an entire executable that parsed an ASCII file on each running and presented what it found, NMENU is really just a batch file (NMENU.BAT), which summons other utilities such as MENUEXE.EXE and MENUREST.EXE

## The NMENU Process

Creating a menu with NMENU is really a three-step process. The first involves generating an ASCII file (just as you do with MENU) that must have the extension .SRC to identify it as a source file. The next step is to run an executable program, MENUMAKE, that outputs a file with same name and a .DAT extension—the data file. Lastly, run NMENU on the .DAT file, and the menu appears.

Older files for MENU can be converted to .DAT format through the MENUCNVT program. It creates a .SRC file from the original that can then be run through MENUMAKE. It is important to note, whether creating new menus or converting old ones, that the .DAT file is not viewable or changeable with any editor. To make changes in the operation of the menu, you must change the .SRC file. Personally, this author recommends that .SRC files be marked as read-only and never deleted. The first time you delete a .SRC file, you will find that when a slight change needs to be made in a menu's operation, there is no way to do so short of re-creating the source file.

# Components

NMENU files consist of several components, each extremely important to the operation of the finished product:

◆ Titles

◆ Options

◆ Submenus

◆ Commands

◆ Prompts

Titles are simply text that appears at the top of the menu. There is a limit of 40 characters, but there are no other restrictions on content. Options are placed within braces { } and denote actions to take place. Titles of options appearing on the menu itself cannot exceed 60 characters in length. Executable options include the following:

◆ **BATCH.** Removes the program from memory before executing the item, freeing up 32 KB.

◆ **CHDIR.** Changes to a specified drive\directory before executing the next command.

◆ **NOCLEAR.** Leaves the present screen display exactly the way it is.

◆ **NOECHO.** Does not echo commands it executes.

◆ **PAUSE.** Stops the display and waits for an acknowledgment.

◆ **SHOW.** Shows the commands being executed (the opposite of NOECHO).

**149**

Submenus are further branches of this menu. One choice on a main menu, for example, might be "Word Processors." When the user chooses that option, a submenu could open, offering choices between Word, WordPerfect, or Lazy Write. The only restriction here is that submenus cannot go more than 10 layers deep.

Commands are the heart of the operation and include—in order of importance—the following:

- ◆ **MENU.** Marks the beginning of a new menu or submenu.

- ◆ **ITEM.** Signifies a menu choice and the title it is to use.

- ◆ **EXEC.** Tells DOS to run an item.

- ◆ **LOAD.** Summons a submenu from a separate .DAT file.

- ◆ **SHOW.** Shows a submenu from the same .DAT file.

Lastly, prompts request additional information from the user that is then used within the operation. There are three types of prompts:

- ◆ **GETO.** Requests optional information before executing the item. If the user presses Enter without giving a value, no harm is done.

- ◆ **GETR.** Requests required information. A value *must* be given before processing continues.

- ◆ **GETP.** Converts the input into a parameter and saves the value.

## Layout

The first line of the menu routine must identify it as a menu, giving a number and title. An example:

```
MENU 1, Main Menu
```

The first menu (bear in mind that one menu can contain multiple submenus) must always use the number 1 for legibility's sake. Successive submenus do not have to be sequentially numbered, as the number is used only as an identifier. An example of the layout, then, is

```
MENU {number}, {title}
   ITEM {title}
        {commands}
   ITEM {title}
        {commands}
```

Following the menu line are the items that are to appear as selections and the commands to execute them. The following is a simple menu for purposes of illustration. The same operation was performed earlier in the MENU discussion.

```
MENU 1, William's Choices
     ITEM Q&A Version 4
          EXEC P:
          EXEC QA
          EXEC F:
     ITEM Lotus 1-2-3
          EXEC S:
          EXEC 123
          EXEC F:
     ITEM Additional Choices {NOCLEAR}
          SHOW 10
MENU 10, Choices
     ITEM Print Shop
          EXEC MAP G:=SYS:APPS\PS
          EXEC G:
          EXEC PS
          EXEC F:
     ITEM QUIT
          EXEC LOGOUT
```

The example consists of one menu and one submenu. On the main menu, with a heading of William's Choices, there are three choices. The third selection, Additional Choices, summons the submenu. Then the command SHOW 10 summons MENU 10. Menu 10, the submenu, follows the main menu in the listing. Notice {NOCLEAR} for the submenu, which leaves the original menu on the screen and places the submenu on top of it, in much the same way as NetWare does most of its system menus.

With MENU you can control the exact position of a menu on the screen by specifying centered parameters. With NMENU, there is no equivalent option. NetWare itself determines where the menus appear on the screen.

It is important to remember that during generation of the data file, the submenu will continue on until another MENU command is encountered. The next submenu could be MENU 11, MENU 20, or any other valid number.

## Three Special EXECs

There are three special EXEC statements that sound alike, but behave very differently. In the last example, the Quit menu choice calls EXEC LOGOUT. This command logs the user completely out of the network, canceling any mapping and any other conditions that might have been created during the network session.

EXEC EXIT leaves the menu completely and returns the user to a DOS prompt. The menu is completely unloaded and must be summoned again to be used.

EXEC DOS opens a DOS session with the menu still active. The user can continue with normal operations, but the menu is still resident in memory. Typing **EXIT** cancels the DOS session and returns to the menu where processing left off.

## Menu Key Assignments

When choices are presented on a menu, the default is for successive alphabetic lettering of the entries to be assigned as keys to press to summon the entry. In the previous example, the choice Q&A Version 4 would appear as a selection as A. Q&A Version 4, and the next would be B. Lotus 1-2-3.

This default scheme can be overridden by placing the desired key in braces, along with an up-carat (^), following the menu choice. The following example shows numbers being added for the menu choices. The actual entries will now appear on the menu as 1. Q&A Version 4, and the next as 2. Lotus 1-2-3.

```
MENU 1, William's Choices
    ITEM Q&A Version 4{^1}
        EXEC P:
        EXEC QA
        EXEC F:
    ITEM Lotus 1-2-3{^2}
        EXEC S:
        EXEC 123
        EXEC F:
    ITEM Additional Choices {NOCLEAR}{^3}
        SHOW 10
MENU 10, Choices
    ITEM Print Shop{^1}
        EXEC MAP G:=SYS:APPS\PS
        EXEC G:
        EXEC PS
        EXEC F:
    ITEM QUIT{^2}
        EXEC LOGOUT
```

A useful variation on this scheme is to assign the first letter of each choice as the hot key. The following example shows a slight modification that enables the selections to now appear as Q. Q&A Version 4 and L. Lotus 1-2-3.

```
MENU 1, William's Choices
    ITEM Q&A Version 4{^Q}
        EXEC P:
        EXEC QA
        EXEC F:
    ITEM Lotus 1-2-3{^L}
        EXEC S:
        EXEC 123
        EXEC F:
    ITEM Additional Choices {NOCLEAR}{^A}
        SHOW 10
MENU 10, Choices
    ITEM Print Shop{^P}
        EXEC MAP G:=SYS:APPS\PS
        EXEC G:
        EXEC PS
        EXEC F:
    ITEM QUIT{^Q}
        EXEC LOGOUT
```

**153**

# Accepting Input

There are three different ways to accept input into a menu: GETO, GETR, and GETP. They are interchangeable and all use the same format:

```
GETx {prompt up to 40 characters} {value}
{length},{default},{SECURE or not},{append}
```

GETO is used if the variable value is optional. You can continue processing without it—if, for example, you need to do a CHKDSK operation and prompt the user to enter the drive letter. If the user enters a drive letter, the operation is performed on that drive. If the user does not enter a value, CHKDSK is not fed a drive letter and performs its operation on the current drive.

GETR is used when the user *must* enter a value. If all files are being copied from a source drive to a target, for example, and the user's computer has a disk drive for both A and B, then the user *must* specify which is the target.

GETP works similarly to GETR. The difference is that GETR retains its value only for the operation it is carrying out. Values input to GETP are assigned numbers (%1, %2, %3, and so on), and they are retained for as long as the menu session is active. A drive letter read in with GETP can have multiple operations performed on it (CHKDSK, FC, and so forth) without the user having to enter the drive letter for each operation.

The prompt can be between 1 and 40 characters in length, and the value (also known as the *prepend*) can be blank, or a valid entity (this confusing concept will become clearer in the examples). Length is the number of characters the variable can be, and the default is what will be taken if no entry is made. The word SECURE in the designated position makes asterisks appear on the screen when the value is entered (as with a password). Lastly, append is any value that you want to tack on to the end of the given variable. If you want to copy files from the APPL directory, for example, ask the user to enter the drive (F) then append :\APPL\ to the user's variable.

One very important rule to remember is that not all values need to be given. Parameters can be left blank by putting two commas together in the fields separated by commas (,,), or blank braces in those fields that need them ({}).

## Some Illustrations

The following is a very simple example. The menu choice that appears is for a directory listing. When the user chooses that, they are prompted for a drive on which to do the operation—Which Drive:. GETO means the response is optional, so pressing Enter without specifying a value is acceptable. The empty braces {} indicate that no prepend information is needed. The length of the entry the user makes is limited to one character, and there is no default ,,. The word SECURE does not appear in the last field so what the user types will appear. Finally, {:} puts a colon on the end of the entry, if there is one.

```
ITEM Directory Listing
    GETO Which Drive: {}1,,{:}
    EXEC DIR %
```

If the user presses Enter without entering a value, EXEC DIR does a directory listing on the current directory. If the user enters **C**, EXEC DIR becomes EXEC DIR C. Notice that nowhere on the EXEC line is the variable mentioned by name. The % uses the value of the last GETx operation.

The following example is using GETP to read and keep the value of two variables for a DISKCOPY operation. Again, there is no prepend {}. The length is now set at two characters, and defaults have been assigned as A: and B:. These values appear in each prompt. Pressing F10 keeps the default, or it can be typed over with different values. No append information is given.

```
ITEM Copy one diskette to another
    GETP Enter the source drive: {}2,A:,{}
    GETP Enter the target drive: {}2,B:,{}
    EXEC DISKCOPY %1 %2
```

By using GETP, the values assigned here can be used later on in the same routine. After the DISKCOPY is done, for example, a few more lines can be added.

```
FC %1:\appl\kristin %2:\appl\kristin
CHKDSK %2
```

will compare one file on each drive and see that they are the same, then do a CHKDSK of the target drive to verify there are no problems with it.

The following example shows an example of GETR that requires a value to be entered. The prepend is Q=, which is equivalent to the information necessary on a command line to capture a queue. The length is set at 8, and there is no default and no append information. It is important to note that there is a difference between append information of {} and { }. The former does not append anything; the latter puts a blank space at the end (not good if you are then going to specify a file name after a drive letter).

```
ITEM Capture Network Printer
    GETR Enter Queue Name: {Q=}8,,{}
    EXEC CAPTURE
```

# Real World

Depending on which version of NetWare you are using, create some simple menus, as outlined, with either MENU or NMENU. Experiment with palette colors and embedded menus (menus within menus). Think of mundane operations that occur at your site that would benefit greatly if their operation could be simplified with a menu. Some examples include the following:

◆ Capturing and recapturing a printer.

◆ Changing printing parameters to suddenly print multiple copies of a document, then switching back.

◆ Checking to see how many members of a group are logged in and sending them messages.

# Summary

The NMENU utility is supplied with Novell NetWare 3.12 and greater. It replaces MENU by offering far more options and greater flexibility. Using it, you can create menus that simplify tasks for users and perform multiple operations with a single keystroke.

The following chapter looks at one of the more classic examples of a menu utility, the SBACKUP routine. It is the responsibility of all administrators to ensure the integrity of data on their systems, and one way of doing so is with regular backups.

**CHAPTER 11**

# Performing Backups with the SBACKUP Utility

Beginning with NetWare Version 3.11, the SBACKUP utility has been included with every subsequent NetWare version. As the name implies, SBACKUP enables you to perform backups of the server to a variety of removable media. What the name does not imply is that it also enables you to create backups of client machines as well. The media to which the backup is being done must be attached to the server (rather than to a workstation), allowing backups to take place locally and reducing the amount of network traffic.

Lacking in glamour and glitz, SBACKUP provides the absolute bare-minimum backup features that should be considered when ensuring the sanctity of your data. On the undeniable plus side, it is free and included with the base operating system installation. It also can back up a variety of operating systems (DOS, OS/2, Unix,

Macintosh) and supports tape drives and disk drives. It is highly recommended that at your own site, you consider other backup software with more features and a more intuitive interface. At a customer's site, or one that you must remotely support, SBACKUP enables you to back up their system without the need of convincing them to make an additional purchase.

A few changes were made to the utility with the release of NetWare 4.x, but primarily they consist of the incorporation of the NBACKUP utility, which has been a stand-alone utility since NetWare 2.x. This chapter focuses on SBACKUP as it exists prior to 4.x, and concludes with a short discussion of NBACKUP. All administrators should know the importance of backups and reasons why they are done, so this chapter will not discuss backup hierarchies or rotational methods. You can work out these items for yourself, as the focus here is on how the SBACKUP utility is employed to its maximum capabilities.

# SMS and SBACKUP

The problem inherent in many backup routines is that they require a restore routine to be present on the target drive in order to restore the contents. After the total decimation of a server, whether by fire, flood, or any other disaster, you are starting from scratch when you rebuild the network. Although a disaster situation is not an everyday occurrence, and most restores are necessary because Bill deleted a file he should not have, this is the scenario for which you must always plan.

Novell has addressed this possibility with NetWare 3.12 and later by adhering to a software architecture known as *Storage Management Services* (SMS). NetWare 3.11 contains an SBACKUP utility, but it does not use SMS. Being software and hardware independent, SMS enables backups to tape drives, disk drives, or hard drives. Through the use of SMS, files travel directly from the source to the target, and there is support for multiple protocols and name spaces.

When implemented on NetWare, SMS enables you to choose among backing up all files on the server (including the bindery and system files), only files that have been modified since the last backup, or only files matching a given extension or in specified directories. These choices can be referred to as a *full backup*, an *incremental backup*, or a *differential backup*, respectively.

# Required SBACKUP Files

To use SBACKUP, it must be loaded as a series of NetWare Loadable Modules (NLMs). Both the server and a target file server (if you are backing up to another server) must have the appropriate NLMs loaded on them before you commence. The required files are dependent on the action you are doing, but can include the following:

- **SBACKUP.NLM**. The interface. It also ascertains, from the menu selections made, which other modules need to be activated.

- **SIDR.NLM**. The data requester. It passes the requests for data to and from the server and TSA.NLM.

- **TSA.NLM**. The Target Service Agent module. It is the link between the requester and the module loaded specifying the target.

- **TSA-31x.NLM**. The target-specific portion of the backup routine. This file is loaded to process data using the data structure of the client.

- **WANGTEK.NLM**. The driver for the backup device.

- **TSA_DOS.NLM**. The utility loaded at the server in conjunction with SBACKUP to back up a DOS client.

- **TSA_DOS.COM.** The file that must be loaded on a DOS client if you are backing up files from it.

- **TSA_OS2.COM.** The file that must be loaded on an OS/2 client if you are backing up files from it.

Although it should be obvious, it is worth stating that the utilities ending with .NLM are loaded on the server—both host and target if the backup is to another sever. The utilities ending in .COM are loaded on client machines only if the backup is of that client and not of the server. These procedures are explained in the next two sections.

# Seven Steps to Backing Up a Server

Though rather intuitive in nature once the interface is loaded, you must follow a set routine exactly in order to ensure that SBACKUP will see the available devices and drivers. To back up a server, the following seven steps are required:

1. At the server, load the Target Service Agent. The command is

   **LOAD TSA**

2. Load any special drivers that are not standard to your target (for example, a special tape device). Normally, this step need not be followed because TSA loads all applicable modules.

3. At the server, type

   **LOAD SBACKUP**

   You will be prompted for a username and password, providing needed security to the backup tape. Entering the information for a regular user limits the amount of data that SBACKUP can back up. For a complete backup, enter the name of the supervisor, or the name of a person with supervisor-equivalent rights.

4. Select the backup target. A box appears with recognized drivers within it. If no drivers have been loaded, the box is empty. Move the cursor to the device you want and select it. This action establishes the connection between the target and the host, linking them together, and enabling communication between them.

5. The SBACKUP main menu appears. From it, choose Select Target to Backup/Restore (other choices include Backup and Restore). Select the appropriate entry. Figure 11.1 shows the choice for backing up the entire server.

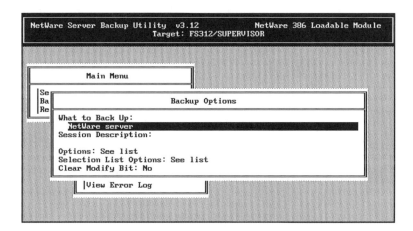

**Figure 11.1**

The main backup menu within SBACKUP.

If you want to exclude certain files from the backup, then go to the Options list, as depicted by figure 11.2.

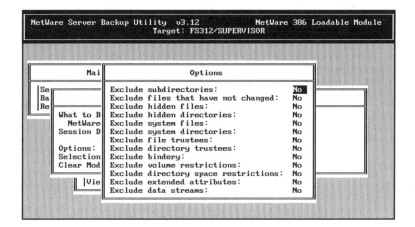

**Figure 11.2**

The Exclude options enable you to customize the backup.

6. At the main menu once more, select Backup, then choose Select a Working Directory. The working directory is where the error log and any other files created by the process will be stored. Be sure to put them in a location where you will

**163**

recognize what they are and act appropriately, even if you do nothing more than delete them so they don't use up server disk space.

It is highly recommended, however, that you not delete them. A log file for each backup session is stored as a separate file within the working directory. Within that file, information is stored, including the date and time of the session, the host and target, and details on the data that was backed up. The details include a complete list of the files, their name space type, and where exactly they reside on the backup media. Needless to say, this is important information to keep readily locatable.

7. Answer a few more questions (such as whether you want to start the backup now or later, and whether you want a full, incremental or differential backup), and the backup will commence.

# Seven Steps to Backing Up Client Files

To back up the files located on a client machine, the steps are similar to the server routine, but with a few modifications. Perform the following seven steps:

1. At the file server, enter the command

   **LOAD TSA_DOS**

   for DOS-based client machines; or

   **LOAD TSA_OS2**

   for OS/2, High Performance File System client machines.

   Regardless of which one you enter, the LOAD command automatically loads a handful of other needed modules, including the following:

   ◆ STREAMS

   ◆ NUT

- ◆ CLIB
- ◆ TLI
- ◆ SPXS or IPXS

2. Load the TSA_SMS.COM file on the client machine. For automated action, add this command to the AUTOEXEC.BAT file of the machine and then have the user reboot the machine.

3. At the server, enter

   **LOAD SBACKUP**

4. Select the client machine that now appears as a selection. Enter the appropriate username and password—these can be of the supervisor or the user.

5. Select the target device.

6. Select Backup from the main SBACKUP menu.

7. Commence the backup.

Network traffic is increased somewhat as the server acts as a go-between for the client machine and the backup device. Though slower than backing up to a locally connected tape device, this procedure provides an inexpensive means of backing up all workstations with only one device.

# Seven Steps to Restoring Backups

It is incredibly easy to restore a backup. With SMS technology, the restore need not be done on the machine from which the backup was conducted. Thus, you can back up files on a 3.12 server and restore them on a 4.x server using the following seven steps:

1. Load the appropriate TSAs as if you were doing a backup.

2. Load the SBACKUP.NLM as detailed earlier.

**165**

3. Select Restore from the main menu.

4. Define a working directory.

5. Enter the path of the directory for the files you want to restore.

6. Select Restore, and change any options that you want to be different from the default. Figure 11.3 shows the default settings.

**Figure 11.3**

The Restore Options list.

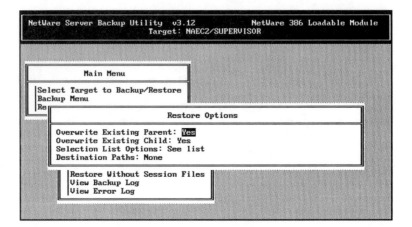

```
NetWare Server Backup Utility  v3.12          NetWare 386 Loadable Module
                         Target: NAEC2/SUPERVISOR




          ┌──────────────────────────────┐
          │          Main Menu           │
          ├──────────────────────────────┤
          │ Select Target to Backup/Restore
          │ Backup Menu
          │ Re┌─────────────────────────────────────────────┐
          │   │              Restore Options                │
          │   ├─────────────────────────────────────────────┤
          │   │ Overwrite Existing Parent: Yes              │
          │   │ Overwrite Existing Child: Yes               │
          │   │ Selection List Options: See list            │
          │   │ Destination Paths: None                     │
          │   └─────────────────────────────────────────────┘
          │   │Restore Without Session Files
          │   │View Backup Log
          │   │View Error Log
```

7. Choose Yes to proceed with the restore.

# Other Points to Ponder

The log files (error and backup) can be viewed by choosing the Backup Menu from the main SBACKUP menu. This menu provides four choices: Select Working Directory, Backup Selected Target, View Backup Log, and View Error Log. The error log contains information about any files that were opened when the backup routine tried to access them, or other errors that could affect the reliability of a restore operation.

Novell quickly recognized that hard drives are growing in capacity at rates greater than backup media. For that reason, backups can span more than one tape. Though multiple media has been needed since the days when backups used to be done to tapes, it has not been all that long ago that you could only back up one tape. It is highly recommended that spare tapes be kept around and handy so that you don't find yourself in a pinch when a backup that always used to fill only x number of tapes now needs x+1 to complete.

You need not use one tape per backup session. Sessions can be appended to the end of an existing tape, and this makes perfect sense to do with incremental backups.

NetWare 4 allows for file compression. If compression is turned on, the speed of restore operations will be lengthened if you are overwriting existing files, because the files are decompressed for examination before being overwritten. If you have compressed files and are doing a complete restore of a directory, speed can be increased by deleting the files prior to the restoration.

# What Happened to NBACKUP?

NBACKUP is a utility that was included with NetWare starting with version 2.2. Though a step in the right direction, it was significantly lacking in fundamental features. It could back up only DOS and Macintosh name spaces, for example, and could not be used to back up other servers. The backup format used with NBACKUP is not compatible with SBACKUP, and the appropriate utility must be running to do a restore.

Further, NBACKUP did not allow appending additional backups to a single tape, and it could restore files only to the same storage device from which they were originally backed up. In other words, 2.2 files could not be backed up and restored on a 3.11 server.

NetWare 2.2 included only NBACKUP; 3.11 had NBACKUP and SBACKUP. An important note, however, is that 3.11's SBACKUP did not feature SMS technology. NetWare 3.12 has SMS technology in SBACKUP and no longer includes NBACKUP. The same is true with NetWare 4.x.

# Real World

The system administrator alone bears the responsibility for maintaining the integrity of the system data, and there is no better way of so doing than by making certain that good, routine backups are performed and maintained on a regular basis.

Make certain that backups are being performed on your system on at least a daily basis. Make certain that the media being used is being rotated so that if your last backup turns out to be degraded, you have another one to fall back on. Further, make certain that some of the backups are stored off-site, in case a tornado or hurricane damages your building.

Always prepare for the worst-case scenario and hope that it never happens. Have in place a contingency plan for every error or problem that can occur, and make certain that key players are familiar with it. As part of that plan, make certain that several people at your site know how to perform backups and restores and have access to where the tapes are stored. Although keeping all this knowledge to yourself makes for good job security, it also makes for a lousy way to ensure the future of a business.

# Summary

SBACKUP is a useful utility that provides a bare-bones approach to backing up the files on a network. Not only will it work for backing up a server, it also enables you to back up the files on a client machine. When using SMS technology—which began with 3.12—the host and target can communicate directly, and network traffic can be significantly reduced during the operation.

# The Elements of Printing

One of the most complicated components of running (or administering) a network is print management. Print management can be broken into two smaller elements, the first of which includes submitting print jobs and performing printing functions. The second element involves configuring printing on the network.

This chapter looks at the various command-line utilities you use to submit print jobs. Chapter 13, "Advanced Printing Concepts," addresses printing configuration.

## Using the CAPTURE Command

The CAPTURE utility redirects printed output from applications that aren't designed to run on a network, or from the screen to a NetWare print queue. A plethora of options can be used with it, including those shown in the following list:

◆ **/?.** Displays basic syntax help.

◆ **AU.** Autoendcap automatically closes a print job when you exit an application. By default, autoendcap is enabled.

◆ **NA.** No Autoendcap requires the use of the ENDCAP utility to end the capture.

◆ **B.** Enables you to define a banner. A banner name can be any word or phrase up to 12 characters that you want to appear on the lower part of the banner page.

◆ **NB.** Stops NetWare from printing a banner page.

◆ **C.** Used as c=n, where n is the number of copies you want to print (the default is 1).

◆ **FF.** FormFeed sends a form-feed code to the printer at the end of the job, so the next job starts at the top of the next sheet of paper. (By default, form feeding is enabled.)

◆ **NFF.** NoFormFeed does not send a form-feed code at the end of a print job.

◆ **K.** Keeps all the data received during a print capture, in case the workstation locks up or loses power while capturing data.

◆ **L.** Used in the syntax L=n, where n is the LPT port you want to capture. The default is 1, and CAPTURE cannot redirect output from serial ports.

◆ **NAM.** Enables you to specify a name or phrase, up to 12 characters long, to appear in the upper part of the banner page.

◆ **NOTI.** Notifies the user when the print job has cleared the print queue.

◆ **NNOTI.** Does not notify the user when the print job has been printed (the default).

◆ **Q.** Syntax is Q=queuename, where queuename is the file server queue you want to send a print job to.

◆ **S.** Syntax is s=n, where n is the name of a file server other than your default to which you are sending the print job.

◆ **SH.** The most useful troubleshooting option of all. It shows a list of the currently captured LPT ports.

◆ **T.** Syntax is T=n, where you choose to override the default tab setting of 8 spaces to something else. The acceptable tab range is from 0 to 18.

◆ **NT.** Signifies NoTabs and makes all tabs arrive at the printer unchanged.

◆ **TI.** The syntax is TI=n, where n is a specified number of seconds to wait after the application finishes writing to the file. After the specified amount of time, CAPTURE begins again. For best results, TI should not be set to less than 5 seconds or greater than 60. Setting it to 0 disables the Timeout feature.

If the TI setting is too low, you can have problems printing graphic files. Changing it to a higher number corrects only parts of files being printed.

To capture print jobs to the ADMIN queue on the PRIMER server, for example, the command is

```
CAPTURE S=PRIMER Q=ADMIN_Q NB NFF TI=10
```

The command shown also keeps a banner page from printing, doesn't print a form feed, and sets the time-out to 10 seconds.

To see the status of your current capture, use the following command:

```
P:\>CAPTURE /SH
LPT1:   Capturing data to server PRIMER queue ADMIN.
  User will not be notified after the files are printed.
  Capture Defaults:Enabled        Automatic Endcap:Enabled
  Banner :(None)            Form Feed     :No
  Copies :1                 Tabs          :No conversion
  Form   :0                 Timeout Count :10 seconds
LPT2:   Capturing data to server PRIMER queue LASER.
  User will not be notified after the files are printed.
  Capture Defaults:Enabled        Automatic Endcap:Enabled
  Banner :(None)            Form Feed     :No
```

**171**

```
        Copies :1              Tabs         :No conversion
        Form   :0              Timeout Count :10 seconds

LPT3:   Capturing data to server PRIMER queue ADMIN_2.
    User will not be notified after the files are printed.
    Capture Defaults:Enabled          Automatic Endcap:Enabled
    Banner :(None)            Form Feed     :No
    Copies :1                Tabs           :No conversion
    Form   :0                Timeout Count  :10 seconds
```

 A problem can occur at the workstation if you press Shift+Print Screen when no LPT ports are captured and no local printers are attached to your workstation. Invariably, the workstation hangs, and requires rebooting. To solve this problem, add the following line to the workstation's NET.CFG file:

**LOCAL PRINTERS = 0**

# Using the ENDCAP Utility

The ENDCAP utility terminates the capturing of one or more of your workstation's LPT ports. Using it alone ends the capture of all ports, or it can be used with any of the options shown in the following list:

◆ **L=n.** Ends the capture of whichever port is specified by n. ENDCAP L=3, for example, ends the capture of port 3.

◆ **ALL.** Ends the capturing of all LPT ports.

◆ **Cancel.** Ends the capturing of LPT1 and deletes data without printing it.

◆ **Cancel Local n.** Ends the capturing of the specified LPT port and deletes data without printing it.

◆ **Cancel ALL.** Ends the capturing of all LPT ports and deletes the data without printing it.

# Submitting Jobs with NPRINT

NPRINT works the same as the PRINT command in DOS. It submits a text file to the NetWare print queue. Unfortunately, the file must be a text file. Fortunately, a large number of parameters can be given with the job. (Many are similar to those given on a global scale with CAPTURE, but on an individual scale here.) The parameters are included in the following list:

- **Banner=banner name**
- **Copies=n**
- **Delete.** Deletes a file immediately after it is printed.
- **Form=name.** Specifies the name or number of a previously defined form.
- **FormFeed**
- **Job=jobname.** Specifies which print job configuration to use (which must have been previously created with PRINTCON).
- **NAMe=username**
- **NoBanner**
- **Details.** Displays a job's printing parameters.
- **NoFormFeed**
- **NoNOTIfy**
- **NoTabs**
- **NOTIfy**
- **Queue=queuename**
- **Server=servername**
- **Tabs=n**

To print seven copies of the AUTOEXEC.BAT file to the ADMIN queue, without a banner page, the command is

```
NPRINT AUTOEXEC.BAT Q=ADMIN C=7 NB
```

**173**

NPRINT is a useful utility enabling you to submit print jobs directly from the command line.

# Using PSC

Chapter 13 talks about PCONSOLE, a menu-based utility that can be used for numerous things—one of which is checking printer status. PSC is a command-line utility offering those same features. The syntax is

```
PSC PS=printservername P=printernumber options
```

The valid options are shown in the following list:

- ◆ **AB.** Aborts the current print job and continues with the next job in the queue.

- ◆ **STAT.** Shows the status of the printer.

- ◆ **PAU.** Pauses printing temporarily.

- ◆ **STO.** Stops the printer.

- ◆ **STAR.** Starts the printer after it has been paused or stopped.

- ◆ **MA Character.** Marks a line of characters on the current line.

- ◆ **FF.** Form-feeds the printer to the top of the next page.

- ◆ **MOF=n.** Mounts a form.

- ◆ **PRI.** Privatizes a remote printer by making it a local printer, so network users cannot access it.

- ◆ **SH.** Changes a private printer back to shared status.

PSC offers a number of parameters, well worth memorizing, for controlling printing and print jobs.

# Using PSTAT

The PSTAT utility is a simple one that shows printer status information. The syntax is

```
PSTAT S=servername P=printer
```

The servername is optional if you're checking a printer connected to the default server.

 **Note** An offline printer is listed as online until you attempt to print to it.

The printer must be connected directly to the server for the PSTAT utility to work.

# Understanding SPOOL

The SPOOL utility is rarely used these days, but it can definitely come in handy in troublesome situations. It creates, and lists, spooler mappings to print queues that are required to set up default print queues for CAPTURE and NPRINT. It also supports applications written to printer numbers rather than print queues. The syntax is

```
SPOOL printernumber TO QUEUE queuename
```

Numbers for the `printernumber` range from 0 through 4, and the `queuename` is any existing print queue name.

## PRACTICE EXERCISE

Using the software that comes with this book, you can emulate a running network without needing access to it. Because the executable file is called PRIMER, you can execute any command by preceding it with that call. If, for example, there were a command called XYZ, the command would be PRIMER XYZ.

Using this software, examine some features of the utilities discussed in this chapter using the following steps:

1. Type **PRIMER CAPTURE /?**

2. Notice the information that it gives you. Rather than attempting to remember every single parameter available, the /? parameter quite often can be a lifesaver.

3. Type **PRIMER CAPTURE /SH**

4. Notice the setup for each of the captured ports.

5. Type **PRIMER PSC**

6. Note that when the /? option is not available, typing the command by itself provides online help about what the available parameters are.

# Summary

This chapter explores the basic command-line utilities used to capture network printers and submit print jobs. Chapter 13 delves further into printing, looking at the ways of configuring the services and the utilities used to do so.

# Advanced Printing Concepts

Five utilities make up the necessary tools for configuring and managing network printing, including the following:

- ◆ PCONSOLE
- ◆ PRINTCON
- ◆ PRINTDEF
- ◆ PSERVER
- ◆ RPRINTER

With the exception of PCONSOLE, rarely are the other utilities thought about on a daily basis. That doesn't mean they don't run, or aren't crucial to operations. It just means that after your scripts and configurations are configured, you have few occasions where you need to change them.

This lack of contact can be good and bad. It's good because, after you get everything up and running, you can walk away and let things tend to themselves. It's bad because, when you do make a change, rarely can you remember the syntax and idiosyncrasies of the utilities allowing you to do so.

This chapter looks at all five, and explores where, why, and how they are used.

# Understanding PCONSOLE

PCONSOLE, or print console, enables you to view information about print jobs, add them, and delete them from the print queues. Users can add, delete, and change the order of jobs in the queue they've scheduled, and the supervisor can do so for everyone. Figure 13.1 shows the main menu.

**Figure 13.1**

The main PCONSOLE menu.

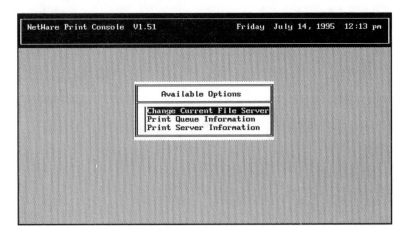

Three choices are available from the main menu, and all three are discussed in the following sections.

## Change Current File Server

Selecting Change Current File Server shows a list of active file servers on the network, as shown in figure 13.2. Highlight the file server you want and press Enter.

**Note** If the server you want is not listed, press Insert. NetWare searches for any additional file servers.

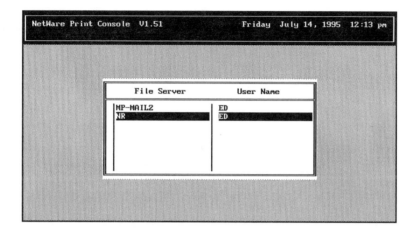

**Figure 13.2**

The list of available file servers.

# Print Queue Information

Selecting Print Queue Information from PCONSOLE's main menu shows the print queues on the current file server, as shown in figure 13.3. From here, you can add, delete, or rename a queue (if you have Supervisor rights).

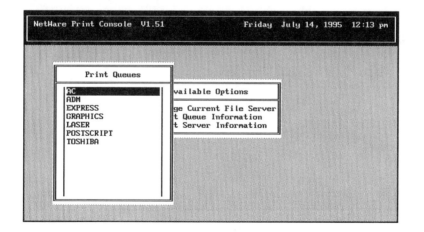

**Figure 13.3**

The list of print queues on this file server.

You see print queue information by highlighting the queue and pressing Enter, as shown in figure 13.4. Here, a different set of options is shown to users based on their security equivalents. The list shown in figure 13.4 is all of those available, and requires supervisor rights.

**Figure 13.4**

The queue information options.

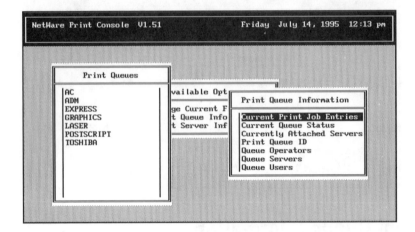

Selecting Current Print Job Entries shows a list of the current print jobs, as shown in figure 13.5. These are the jobs currently waiting to be serviced—or presently being serviced. The two entries in figure 13.5 are both being printed at the current time, as witnessed by the word *Active* in the status field.

**Figure 13.5**

The current queue entries.

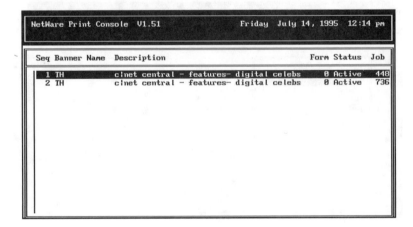

To delete one of these jobs, highlight the job and press Delete. A dialog box appears, prompting you to verify the deletion. To add a job to the queue, press Insert and fill in the appropriate information. If you press Enter on an entry, additional information about the print job appears, as shown in figure 13.6.

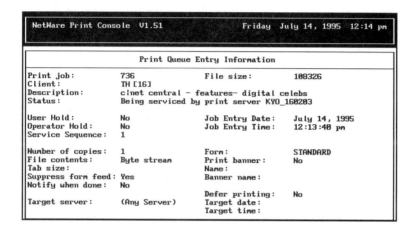

**Figure 13.6**

Additional information for the selected print queue entry.

## Current Queue Status

Figure 13.7 shows how you can see the current queue status, and figure 13.8 shows an example of the display. The bottom three fields on the screen are the most important because they dictate the following:

◆ Whether users can place entries in a queue.

◆ Whether the server can service entries in a queue.

◆ Whether a new server can attach to a queue.

The default for each print queue status field is Yes. To change the status of an option, highlight the option and press Enter; then change the status by typing **N**.

**Figure 13.7**

Selecting Current
Queue Status.

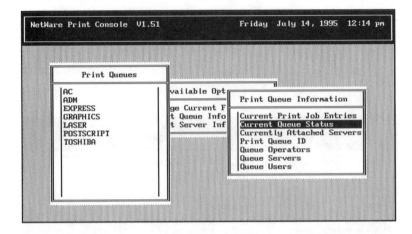

**Figure 13.8**

The status of a
selected queue.

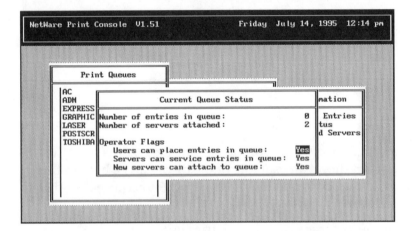

## Currently Attached Servers

The Currently Attached Servers option, shown being selected
from the menu in figure 13.9, shows, as its name suggests, which
print servers are currently attached. A sample of the display is
shown in figure 13.10.

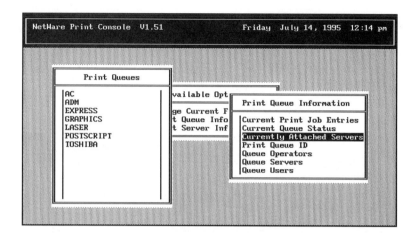

**Figure 13.9**

Selecting Currently
Attached Servers.

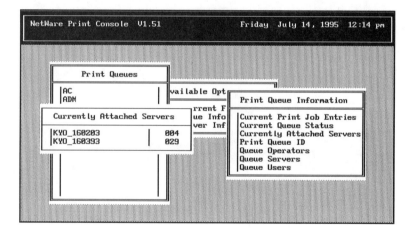

**Figure 13.10**

Those print servers
currently attached to
the queue.

# Print Queue ID

The physical object ID number of the queue, as well as the server
to which it is attached, is shown when you select Print Queue ID
from the Print Queue Information menu. The object ID number is
a link to the directory created with the same object ID number as
its name in SYS:SYSTEM. This directory is where files and print
jobs are stored during printing. Only after they have completely
printed are they removed.

## Queue Operators

The Queue Operators are accessed by choosing that option from
the Print Queue Information screen shown in figure 13.11. A
complete list of users and groups defined as operators appears,
as shown in figure 13.12.

**Figure 13.11**

Selecting the Queue
Operators option.

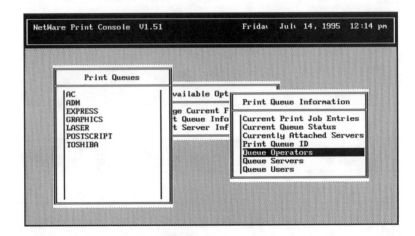

**Figure 13.12**

The defined queue
operators.

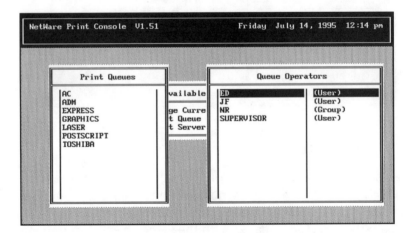

Queue operators are users and groups who can manage the print
queue. You can add someone to the list by pressing Insert and
selecting the new operator from the Queue Operator Candidates
dialog box. You can delete someone by highlighting their entry
and pressing Delete.

# Queue Servers

Queue Servers, chosen from the Print Queue Information dialog box, shows a list of print servers that should attach to the queue. Every print queue has to be serviced by a print server, or multiple print servers.

Selecting this option lists the servers, as shown in figure 13.13. If you press Insert, you can add another server from the list of candidates that appear, as shown in figure 13.14.

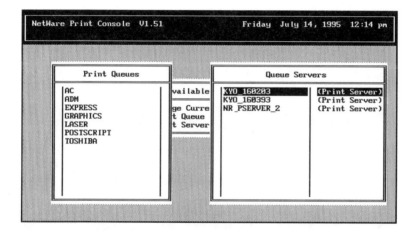

**Figure 13.13**

The current queue servers.

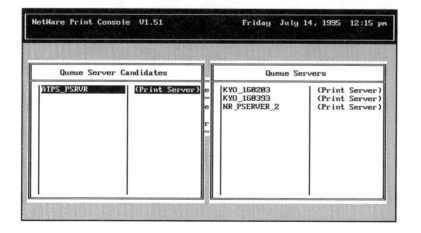

**Figure 13.14**

The candidates that can be added to the server list.

185

## Queue Users

The last option on the Print Queue Information menu is Queue Users. Selecting this option shows a list of users able to use the selected print queue. Group EVERYONE is assigned by default when a print queue is created. To add a user (or group of users) to this list, press the Insert key. A screen listing all candidate queue users appears.

## Print Server Information

To see information about a print server (as opposed to a print queue), select Print Server Information from the main PCONSOLE menu, as shown in figure 13.15.

**Figure 13.15**

The Print Server Information option.

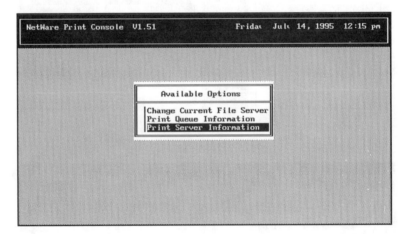

A list of current print servers appears. Select one from the list, and the Print Server Information screen appears, as shown in figure 13.16.

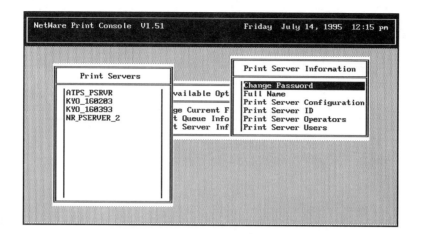

```
NetWare Print Console  V1.51                Friday  July 14, 1995  12:15 pm

          Print Servers                     Print Server Information

  ATPS_PSRVR             vailable Opt      Change Password
  KYO_160203                               Full Name
  KYO_160393            ge Current F       Print Server Configuration
  NR_PSERVER_2          t Queue Info       Print Server ID
                        t Server Inf       Print Server Operators
                                           Print Server Users
```

**Figure 13.16**
Current servers and the Print Server Information menu.

## Change Password

This menu choice is self-explanatory; it prompts you to type the new password, then retype it to verify that no mistakes were made. If it exists, the password is used when loading and unloading the print server.

## Full Name

This menu choice enables you to give free text that helps identify the print server.

## Print Server Configuration

The Print Server Configuration choice, highlighted in figure 13.17, brings up another menu of choices, as shown in figure 13.18.

Each option in this menu also can be found in other portions of PCONSOLE, except Printer Configuration, which brings up a dialog box enabling you to identify each printer hooked to the print server. This menu selection brings up a list of the configured printers, as shown in figure 13.19.

**187**

**Figure 13.17**

The Print Server Configuration menu choice.

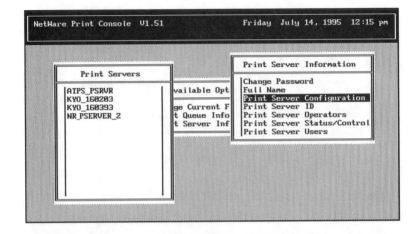

**Figure 13.18**

The available configuration options.

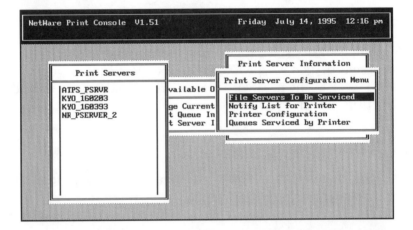

**Figure 13.19**

The currently configured printers.

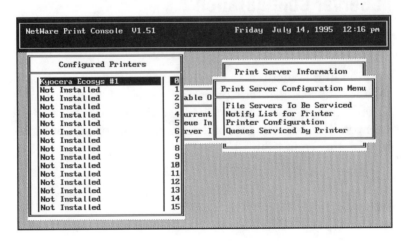

## Print Server ID

The Print Server ID menu option shows you the print server ID, as well as the name of the file server.

## Print Server Operators

Selecting this option, as shown in figure 13.20, shows a list of all the current operators (see fig. 13.21).

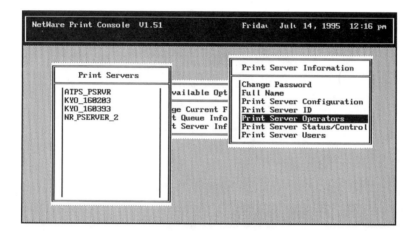

**Figure 13.20**

The Print Server Operators menu selection.

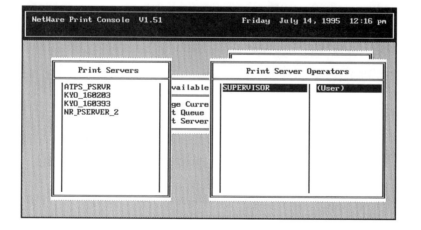

**Figure 13.21**

The currently defined server operator list.

As with any other listing, you can add names by pressing Insert and selecting them from the Candidate Operators screen. Adding multiple operators is done by marking them; you can mark them by pressing F5, then pressing Enter.

## Print Server Status/Control

The Print Server Status/Control option activates another menu—the Print Server Status and Control menu shown in figure 13.22.

**Figure 13.22**

The Print Server Status and Control menu.

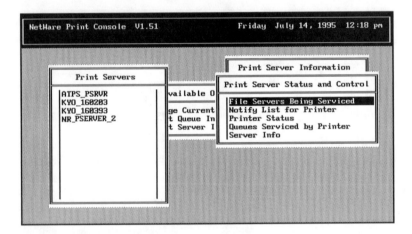

The menu choices include the following:

- ◆ **File Servers Being Serviced.** Shows the file servers to which the print server is attached.

- ◆ **Notify List for Printer.** Shows a list of users or groups that will be notified if the printer has problems. You can add or delete users and groups from this option.

- ◆ **Printer Status.** Shows the status of the current printer.

- ◆ **Queues Serviced by Printer.** Shows a list of print queues serviced by the printer.

- ◆ **Server Info.** Displays the information shown in figure 13.23. In addition to general information, it enables you to change the status of the current print server.

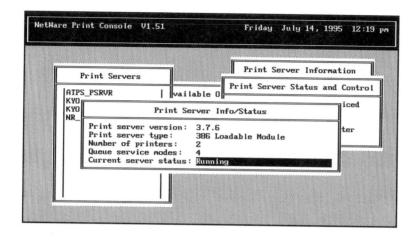

**Figure 13.23**
The server status information.

## Print Server Users

Selecting Print Server Users shows a list of users and groups with rights to use the print server. The default entry is the group EVERYONE. To add more users, press Insert and select the new users from the Print Server User Candidate list. Likewise, to delete a user, highlight the user and press Delete.

# Configuring Print Jobs with PRINTCON

The PRINTCON utility creates special printer setup configuration files. Figure 13.24 shows the main PRINTCON menu.

From here, you can do three things:

- ◆ **Edit Print Job Configurations.** Modify or create print job configurations from here. A list of exiting ones appears, and to define a new print job configuration, press Insert. To delete a print job configuration, highlight the entry and press Delete.

◆ **Select Default Print Job Configuration.** Enables you to specify which print job configuration is used as the default configuration.

◆ **Copy Print Job Configurations.** Enables the supervisor to distribute a print job to specific users, or to let users share a print job configuration with other users.

**Figure 13.24**

The main PRINTCON menu.

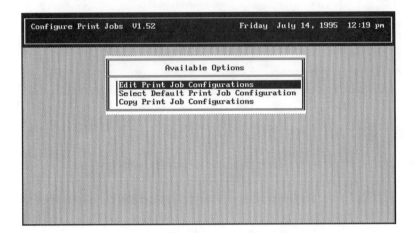

# Defining Forms with PRINTDEF

The PRINTDEF utility enables you to define forms—that are of different size and shape—to be printed on. Figure 13.25 shows the main menu, and you can see the simplicity of it.

Print Devices enables you to import, export, and edit printer names and definitions. Forms enable you to create, delete, or modify the form names and their definitions.

Figure 13.26 shows the form created by default: STANDARD. Figure 13.27 shows the definitions for it. All can be edited from this menu.

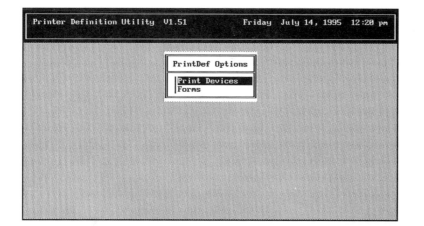

**Figure 13.25**

The main PRINTDEF menu.

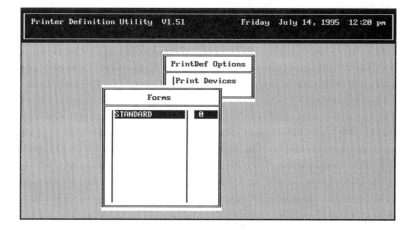

**Figure 13.26**

The default form.

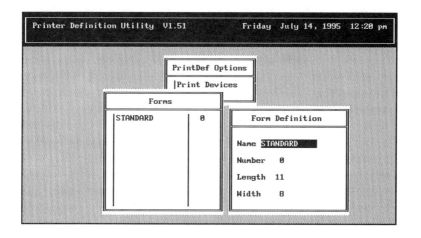

**Figure 13.27**

The definitions for the STANDARD form.

# Using PSERVER.NLM and PSERVER.EXE

The PSERVER utility is what you run on a computer to make it a print server. If the computer in question also functions as a file server, then you use PSERVER.NLM. If the computer in question is not a file server, however, PSERVER.EXE is the utility you load.

## PSERVER.NLM

PSERVER.NLM is the module loaded on a file server to make it a print server as well. The syntax is

`LOAD PSERVER printservername`

The NLM is stored in the SYSTEM subdirectory. If it has been moved from there, then the path to it must be given between the LOAD and PSERVER elements in the command.

To load PSERVER automatically each time you boot the file server, add the command to the server's AUTOEXEC.NCF file.

## PSERVER.EXE

Print servers running on a dedicated workstation run the PSERVER.EXE command. They can support up to 16 printers, and can service queues for up to 8 file servers. The syntax for the command is

`PSERVER fileservername printservername`

To run PSERVER, you need access to IBM$RUN.OVL, SYS$ERR.DAT, SYS$HELP.DAT, and SYS$MSG.DAT, which are in the PUBLIC directory.

# Remote Printing with RPRINTER

If you need to connect a workstation printer to the network as a remote printer, without making it a dedicated workstation (PSERVER.EXE), RPRINTER.EXE is the utility of choice. The syntax for it is

```
RPRINTER printservername printer flag
```

The flags can be:

- ◆ -R (to disconnect the remote printer)
- ◆ -S (to show the status of the remote printer)

Once loaded, RPRINTER runs as a TSR on the workstation; and if more than one remote printer is attached to the workstation, a separate TSR must be loaded for each printer.

As with PSERVER, RPRINTER must have access to a number of files before it can run. These are IBM$RUN.OVL, SYS$ERR.DAT, SYS$HELP.DAT, and SYS$MSG.DAT.

# Real World

Configuring printing is one of the most difficult components of networking, be it with NetWare or any other network operating system. Become extremely familiar with every one of the utilities discussed here, and know the parameters that they offer. Know how to check the status of each printing component, and how to modify it if need be.

What makes managing network printing so confusing is that though it is rarely equaled in importance, it is also something that you do not mess with every day. Once you have the printing functions properly configured, you tend to leave it alone and not worry about it. This hands-off method can lead to a false sense of security; you will need to know everything there is to know about it when an error occurs.

Use the time between errors to familiarize yourself with your setup and all components therein.

# Summary

This chapter examines printing from the perspective of configuration and installment. The five main utilities are discussed, and all available parameters introduced.

Chapter 14, "Managing Volumes and Directories," turns attention to the directory structure and utilities used to manage it.

# Managing Volumes and Directories

Manipulating and managing the directories and subdirectories on your server is crucial when fully administering the network. Essentially, eight utilities fit into this category:

- ◆ CHKDIR
- ◆ CHKVOL
- ◆ NDIR
- ◆ LISTDIR
- ◆ PURGE
- ◆ RENDIR
- ◆ SALVAGE
- ◆ VOLINFO

Some of these do little more than show you information about the volumes or directories; others let you change factors of them. This chapter looks at all eight and discusses the options they provide.

# Using CHKDIR

CHKDIR shows several things about a particular directory, including the following:

- ◆ Directory space limitations for the file server, volume, and directory

- ◆ The volume's maximum storage capacity in kilobytes, and the directory's maximum storage capacity (if the directory has a space restriction in effect)

- ◆ Kilobytes currently in use on the volume and in the specified directory

- ◆ Kilobytes available on the volume and in the specified directory

The following example shows a simple running of the utility:

```
P:\>chkdir

Directory Space Limitation Information For:
PRIMER\VOL1:PROJECTS

    Maximum        In Use      Available
 2,360,808 K   1,736,800 K     624,008 K   Volume Size
               1,352,744 K     624,008 K   \PROJECTS
P:\>
```

The following example shows specifying another path:

```
P:\>chkdir f:

Directory Space Limitation Information For:
PRIMER\SYS:LOGIN

   Maximum        In Use      Available
   410,000 K    289,972 K     120,028 K   Volume Size
                  1,124 K     120,028 K   \LOGIN
P:\>
```

CHKDIR shows several things about a directory, much of which is available from no other utility.

# Using CHKVOL

CHKVOL is similar to CHKDIR, and used to see the amount of space in use and available on the volume. The syntax is:

```
Chkvol fileserver_name\volume_name
```

 **Note** Specifying * for the volume name shows all the volumes that are present; using the same character for the file server shows all file servers you are attached to. This utility is a little dangerous, because it is not limited by security level. Viewable information can be obtained by any user.

An example of using CHKVOL on the current volume is

```
P:\>chkvol

Statistics for fixed volume PRIMER/VOL1:

Total volume space:                    2,360,808  K Bytes
Space used by files:                   1,736,900  K Bytes
Space in use by deleted files:            97,800  K Bytes
Space available from deleted files:       97,800  K Bytes
Space remaining on volume:               623,908  K Bytes
Space available to WSTEEN:               623,908  K Bytes


P:\>
```

The preceding code shows the volume space in bytes, the byte count taken by files, the number of bytes available on the volume, and the number of directory entries left. The following example shows the use of the asterisk wild card character to see the information for all volumes:

```
Statistics for fixed volume PRIMER/SYS:

Total volume space:                      410,000  K Bytes
Space used by files:                     289,632  K Bytes
Space in use by deleted files:            92,328  K Bytes
Space available from deleted files:       92,328  K Bytes
Space remaining on volume:               120,368  K Bytes
Space available to WSTEEN:               120,368  K Bytes
```

**199**

```
Statistics for fixed volume PRIMER/ADMIN:

Total volume space:                         496,660  K Bytes
Space used by files:                          1,964  K Bytes
Space in use by deleted files:                    0  K Bytes
Space available from deleted files:               0  K Bytes
Space remaining on volume:                  494,696  K Bytes
Space available to WSTEEN:                  494,696  K Bytes

Statistics for fixed volume PRIMER/VOL1:

Total volume space:                       2,360,808  K Bytes
Space used by files:                      1,736,900  K Bytes
Space in use by deleted files:               97,800  K Bytes
Space available from deleted files:          97,800  K Bytes
Space remaining on volume:                  623,908  K Bytes
Space available to WSTEEN:                  623,908  K Bytes
```

# Using NDIR

The NDIR command works much like the DIR command in DOS. It shows you the files and subdirectories that are present, but it has more options than you would ever expect to use in a lifetime. It can be used with several options, including the following categories:

◆ Display options

◆ Attribute options

◆ Format options

◆ Restriction options

◆ Sort options

## Display Options

The following list describes the display options:

◆ **/Files Only.** Sorts and displays only files.

◆ **/SUB.** Sorts and displays all subdirectories from your current path.

◆ **/Directories Only.** Sorts and displays only directories.

◆ **/Continuous.** Scrolls display continuously.

◆ **/?.** Displays help.

These options enable you to change the display on your screen.

## Attribute Options

The following list describes the attribute options:

◆ **RO.** Lists files that have the read-only attribute set.

◆ **SH.** Lists files that have the shareable attribute set.

◆ **A.** Lists files that have their archive attribute set. Files are displayed in the backup format, which lists the last modified and last archived dates. The archive flag is set whenever a file is modified.

◆ **X.** Lists files that are flagged as execute only.

◆ **H.** Lists files or directories that have the hidden attribute set.

◆ **SY.** Lists files or directories that have the system attribute set.

◆ **T.** Lists files that have been flagged as transactional.

◆ **P.** Lists files or directories that have the purge attribute set.

◆ **CI.** Lists files flagged as copy inhibited. Restricts Copy rights of users logged in from Macintosh workstations. Only valid for files.

◆ **DI.** Lists files or directories flagged as delete-inhibited. Prevents users from erasing directories or files even if they have Erase rights.

◆ **RI.** Lists files and directories flagged as rename-inhibited. Prevents users from renaming directories and files even if they have modify rights.

◆ **[NOT].** Can be used with all the previous attribute options to look for files that don't have the specified qualities.

The attribute options force the files listed to fall within certain ranges of what their status is.

## Format Options

The following list describes the format options:

◆ **/R.** Lists inherited and effective rights on files and subdirectories; lists rights filters, compression and migration status, and file attributes.

◆ **/D.** Lists date and time information for files and directories.

◆ **/MAC.** Lists Macintosh subdirectories or files in a search area. When you list only Macintosh files or subdirectories, they appear with their full Macintosh names.

◆ **/LONG.** Lists all Macintosh, OS/2, and NFS long file names for the file under all loaded name spaces in a given search area.

The format options change the amount of information shown to you on files matching your search specifications.

## Restriction Options

The restriction options, all of which can be used with [NOT], are described in the following list:

◆ **/OW[NOT] EQ user.** Lists files not created by a specific user.

◆ **/SI[NOT] GR I EQ I LE number.** Lists file sizes that are not greater than, equal to, or less than a certain number.

◆ **/UP[NOT] BEF I EQ I AFT mm-dd-yy.** Lists files not last updated on, before, or after the date specified.

◆ **/CR[NOT] BEF I EQ I AFT mm-dd-yy.** Lists files not created on, before, or after the date specified.

◆ **/AC[NOT] BEF I EQ I AFT mm-dd-yy.** Lists files not last accessed on, before, or after the specified date.

◆ **/AR[NOT] BEF | EQ | AFT mm-dd-yy.** Lists files not archived on, before, or after the specified date.

The restriction options restrict the file matches that are found.

## Sort Options

The following list describes the sort options:

◆ **/SORT SI.** Sorts display by file size from least to greatest.

◆ **/SORT CR.** Sorts display by creation date from earliest to latest.

◆ **/SORT OW.** Sorts display alphabetically by owner names.

◆ **/SORT AC.** Sorts display by last accessed date from earliest to latest.

◆ **/SORT AR.** Sorts display by last archive date from earliest to latest.

◆ **/SORT UP.** Sorts display by last update from earliest to latest.

◆ **/SORT UN.** Stops all sorting.

◆ **[REV].** Can be used by all preceding sort options to reverse the sort order.

The sort options take the display and alter it into a pattern before displaying it to you. That pattern can be based on a number of things: owner, archive date, name, and so forth.

# Using LISTDIR

LISTDIR shows subdirectories and information about their creation date, Inherited Rights Mask, and your effective rights in them. The following list describes the options you can use with it:

◆ **/Rights.** Lists the Inherited Rights Masks of all subdirectories in a specific directory.

◆ **/Effective rights.** Lists the effective rights for all subdirectories of the specified directory.

◆ **/Date or /Time.** Lists the date or time or both that a subdirectory was created.

◆ **/Subdirectories.** Lists a directory's subdirectories.

◆ **/All.** Lists all subdirectories, their Inherited Rights Masks, effective rights, and their creation dates and times.

LISTDIR is an extremely useful utility that shows subdirectories and information about their creation date, Inherited Rights Mask, and your effective rights in them.

# Using PURGE

The PURGE utility restores to the system all the space currently in use by deleted files. It can be used to delete an individual file, everything in a directory, or everything that has been deleted on a volume (if you use the /ALL parameter following).

It's important to know that PURGE doesn't remove files that are currently in existence unless you specifically indicate a file to remove. By default, it only removes files that have already been deleted, and prevents them from being recovered with SALVAGE.

# Using RENDIR

RENDIR enables you to rename one directory to another name. RENDIR renames a directory, but it doesn't affect the directory's trustee or user rights.

 Changing directory names with RENDIR doesn't update MAP commands in DOS batch files or NetWare login scripts.

# Using SALVAGE

SALVAGE is a menu utility that enables you to restore files that have been previously deleted but not yet purged. When a file is deleted, it only appears as such when you search a directory. In reality, the space it occupied is not restored to the system, and the file can always be brought back unless the server runs out of disk space, or the supervisor uses the PURGE utility.

 Files must be deleted with DOS utilities, such as DEL or ERASE, for SALVAGE to work. Files removed with PURGE are forever removed from the system.

 Deleted files are stored in the directory from which they were deleted. If that directory itself gets deleted, NetWare stores them in a hidden directory called DELETED.SAV.

# Using VOLINFO

VOLINFO is a quick utility that shows the amount of disk space left on a file server or volume. For up to six volumes, you see the amount of space that originally was available on the volume, as well as how much of that space is free. Figure 14.1 shows an example of the display.

If your server has more than six volumes, press the Down Arrow key or the Up Arrow key to get to the following or preceding volumes.

**Figure 14.1**

The VOLINFO screen.

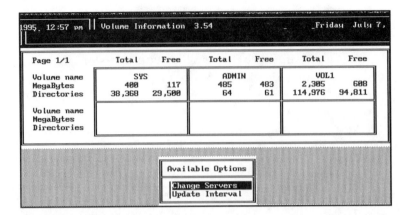

| 1995, 12:57 pm ‖ Volume Information 3.54 | | | | | _Friday July 7, |
|---|---|---|---|---|---|

| Page 1/1 | Total | Free | Total | Free | Total | Free |
|---|---|---|---|---|---|---|
| Volume name | SYS | | ADMIN | | VOL1 | |
| MegaBytes | 400 | 117 | 485 | 483 | 2,305 | 608 |
| Directories | 38,368 | 29,500 | 64 | 61 | 114,976 | 94,811 |
| Volume name | | | | | | |
| MegaBytes | | | | | | |
| Directories | | | | | | |

Available Options

Change Servers
Update Interval

# PRACTICE EXERCISE

Using the software that comes with this book, you can emulate a running network without needing access to it. Because the executable file is called PRIMER, you can execute any command by preceding it with that call. If there were a command called XYZ, for example, the command would be PRIMER XYZ.

Using this software, look at the results of the CHKVOL command:

1. Type **PRIMER CHKDIR**

2. Note the information for \LOGIN directory of SYS volume.

3. Type **PRIMER CHKVOL**

4. Note the additional information given over CHDIR.

5. Type **PRIMER LISTDIR**

6. You now see the subdirectories as well.

7. Type **PRIMER LISTDIR /R**

8. Note what specified rights are there.

9. Type **PRIMER LISTDIR /E**

10. Now see what your real (effective) rights are. Why are they different? Because you are logged in as supervisor.

11. Type **PRIMER LISTDIR /D**

12. Type **PRIMER LISTDIR /T**

13. Note the display between the last two commands to be the same.

14. Type **LISTDIR /S**

15. Look at all information by typing **LISTDIR /A**

# Real World

Examine your system using the utilities discussed here, and complete the following information sheet, which you should keep handy in the event your system requires maintenance:

1. Number of volumes:

2. Name of first volume:

3. Size of the volume:

4. How much space is in use:

5. How much space is available:

6. How much space could be recovered by purging all deleted files:

7. Name of second volume (if applicable):

8. Size of the volume:

9. Amount of space in use:

10. Amount of space available:

11. Amount of space that could be recovered by purging all deleted files:

12. How often you run Purge:

# Summary

This chapter explores eight utilities that return information about the volumes and directories on the server. Chapter 15, "Managing Files," takes this same concept down to the file level.

15
CHAPTER

# Managing Files

Files are the lowest common denominator on a network. Disks become partitions and volumes. Volumes become directories, which then birth subdirectories, and so on. The lowest level you can go is the file. Files are unique entities beneath all the other options on your PC.

Files are also the most important entity on your network. They contain—or manipulate (if they are executables)—data. Without files, it wouldn't matter how many volumes or directories you had; you would still be out of business within a week.

This chapter picks up where Chapter 14, "Managing Volumes and Directories," leaves off. It focuses on directories and subdirectories and the components therein. This chapter continues that discussion down to the file level, looking at two utilities: FILER and NCOPY.

# Understanding FILER

FILER is a simple, menu-based utility that enables you to control directory, file, and volume information. Using it, you can perform the following tasks:

◆ List files

◆ Copy files

◆ Rename files

◆ Delete files

To start the utility, type **FILER** at a command line; the menu shown in figure 15.1 appears.

**Figure 15.1**

FILER's main menu.

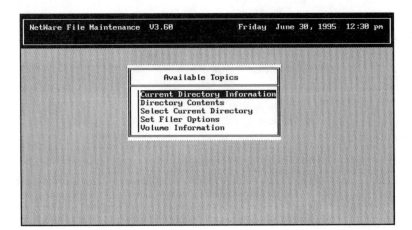

## Current Directory Information

Figure 15.2 shows the information the Directory Information for PUBLIC screen presents. It shows information about the directory, including creation date, owner, current effective rights, Inherited Rights Mask, directory attributes, trustees, and current effective rights.

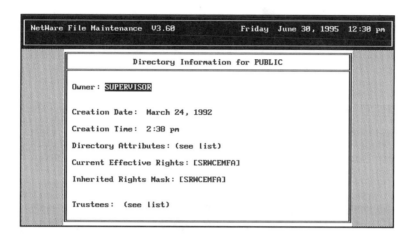

**Figure 15.2**
Directory information.

You also can see and assign trustees for the directory from this option by choosing the bottom entry: Trustees. A screen similar to the one shown in figure 15.3 appears. From here, to delete a trustee, highlight it and press Delete. To add a new trustee, press Enter and type in the new name.

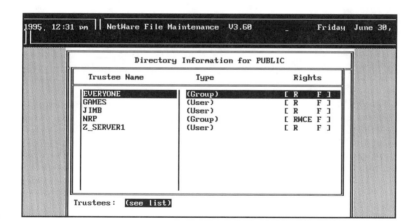

**Figure 15.3**
The list of current trustees.

When you press Enter on a field, a list of available selections appears. If nothing is shown in the box, press Insert, and you see a list of available options. Mark a specific option by highlighting it and pressing Enter, or mark several options by pressing F5. After marking the options you want to add to the list, press Enter to make them applicable.

You can delete existing entries by moving the highlight to them and pressing Delete; or you can add more options by following the steps just described.

## Directory Contents

Figure 15.4 shows the highlight moved to the Directory Contents option. The option shows the files and subdirectories of the current directory.

**Figure 15.4**

The Directory Contents menu choice.

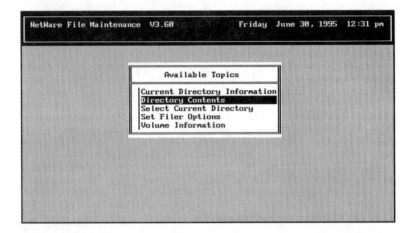

```
NetWare File Maintenance  V3.60              Friday  June 30, 1995  12:31 pm


                        Available Topics

                 Current Directory Information
                 Directory Contents
                 Select Current Directory
                 Set Filer Options
                 Volume Information
```

**Note** When a directory is selected, pressing Enter enables you to make that directory your current directory. The rights you currently have determine which options you see.

When a file or a directory is selected, it can be copied, moved, or viewed. Users also can view or set file and directory information such as copy inhibit, delete inhibit, and so on.

One word of warning: Depending on the size of the directory, you often will need a considerable amount of free memory on the workstation to be able to use this option. Should you lack sufficient memory, a screen similar to that shown in figure 15.5 appears.

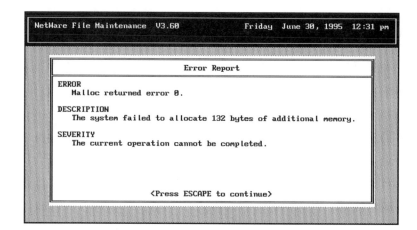

**Figure 15.5**

The error screen that appears when a workstation has insufficient memory.

 **Note** Multiple files and subdirectories can be moved or deleted, but directories and files have to be deleted separately.

The Copy File option copies the file to the new location and leaves the original file; the Move File option copies the file to the new location and then deletes the moved file from its original location.

File information can be changed by moving to the field and pressing Enter. You can type the new information, or choose from a provided list. To add a new right, for example, press Insert, select the right to add by highlighting it, and press Enter. To remove or revoke a right, highlight it and press Delete. Multiple rights can be marked for addition or deletion with the F5 key.

## Select Current Directory

The Select Current Directory option, shown being chosen from the main menu in figure 15.6, enables you to change your current directory and move about the NetWare system. To make another directory current, enter the path as shown in figure 15.7.

**Figure 15.6**

The Select Current Directory menu option.

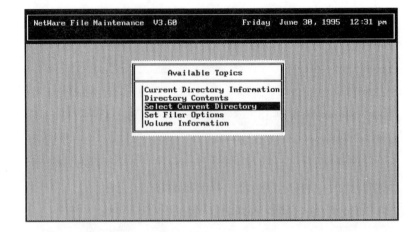

**Figure 15.7**

Entering a new directory path.

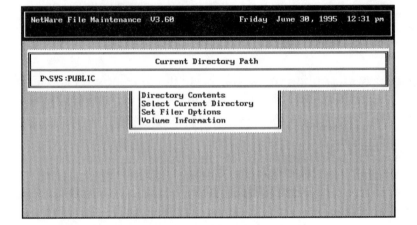

## Set FILER Options

The FILER options determine how this utility functions. To access the options, select the menu choice shown in figure 15.8. A screen of options appears, as shown in figure 15.9.

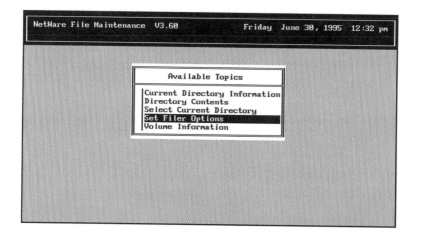

**Figure 15.8**

Selecting Set Filer Options.

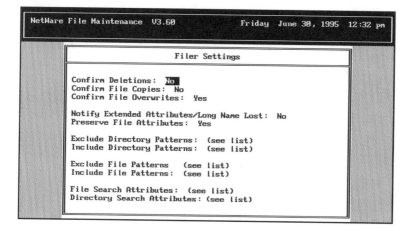

**Figure 15.9**

The existing FILER settings.

Two important sets of options are those specified as patterns to be included or excluded in searches of files and directories (see the middle section of figure 15.9). Figure 15.10 shows the default exclusion pattern for directories (the same would be true for files); figure 15.11 shows the inclusion pattern of everything (again, the same would be true for files). Exclude patterns always override include patterns.

**Figure 15.10**

The exclusion list.

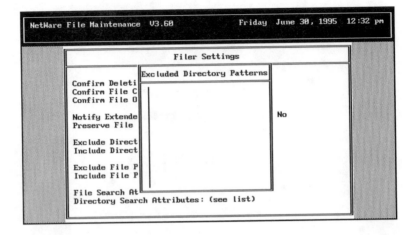

**Figure 15.11**

The inclusion list.

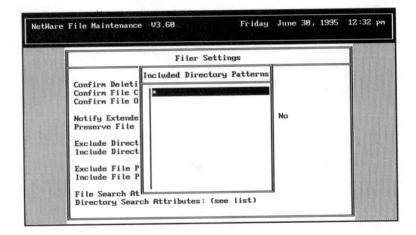

Table 15.1 shows the options in FILER and what the default for each option is and how it affects operations.

**Table 15.1**
*Filer Options*

| Option | Default | Setting Explanation |
|--------|---------|---------------------|
| Confirm Deletions | No | Each file deletion does not need to be confirmed. |
| Confirm File Copies | No | Each file copied does not need to be verified. |

| Option | Default | Setting Explanation |
|---|---|---|
| Confirm File Overwrites | Yes | If a file exists in the target directory, verification will take place before the file being copied will overwrite the one already in that location. |
| Notify Extended Attributes/Long Name Lost | No | You are not notified when the attributes and long file names are not preserved. |
| Exclude Directory Patterns | Blank list | A list can be created by pressing Insert and entering a desired pattern. To remove a pattern, press Delete. To remove multiple patterns, use the F5 key to mark a list of patterns and then press Delete. |
| Include Directory Patterns | | An asterisk represents all possible subdirectories, which is the default setting. |
| Exclude File Patterns | Blank list | A list can be created by pressing Insert and entering a desired pattern. |
| Include File Patterns | | An asterisk is used to display all files. |
| File Search Attributes | Blank list | To add an attribute to the list, press Insert. To remove an attribute, highlight it and press Delete. To remove multiple attributes, use the F5 key to mark them and then press Delete. |
| Directory Search Attributes | Blank list | To add an attribute to the list, press Insert. To remove an attribute, highlight it and press Delete. To remove multiple attributes, use the F5 key to mark them and then press Delete. |

# Volume Information

Volume Information is accessible from the last menu choice, as shown in figure 15.12. It enables you to view information about the volume on which the current directory is located. You can see the volume's total size, the free space that is left on the volume, the maximum number of directory entries, and how many directory entries the volume has remaining (see fig. 15.13).

**Figure 15.12**

Choosing the Volume Information option.

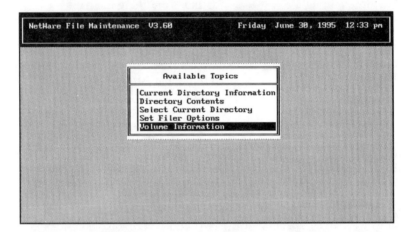

**Figure 15.13**

The information presented by choosing the Volume Information option.

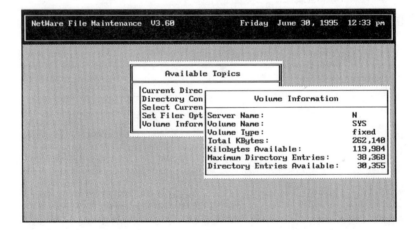

# Using NCOPY

NCOPY is a utility in the PUBLIC directory that works like the DOS COPY command. A key difference between the two is that NCOPY performs the copy at the file server, and COPY reads data from the file server and then writes the data back to the file server over the network. Because of this critical difference, NCOPY is always faster and does not slow down the network as much.

The syntax for the command is as follows:

```
NCOPY path FILENAME to path FILENAME option
```

Wild card characters are supported, and you can go up to as many as 25 directory levels. A minor difference with COPY, as well, is that the copied file retains the original's date and time. The following list describes the NCOPY options:

- ◆ **/A.** Copies only files that have the archive bit set. Will not reset the archive bit.

- ◆ **/C.** Copies files without preserving the attributes or name space information.

- ◆ **/E.** Copies empty subdirectories when you copy an entire directory with the /S option.

- ◆ **/F.** Forces the operating system to write sparse files.

- ◆ **/I.** Notifies you when attributes or name space information cannot be copied.

- ◆ **/M.** Copies only files that have the archive bit set, and resets the archive bit after copying.

- ◆ **/P.** Preserves the current file attributes in version 2.2. If NCOPY is used without the /P, then attributes on the copied files are set to Non-Shareable, Read/Write.

- ◆ **/S.** Copies all subdirectories and files in them.

- ◆ **/V.** Verifies that the original file and the copy are identical.

- ◆ **/?.** Displays help.

- ◆ **/VER.** Shows the version information for this utility, and a list of files needed to run.

**PRACTICE EXERCISE**

Using the software that comes with this book, you can emulate a running network without needing access to it. Because the executable file is called PRIMER, you can execute any command by preceding it with that call. If there were a command called XYZ, for example, the command would be **PRIMER XYZ**.

Using this software, look at the FILER utility:

1. Type **PRIMER FILER**

2. Select Current Directory Information.

3. Note how this selection reveals information about the LOGIN directory. Press Esc.

4. Select Directory Contents.

5. After viewing the files and subdirectories beneath LOGIN, press Esc.

6. Choose Select Current Directory.

7. Here, you can change from the LOGIN directory to another directory. Press Esc.

8. Select Set Filer Options.

9. Note the default settings governing how FILER operates; press Esc.

10. Select Volume Information.

11. Note the information given. Press Alt+F10 to exit the utility.

# Real World

Practice moving files about with both FILER and NCOPY. The two utilities share much in common, and the key difference, in terms of their capability to move and copy files, is that FILER is menu based, and NCOPY is command-line based.

Practice using FILER for its other features as well, such as selecting your current directory, changing creation dates, and adding and removing trustees.

# Summary

This chapter examines two utilities used to manipulate files—FILER and NCOPY. NCOPY is the command-line utility that holds a major advantage over the DOS COPY command—it can perform the operation directly on the file server without the need to read it back to the workstation. FILER is the menu-driven utility that gives you full access to file and directory manipulation.

Chapter 16, "Rights and Attributes," moves into a very important aspect of directory and file properties.

**16 CHAPTER**

# Rights and Attributes

*Rights* and *attributes* are two of the most important components of NetWare security. They can be applied to files and directories alike. They can prevent users from seeing files or directories, from reading their contents, from changing their contents, or even from deleting them entirely.

This chapter looks at the concepts behind rights and attributes, then looks at the eight utilities that allow creation and modification of them:

- ◆ ALLOW
- ◆ FLAG
- ◆ FLAGDIR
- ◆ GRANT
- ◆ REMOVE
- ◆ REVOKE
- ◆ RIGHTS
- ◆ TLIST

These utilities are examined here, in addition to the basic structure behind the rights and attributes of a NetWare file system.

# Understanding Rights

Rights apply to files and directories, and restrict (or allow) users to do something with the entity. The *Read* right, for example, allows users to read the contents of a file. When the right is removed, users cannot read the file.

Rights to a file or directory can be granted to an individual user or to a group (thus giving it to all members of the group). If you want all users to have similar rights to an entity, grant those rights to group EVERYONE, because all users are members of that group.

The rights that can be granted include the following:

◆ Access Control

◆ Create

◆ Erase

◆ File Scan

◆ Modify

◆ Read

◆ Supervisory

◆ Write

*Access Control* enables a user to modify the rights to a file or directory and change the Inherited Rights Mask (IRM), which is discussed later in this chapter.

 Giving a user Access Control rights—and then withholding any other rights—is mindless. Users with Access Control rights can change the other right assignments. The only one they cannot assign themselves is Supervisory.

*Create* within a directory enables a user to make a new file or directory. Create for a file enables the user to recover that file with SALVAGE after it has been deleted.

*Erase* gives the user the necessary permissions to delete the file. For a directory, it enables the user to delete files, subdirectories, and even the directory itself.

*File Scan* on a directory enables a user to see the files within the directory. Without this right, the user sees only an empty directory. File Scan on a file specifically gives permission to see that file in a listing.

*Modify* on a directory allows the changing of file attributes, as well as file and subdirectory names. On a file, Modify implicitly grants the rights for that file. In other words, you can remove Modify from the directory, but leave it in place on one file; only that file within that directory can be modified.

 Modify works only on names and attributes. To change or alter contents of a file, the user also needs Write permissions.

*Read* is the right needed to open files and look at what's in them. This right is also what a user *must* have to be able to execute an executable program.

*Supervisory* gives all rights to the user. This right enables the user to get past all other restrictions, and avoid Inherited Rights Masks (discussed in the next section).

*Write* rounds out the lists of rights, and enables a user to open a file and modify its contents.

Figure 16.1 shows an example of the rights as you're used to seeing them: in a SYSCON window. Figure 16.2 continues by showing the rights not yet granted for the directories.

**Figure 16.1**

The current rights for directories WSTEEN (a trustee).

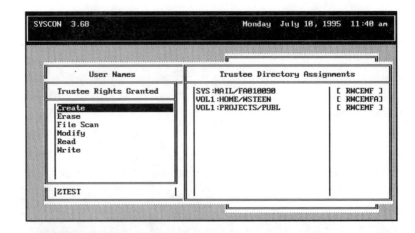

**Figure 16.2**

All available rights for the directories.

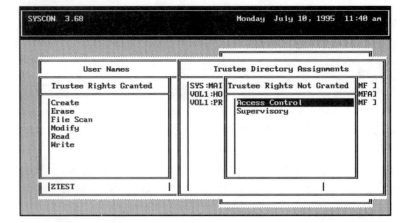

# Understanding Inherited Rights Masks

By default, when rights are placed on a directory, those same rights are inherited by every file and subdirectory beneath it. If you create a directory, therefore, and call it PROJECTS, assign RWC rights to EVERYONE, and create a subdirectory of PROJECTS called HOUSING, all users on the system have RWC (Read, Write, and Create) rights to the new subdirectory and the files contained within. Likewise, if a subdirectory of HOUSING is created called REDLIGHT, the same rights carry on down—these are *inherited* rights.

An Inherited Rights Mask (IRM) sits in one of the subdirectories beneath the main directory and filters out (that is, masks) rights that you don't want to be inherited. If HOUSING had a mask of C, the effective rights in that directory for EVERYONE would be RW (Read and Write, only).

**Note** The most important thing to remember about IRMs is that they are masks (filters). They cannot grant rights. They can only prevent rights you already have from filtering down. If the mask in HOUSING is CM, for example, the effective rights for EVERY-ONE are RW. The fact that they do not have M in the first place never figures into it.

The only right that cannot be filtered out by an IRM is Supervisory. The Supervisory right enables you to completely circumvent any IRM and effectively gives you all rights.

# Understanding Attributes

Attributes differ from rights in that they describe the information contained in the file or directory but don't necessarily relate to individual security. Rather, they relate to the security of the entity in question. With a right, you grant the right to a certain group of individuals to be able to do something with a file or directory. With an attribute, you limit the file or directory specifically to what it can do—regardless of who's trying to do it.

The attributes are

◆ Archive (A)

◆ Copy Inhibit (C)

- Delete Inhibit (D)
- Execute Only (X)
- Hidden (H)
- Indexed (I)
- Purge (P)
- Read Only (Ro)
- Read Write (Rw)
- Rename Inhibit (R)
- Shareable (S)
- System (Sy)
- Transactional (T)

The *Archive* attribute (A), as with DOS, means that the file has changed since the last backup and it should now be backed up to be consistent with your last good copy.

The *Copy Inhibit* attribute (C) keeps Macintosh users from copying the file. This attribute applies only to Mac users and has no bearing on anyone else.

*Delete Inhibit* (D) keeps users from deleting files or directories.

*Execute Only* (X) keeps any .EXE or .COM file from being copied to any other source. You can do absolutely nothing with the file other than run it, and there is no way of removing this attribute after it has been set.

*Hidden* (H) keeps the file or directory from appearing if you use the DIR command, but it still appears in NDIR lists if the user running it has the File Scan right.

*Indexed* (I) makes NetWare keep a separate index of where to find the file for easier access and is useful only for larger files, such as databases.

The *Purge* attribute (P) signifies that if the file is ever deleted, all traces of it will be deleted as well, and SALVAGE cannot be used to recover the file.

*Read Only* (Ro) and *Read Write* (Rw) are self explanatory. The latter attribute also enables you to modify, delete, or rename the file.

*Rename Inhibit* (R) keeps the file from being renamed.

*Shareable* (S) allows more than one user to access the file.

*System* (Sy) marks the file or directory as being necessary for operation. More importantly, it keeps the file from appearing in DIR listings. Like Hidden, however, the entities still show up in NDIR listings if the user has the File Scan right.

*Transactional* (T) enables monitoring of the file's activity with the Transactional Tracking System (TTS).

# Understanding ALLOW

The ALLOW command-line utility enables you to change the Inherited Rights Mask (IRM) of a file or directory. The syntax is as follows:

```
ALLOW directory_or_file_name rights
```

The rights can be the following:

- ◆ **ALL.** Specifies all rights.
- ◆ **No Rights.** Specifies no rights, does not remove Supervisory.
- ◆ **Read**
- ◆ **Write**
- ◆ **Create**
- ◆ **Erase**
- ◆ **Modify**
- ◆ **File Scan**
- ◆ **Access Control**

**Note** When you use ALLOW, specify exactly what the IRM should be—not just what you want to add. Each time you use it, it overrides the previous mask.

To change the IRM of the HOUSING subdirectory to Read and File Scan, for example, type the following:

`ALLOW HOUSING R F`

To change the IRM of the file POSSIBLE in HOUSING to Read, Write, and File Scan, type the following:

`ALLOW HOUSING\POSSIBLE R W F`

When typed without any parameters at all, ALLOW shows you those that exist. The following is a sample of the display that's generated:

```
Files:

        VOL$LOG.ERR                   [SRWCEMFA]
        TTS$LOG.ERR                   [SRWCEMFA]
        BACKOUT.TTS                   [S       ]
        DIRSIZE.DAT                   [SRWCEMFA]

Directories:

        DELETED.SAV                   [S       ]
        LOGIN                         [SRWCEMFA]
        SYSTEM                        [S       ]
        PUBLIC                        [SRWCEMFA]
        MAIL                          [S       ]
        ETC                           [SRWCEMFA]
        ARCSERVE                      [SRWCEMFA]
        MHSUPDT                       [SRWCEMFA]
        MHS                           [SRWCEMFA]
        PWRCHUTE                      [SRWCEMFA]
        HOME                          [SRWCEMFA]
        DB                            [SRWCEMFA]
        LANMEMOS                      [SRWCEMFA]
        DESKTOP.AFP                   [S       ]
        NETWORKT                      [S       ]
        AUTOEXEC                      [S       ]
```

ALLOW shows you the existing rights for file and directories, and enables you to change them. It is also the only command-line utility that enables you to change Inherited Rights Masks.

# Using FLAG and FLAGDIR

The FLAG utility shows and changes file attributes; FLAGDIR does the same for directories. You also can use FLAG and FLAGDIR to change a file's or directory's owner, or to modify how search drives are used to find executable files. The syntax for either is as follows:

```
FLAG[DIR] path list
```

The options include the following:

- ◆ **Archive**
- ◆ **Copy Inhibit**
- ◆ **Delete Inhibit**
- ◆ **Execute Only**
- ◆ **Hidden**
- ◆ **Indexed**
- ◆ **Purge**
- ◆ **Read Only**
- ◆ **Read/Write**
- ◆ **Rename Inhibit**
- ◆ **Shareable**
- ◆ **System**
- ◆ **Transaction**
- ◆ **SUBdirectory.** Displays or changes file attributes in the specified directory and its subdirectories.
- ◆ **All.** Causes all available attributes to be assigned.

**231**

To change file attributes with FLAG or FLAGDIR, your effective rights in that directory *must* include Read, File Scan, and Modify rights.

For example, to flag as Shareable Read Only every file on PRIMER in the DOS 6 directory, type the following:

```
FLAG PRIMER\SYS:PUBLIC\IBM_PC\MSDOS\V6.22\*.* SRO
```

Typing **FLAG** alone, without any parameters, shows you the attributes currently in existence for the files. The following is an example of the display generated:

```
TOKEN.RPL            [ Ro S - - - -- - - -- -- -- DI RI ]
LOGIN.EXE            [ Ro S - - - -- - - -- -- -- DI RI ]
CONSOLE.COM          [ Ro S - - - -- - - -- -- -- DI RI ]
SLIST.EXE            [ Ro S - - - -- - - -- -- -- DI RI ]
RPRINTER.HLP         [ Ro S - - - -- - - -- -- -- DI RI ]
RPRINTER.EXE         [ Ro S - - - -- - - -- -- -- DI RI ]
PSC.EXE              [ Ro S - - - -- - - -- -- -- DI RI ]
PSERVER.EXO          [ Rw S - - - -- - - -- -- -- -- ]
SYS$MSG.DAT          [ Ro S - - - -- - - -- -- -- DI RI ]
IBM$RUN.OVL          [ Ro S - - - -- - - -- -- -- DI RI ]
SYS$ERR.DAT          [ Ro S - - - -- - - -- -- -- DI RI ]
SYS$HELP.DAT         [ Ro S - - - -- - - -- -- -- DI RI ]
SNIPEINI.DAT         [ Ro S - - - -- - - -- -- -- DI RI ]
SNIPESYN.DAT         [ Ro S - - - -- - - -- -- -- DI RI ]
SPACE.COM            [ Ro S - - - -- - - -- -- -- DI RI ]
CHKLIST.MS           [ Ro S - - - -- - - -- -- -- DI RI ]
LOGON.EXE            [ Ro S - - - -- - - -- -- -- DI RI ]
EXPRESSM.INI         [ Rw - - - - -- - - -- -- -- -- ]
DOSAGENT.EXE         [ Rw - - - - -- - - -- -- -- -- ]
BYE.BAT              [ Rw - - - - -- - - -- -- -- -- ]
NLOGOUT.EXE          [ Rw - - - - -- - - -- -- -- -- ]
LOGOUT.BAT           [ Rw - - - - -- - - -- -- -- -- ]
PSERVER.EXE          [ Ro S - - - -- - - -- -- -- DI RI ]
```

The FLAG utility is similar to ALLOW. Whereas ALLOW shows you all the rights for an entity and enables you to change them, FLAG does the same for attributes, and enables you to change them, as well.

# Understanding GRANT

The GRANT utility gives trustee rights to a user or a group, with the following syntax:

```
GRANT rights FOR path TO [USER or GROUP] user_or_group_name
```

The rights are any of those already discussed in this chapter, or

- **All.** Gives all except Supervisory rights.

- **No Rights.** Takes away all rights except Supervisory.

- **ALL BUT or ONLY.** Additional parameters you can use before any specified rights.

The following example grants Access Control, Read, Write, File Scan, and Modify rights for the PUBLIC directory to a trustworthy individual:

```
GRANT A R W F M FOR PRIMER\SYS:PUBLIC TO WSTEEN
```

# Understanding REMOVE

Whereas GRANT adds users and groups to trustee lists, REMOVE deletes them. The syntax is as follows:

```
REMOVE [USER or GROUP] user_or_group_name FROM path option
```

The options are the following:

- **/S.** Removes them from all subdirectories in the path, as well as the files in the specified directory.

- **/F.** Removes them from files in the path.

For example, to remove WSTEEN as a trustee from the PROJECTS directory on volume VOL1 of the PRIMER server, type the following:

```
REMOVE USER WSTEEN FROM PRIMER\VOL1:PROJECTS
```

# Using REVOKE

REVOKE is similar to REMOVE. It enables you to revoke trustee rights for files or directories from users and groups. The syntax follows:

```
REVOKE rights path FROM [USER of GROUP] user_or_group_name
```

EVOKE can be used with the following two options:

◆ /SUB

◆ /FILE

The rights can be any of the existing ones, or any of the following:

◆ **ALL.** Removes all rights.

◆ **/SUB.** Includes files and subdirectories of the selected directory.

◆ **/FILE.** Includes files of the selected directory.

To keep WSTEEN from erasing files in the PROJECTS directory, for example, type the following:

```
REVOKE E PRIMER:VOL1\PROJECTS FROM USER WSTEEN
```

# Understanding RIGHTS

The RIGHTS utility shows your effective rights to a file or subdirectory. The syntax is as follows:

```
RIGHTS path
```

The following example shows the information this utility returns:

```
P:\>rights
PRIMER\VOL1:PROJECTS
Your Effective Rights for this directory are [SRWCEMFA]
    You have Supervisor Rights to Directory.   (S)
  * May Read from File.                         (R)
```

```
    * May Write to File.                        (W)
      May Create Subdirectories and Files.      (C)
      May Erase Directory.                      (E)
      May Modify Directory.                     (M)
      May Scan for Files.                       (F)
      May Change Access Control.                (A)
```

* Has no effect on directory.

```
      Entries in Directory May Inherit [SRWCEMFA] rights.
      You have ALL RIGHTS to Directory Entry.
```

```
P:\>
```

The RIGHTS utility shows you the effective rights that are current for you within a file or directory.

# Using TLIST

The TLIST utility shows a list of trustees for a file or directory. The syntax follows:

```
TLIST path
```

Wild cards can be used, and you must be logged in as a supervisor or be supervisor equivalent to use the utility.

An example of what the utility displays is as follows:

```
P:\>tlist

PRIMER\VOL1:PROJECTS
No user trustees.
Group trustees:
  EVERYONE                              [         ]
➥EVERYONE
  USERS                                 [ R     F ]
  MANAGERS                              [ RWCEMFA]

P:\>
```

TLIST shows the trustee list for directories and can be a useful tool in troubleshooting when there is a question about security.

# Real World

Run the RIGHTS and TLIST utilities on several of your directories. Using a dummy user, grant them permissions to a directory, and to a specific file that they normally wouldn't have access to. Note what each right does, as you add them one at a time, and remove them one at a time. Note the effects of each, and use this knowledge to make your system more secure.

# Summary

This chapter looks at rights and attributes—two often-confused issues of network file and directory security. Chapter 17, "Managing the Server," looks at the server itself and the utilities important to it.

**17**

CHAPTER

# Managing the Server

A *network* consists of physical components that are connected in such a way that individual workstations on that network can share resources. *NetWare* is an operating system that consists of two components. The first is an operating system that runs on a dedicated computer—the server. The second component is a *shell*, which runs on the workstations.

This chapter describes the server and the interactions available through the use of three options:

- ◆ FCONSOLE
- ◆ The server itself
- ◆ Remote management utilities, such as RCONSOLE and ACONSOLE

Before dissecting the preceding options, some background information about the server is necessary.

# The Server

The hard disk is divided into logical structures that consist of *volumes* and *directories*.

Volume names, which must be between two and fifteen characters, are identified—when written—by a colon immediately following the name. Volume names must be unique on a file server.

Volumes can be as large as 32 TB, and can span as many as 32 hard disks. The maximum number of volumes on a file server is 64, and the size of them (when added together) must be equal to (or less than) 32 TB. Only one volume is required by NetWare: SYS.

The directories created when the operating system is first installed include the following:

- DELETED.SAV
- DOC
- ETC (only when TCP/IP installed)
- LOGIN
- MAIL
- PUBLIC
- SYSTEM (houses the NLMs, the bindery, and supervisory utilities)

Other directories are added as additional software packages and applications are installed, but these are the only ones required by the NetWare operating system.

# Using **FCONSOLE**

*FCONSOLE* is a powerful utility, one in which access is limited to users who are specifically granted permission to use it. FCONSOLE enables you to perform several tasks:

◆ Broadcast messages

◆ Change to a different server

◆ See user connection information

◆ Shut down the file server from a workstation

◆ View and change the status of the file server

◆ See the version of NetWare currently running on the server

 **Note** A *console operator* is a user the supervisor has granted FCONSOLE rights to.

Figure 17.1 shows the main FCONSOLE screen. Figure 17.2 shows the message box that appears if you elect to broadcast a message to all users on the network.

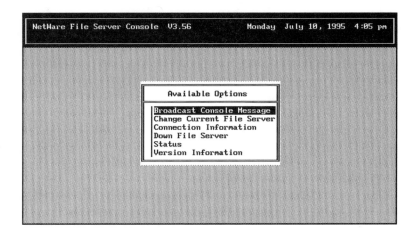

**Figure 17.1**
The main FCONSOLE menu.

**Figure 17.2**

The broadcast message box that appears when you want to send a message to everyone on the network.

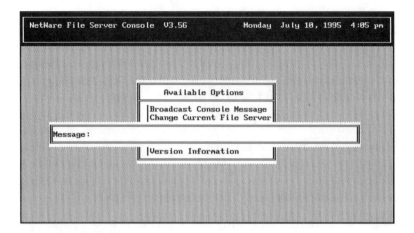

FCONSOLE provides a useful way to notify users when maintenance is about to be performed on the system. When using FCONSOLE to send a message, your message length is limited to 55 characters.

When you select Change Current File Server from FCONSOLE's main menu, a list of the other servers to which you are currently connected appears. Select the server you want, then press Enter. You are prompted to type your user name and, if needed, your password.

To log out of a file server, highlight the server and press Delete. To change the user name that you're logged in with, press the F3 key.

The Connection Information option on FCONSOLE's main menu shows all the connections for the server (see fig. 17.3). The connection information is updated every two seconds by default.

> **Note** You can send or broadcast a message to a specific user by selecting the user from the Current Connection screen and pressing Enter. Next, choose Broadcast Console Message from the Connection Information menu that appears and type your message.

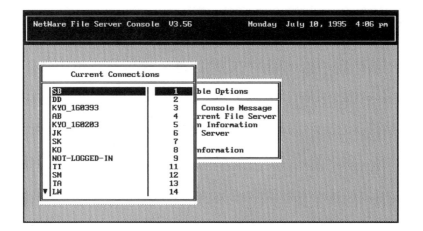

**Figure 17.3**
The list of your current server connections.

Selecting Down File Server from FCONSOLE's main menu enables the network file server to be shut down remotely—from a workstation. A verification dialog box appears; enter **Yes** to complete the task or **No** to back out.

Selecting the Status option from the main FCONSOLE menu shows the following information:

◆ Server date

◆ Server time

◆ Login restriction status

◆ Transaction tracking status

Figure 17.4 shows an example of the data. To change any parameter, use the arrow keys to highlight the field and then press Enter. Type the new information and press the Esc key to save your changes.

The final menu choice in FCONSOLE—Version Information— displays standard information about your version of NetWare, as shown in figure 17.5.

**Figure 17.4**

The File Server Status box shows information about the server.

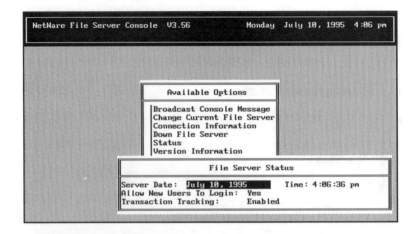

**Figure 17.5**

The standard version information about NetWare.

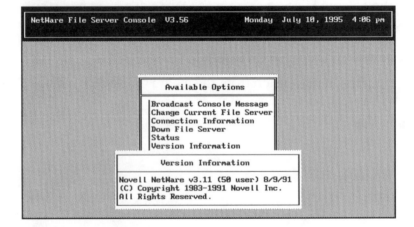

# At the Server

Five types of console commands are available: Configuration, Installation, Maintenance, Screen display, and Other.

Configuration commands include Config (which shows details of current server configuration), Name, Time, UPS Status, and Volumes.

Installation commands include Bind (which links the LAN driver to the communication protocol), Load, and Mount. Maintenance commands are Clear station, Disable login, Down, Enable login, Remove DOS, Unbind, and Unload.

Screen display commands include Broadcast, Cls, Exit, and Send. Other commands are Add name space, Display servers, Modules, Name (shows the name of the file server), Secure Console (which unloads DOS from memory and requires a warm boot), Set, Time, and UPS Time. Secure Console not only removes DOS from memory, but also only allows those NLMs that reside in SYS:SYSTEM to be loaded. All name space modules, incidentally, end with the extension .NAM.

Figure 17.6 shows the monitor screen and a list of options that can be performed from it. It's a good idea to leave the server on the monitor screen, because it also provides a built-in screen saver—commonly known as the *snake* (see fig. 17.7).

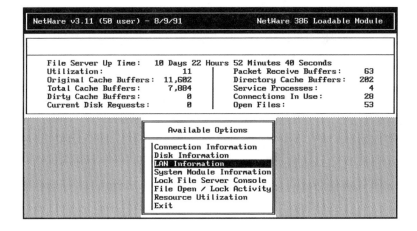

**Figure 17.6**

The monitor screen, showing a list of available options.

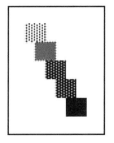

**Figure 17.7**

The monitor screen saver.

The information shown on the main screen includes the following:

- ◆ **Server Up Time.** Amount of time since the file server was last started.

- ◆ **Utilization.** Percentage of processor available cycles currently in use.

- ◆ **Original Cache Buffers.** Original size of the cache-buffer pool when the server was brought up.

- ◆ **Total Cache Buffers.** Amount of buffers currently available for file caching.

- ◆ **Dirty Cache Buffers.** Number of cache buffers storing information in memory that has not been written to disk.

- ◆ **Current Disk Requests.** Number of outstanding requests for all the disks in the system.

- ◆ **Packet Receive Buffers.** Number of buffers used to hold workstation requests so that service processes can handle them.

- ◆ **Directory Cache Buffers.** Number of buffers available to the file system for directory entry caching.

- ◆ **Service Processes.** Number of processes for workstation requests.

- ◆ **Connections in Use.** Number of connections in use, including users attached but not logged in.

- ◆ **Open Files.** Files on the file server that are currently in use.

On the menu of options, Connection Information displays a list showing all current logical connections, as depicted in figure 17.8. Selecting a user and pressing Enter shows how long that user has been logged in, and what files the user has open, as shown in figure 17.9.

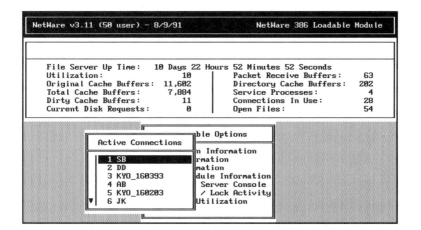

**Figure 17.8**
Current connections.

```
NetWare v3.11 (50 user) - 8/9/91          NetWare 386 Loadable Module

  File Server Up Time:   10 Days 22 Hours 52 Minutes 52 Seconds
  Utilization:               10        Packet Receive Buffers:     63
  Original Cache Buffers: 11,602       Directory Cache Buffers:   202
  Total Cache Buffers:    7,884        Service Processes:           4
  Dirty Cache Buffers:       11        Connections In Use:         28
  Current Disk Requests:      0        Open Files:                 54

              ┌─────────────────────┐  ble Options
              │ Active Connections  │  n Information
              │                     │  rmation
              │   1 SB              │  mation
              │   2 DD              │  dule Information
              │   3 KYO_160393      │   Server Console
              │   4 AB              │  / Lock Activity
              │ ▼ 5 KYO_160203      │  Utilization
              │   6 JK              │
              └─────────────────────┘
```

**Figure 17.9**
Information on user DD's current connection.

```
NetWare v3.11 (50 user) - 8/9/91          NetWare 386 Loadable Module

              Connection Information for DD

  Connection Time:      0 Days  0 Hours  5 Minutes
  Network Address:      000B0FF0:00608C85C72F:4003
  Requests:             1,139          Status:           Normal
  Kilobytes Read:         180          Semaphores:            0
  Kilobytes Written:       44          Logical Record Locks   0

  ┌────────────────────────────────────────────────────┐
  │                    Open Files                       │
  ├────────────────────────────────────────────────────┤
  │ VOL1:PROJECTS/3D                                    │
  │                                                     │
  │                                                     │
  │                                                     │
  │                                                     │
  └────────────────────────────────────────────────────┘
```

Pressing Alt+Esc, you can scroll through the open windows on the server. Every server should have an uninterruptible power supply (UPS) connected to it. One of the screens you should have open, therefore, is the connection to that device, similar to that shown in figure 17.10.

Other open windows include the print services (see fig. 17.11) and the system console (see fig. 17.12).

**Figure 17.10**

The UPS interface.

```
*** PowerChute PLUS Version 4.0 started ***

29-Jun-95 17:10:51  Communications with UPS established
```

**Figure 17.11**

The Print Server interface.

```
                    Novell NetWare Print Server V3.76

0: Not installed                    4: Not installed



1: Admin LaserJet III               5: Not installed
   Waiting for job



2: Acquisitions LaserJet III        6: Not installed
   Waiting for job



3: Not installed                    7: Not installed
```

**Figure 17.12**

The system console.

```
    (C) Copyright 1990-1993 Cheyenne Software, Inc. All Rights Reserved.
[ASDB] E4205 Failed on integrity checking for ASTPSDAT.DB (2)
Loading module MACDB.NLM
  ARCserve Macintosh Workstation Tracker
  Version 5.01    March 11, 1994
    (C) Copyright 1990-1993 Cheyenne Software, Inc. All Rights Reserved.
[ASDB] E4205 Failed on integrity checking for ASTPSDAT.DB (2)
Loading module MACDB.NLM
  ARCserve Macintosh Workstation Tracker
  Version 5.01    March 11, 1994
    (C) Copyright 1990-1993 Cheyenne Software, Inc. All Rights Reserved.
[ASDB] E4205 Failed on integrity checking for ASTPSDAT.DB (2)
Loading module MACDB.NLM
  ARCserve Macintosh Workstation Tracker
  Version 5.01    March 11, 1994
    (C) Copyright 1990-1993 Cheyenne Software, Inc. All Rights Reserved.
[ASDB] E4205 Failed on integrity checking for ASTPSDAT.DB (2)
Loading module MACDB.NLM
  ARCserve Macintosh Workstation Tracker
  Version 5.01    March 11, 1994
    (C) Copyright 1990-1993 Cheyenne Software, Inc. All Rights Reserved.
[ASDB] E4205 Failed on integrity checking for ASTPSDAT.DB (2)
7/10/95 3:56pm: 0.0.0 Remote Console Connection Granted for 000B0FF0:00608C84A8D
D
:
```

From the console, you can load additional NetWare Loadable Modules (NLMs), mount volumes, send messages, or perform other operations. One of the most frequently used NLMs—aside from Monitor—is Install. INSTALL.NLM performs a number of operations; its main menu is shown in figure 17.13.

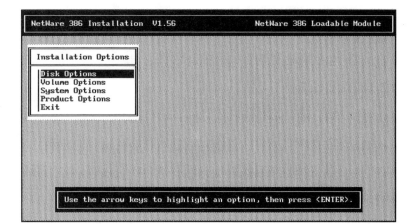

**Figure 17.13**

The main Install menu.

The Disk Options enable you to format the disk, partition it, mirror, or test it. Figure 17.14 shows the menu that appears after selecting this option; figure 17.15 shows the mirroring status.

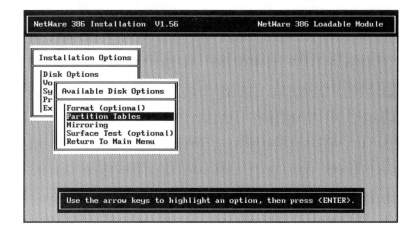

**Figure 17.14**

The Available Disk Options menu.

**Figure 17.15**

The mirroring status of the partitions.

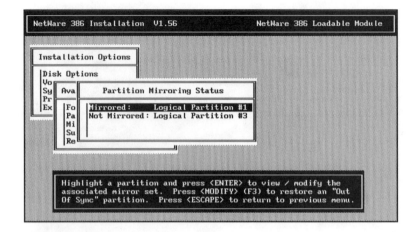

Figure 17.16 shows that the partition is in sync.

**Figure 17.16**

The synchronized status of the current mirrored partition.

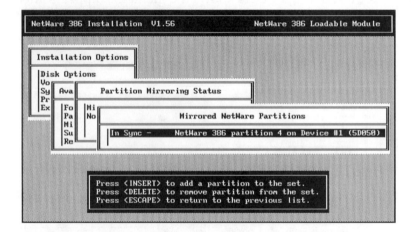

Possibilities that you can see at this screen include the following:

◆ **Mirrored.** The drives or partitions are mirrored and in sync. To delete a partition from a mirrored set, highlight the appropriate partition and press Delete.

◆ **Not mirrored.** The mirroring has not yet been set up on the drive or partition.

◆ **Out of sync.** When out of sync, NetWare doesn't recognize the drives. Changing an out-of-sync partition to a not-mirrored status enables you to access the disk/partition and data on it.

Changing the status of the mirror is done by selecting it and pressing Enter. You then can delete a drive or *partition* (remove it from the mirrored set) by highlighting it and pressing the Delete key. To add a drive to a mirrored set, press Insert. To modify an out-of-sync partition, press F3.

Figure 17.17 shows the list of volumes that appear when you select Volume Options from the main Install menu. Figure 17.18 shows the information available about each volume.

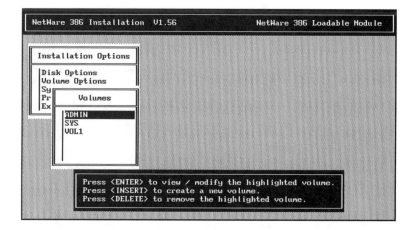

**Figure 17.17**

A list of volumes currently recognized.

If, at any time within Install (or any of the other NLMs), you want to perform an action but can't remember how, press F1 to access online Help. A sample of the information returned from the Help facility is shown in figure 17.19.

**Figure 17.18**

The information available on the selected volume.

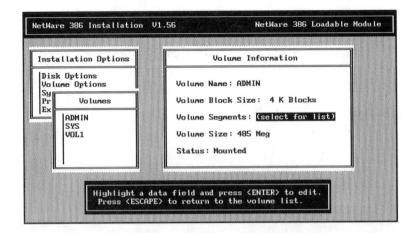

**Figure 17.19**

Pressing F1 brings up online Help.

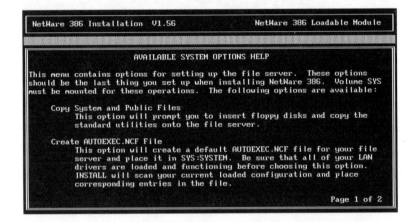

Other tasks you can perform with Install include editing the startup files, as shown in figure 17.20, and installing additional software products, as shown in figure 17.21.

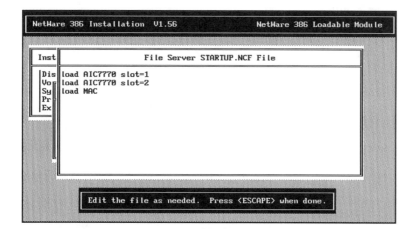

**Figure 17.20**

Install enables
you to edit the
STARTUP.NCF file.

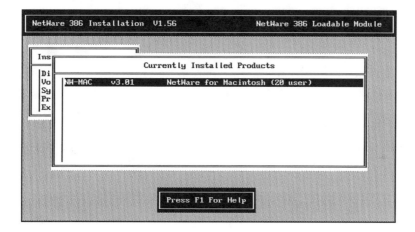

**Figure 17.21**

With Install, you can
add (and delete)
additional software
products.

# Understanding Remote Management

Remote management enables you to access and administer the
server from a workstation (as if you are sitting right at the server).
All the NLMs discussed here can be loaded, executed, and unloaded remotely using the RCONSOLE or ACONSOLE utilities.

RCONSOLE and ACONSOLE enable you to accomplish the same remote task; the only difference is that you use RCONSOLE if you're accessing the server from a workstation, but use ACONSOLE if you're accessing it from a modem.

To use either one, you must first load two NLMs on the server—Remote and Rspx or RS232 (RSPX is used for RCONSOLE, and RS232 for ACONSOLE). When loading Remote, follow it with a password that must be provided if someone uses RCONSOLE or ACONSOLE. An example follows:

```
LOAD REMOTE BILL
```

This line loads the NLM and defines the password as BILL. Next, load RSPX:

```
LOAD RSPX
```

The server functions normally, enabling a user to obtain remote access.

To establish remote server contact (we'll assume from a workstation for the purpose of this discussion), run RCONSOLE from the workstation. A list of available servers appears, as shown in figure 17.22. Select the server you want and press Enter. You are prompted for a password, as shown in figure 17.23. The password is the same as you provided when loading the REMOTE.NLM (BILL).

**Figure 17.22**

The RCONSOLE list of available servers.

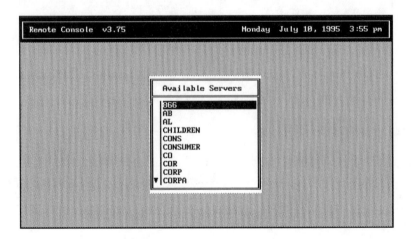

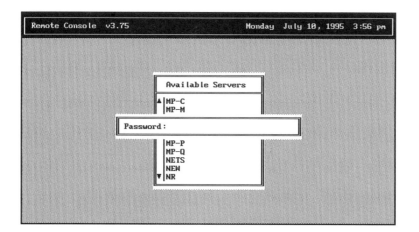

**Figure 17.23**

A password prompt appears.

After the password has been connected, the server's screens appear on your workstation. To toggle between open windows (or to perform any other operation), press the asterisk key on the ten-key keypad of your keyboard. A list of options appears, as shown in figure 17.24. Selecting the first option generates a list of open screens, as shown in figure 17.25.

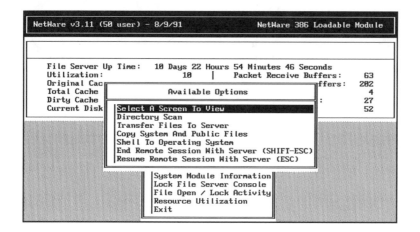

**Figure 17.24**

RCONSOLE available options.

To exit the RCONSOLE utility, use Shift+Esc. A prompt asks for verification that you want to leave the utility (see fig. 17.26). Also, the numeric +– keys toggle between screens.

**Figure 17.25**

A list of available screens.

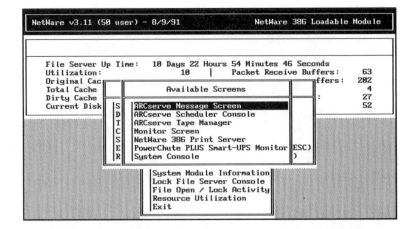

**Figure 17.26**

A prompt that asks you whether you want to leave the RCONSOLE utility.

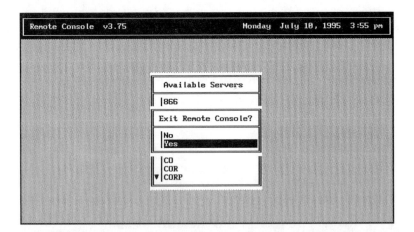

## PRACTICE EXERCISE

Using the software that comes with this book, you can emulate a running network without needing access to it. Because the executable file is called PRIMER, you can execute any command by preceding it with that call. If there's a command called XYZ, for example, the command is **PRIMER XYZ**.

Using this software, examine the FCONSOLE utility using the following steps:

1. Type **PRIMER FCONSOLE**

2. Select Broadcast Console Message.

3. Here, you type a message that is to appear on the screen of every logged-in user. Press Esc.

4. Select Change Current File Server.

5. Note the two shown—PRIMER and GENERAL_COMP. You are known as SUPERVISOR on both. Press Esc.

6. Select Connection Information.

7. Note the two users currently logged in and their connection numbers. Press Esc.

8. Select Down File Server.

9. This is the most dangerous option on the whole system. Were this a live system, choosing YES at this point would bring the network down. Press Esc.

10. Select Status.

11. Note that users can log in, and Transaction Tracking is enabled. Press Esc.

12. Select Version Information.

13. View the information about the NetWare system, then press Alt+F10 to exit the utility.

# Summary

This chapter looks at various utilities and interactions with the network server. Primarily, it explores the FCONSOLE utility, NLMs that can be run at the server, and the remote management utilities RCONSOLE and ACONSOLE.

Chapter 18, "Miscellaneous," looks at utilities that do not fall into any other category, including ATTACH, SEND, CASTOFF, and USERLIST.

# Miscellaneous

The utilities discussed in this chapter are ones that don't fit elsewhere but are essential to NetWare. They include the following:

◆ SEND

◆ CASTOFF and CASTON

◆ ATTACH

◆ SLIST

◆ USERLIST

◆ WHOAMI

These utilities share something in common: each involves interaction with other users or other networks. In addition, they all happen to be command-line utilities. This chapter explores each in detail.

# Using the SEND Utility

The *SEND* utility can be executed from a workstation or the file server console. It enables you to send a short message, of 55 characters or less, to:

◆ Logged-in users

◆ Logged-in groups

◆ The file server console

◆ A single workstation

◆ A set of workstations

The syntax is

```
SEND message TO person(s)_or_place(s)
```

You can send a message to a list of users, a list of groups, the console, a station, a server, or almost any other combination.

 **Note**   The length of the message is limited to 55 characters. Because the workstation and login name of the sender are displayed with the message text, this, in reality, limits the size to 44 characters—depending on the length of the sender's name.

SEND does not leave mail: users must be logged in to receive messages. To send messages to users or groups on another server, you must be attached to that server.

An example of how to send a message to every member of the SALES group follows, reminding those in the group to turn in time sheets:

```
SEND Turn in Time Sheets This Friday TO GROUP SALES
```

To send the note only to WSTEEN, the command is as follows:

```
SEND Turn in Time Sheets This Friday TO USER WSTEEN
```

To send the message to the console operator, type the following line:

```
SEND Turn in Time Sheets This Friday TO CONSOLE
```

Lastly, to send it to everyone currently logged in, type the following line:

```
SEND Turn in Time Sheets This Friday TO EVERYONE
```

Unfortunately, when a message comes in, it stops all workstation processing under DOS. You should be very careful when sending messages to unattended workstations; it prevents the workstation from completing any tasks running while the user is away from the workstation.

# Using CASTOFF and CASTON

SEND and BROADCAST can deliver messages to the workplace and prevent any further processing from happening on that workstation until Ctrl+Enter is pressed. In certain situations, you don't want processing to be interrupted by incoming messages; *CASTOFF* works to prevent any incoming messages. *CASTON* is the opposite; it reenables the workstation to receive messages.

If the CASTOFF utility is used by itself, it prevents incoming messages from other workstations. If the /A or /ALL parameter is also given, it also prevents the file server console from sending messages to the workstation.

# Using ATTACH

The *ATTACH* utility enables you to log in to another file server and use the services provided by it. It differs from LOGIN in one key aspect: When you use LOGIN, all pertinent login scripts run; when you use ATTACH, no scripts are executed.

ATTACH works by assigning a connection number to a workstation and attaching the workstation to an additional file server. You can attach to as many as seven file servers other than the one you initially logged in to.

To attach WSTEEN, for example, to file server PRIMER from another server, issue the following command:

```
ATTACH PRIMER\WSTEEN
```

# Using SLIST

How do you know what file servers you can attach to? *SLIST* shows all the file servers available for your workstation. An example of the output is shown in the following code listing:

```
Known NetWare File Servers          Network  Node Address Status
--------------------------          -------  ------------ ------
866-IST-EXPRESS                     [  705C02][           1]
ABACON                              [    7777][           1]
AL1                                 [ 501109A][           1]
CDROM                               [8CCD3F8A][           1]
CHILDRENS1                          [FACE0FF4][           1]
CONSADMIN                           [FACE0FF3][           1]
CONSUMER_866_INV                    [FACE0FF7][           1]
CORPACCT-EXPRESS                    [    7AB97][           1]
CORPACCT1                           [5026809A][           1]
CORPACCT2                           [5026809B][           1]
CORPACCT3                           [5026809C][           1]
CPROD                               [  123010][           1]
CREDIT1                             [   50149A][           1]
CREDIT2                             [   50149B][           1]
CREDIT3                             [   50149C][           1]
DESIGN1                             [ 501400D][           1]
ECNORTH                             [  112342][           1]
EXEC1                               [     111][           1]
FAC1230                             [1462201A][           1]
FINREP1                             [5026809D][           1]
GENREF02                            [1462271B][           1]
GENREF1                             [1462271A][           1]
GINN450                             [   50809A][           1]
GINN6                               [   50849A][           1]
GINN7                               [   50849B][           1]
GINN_BACKUP                         [   50809B][           1]
GPFS1                               [5023200A][           1]
```

```
GPFS2                      [2D2872F4][              1]
HEST2                      [5026301B][              1]
HEST3                      [5026301A][              1]
HEST5                      [5026301C][              1]
HR1                        [5026519C][              1]
HR1_STORAGEEXPRESS         [  A82D0D][              1]
HR2                        [    2002][              1]
HR3                        [5026519A][              1]
HYPERION-EXPRESS           [   81B1E][              1]
INTERNATIONAL1             [5026519B][              1]
LEGAL-NJ                   [5026819A][              1]
LEGAL-NY                   [  50499A][              1]
MACMILLAN_01               [DEADFACE][              1]
MACMILLAN_ETM              [25202971][              1]
MAC_DIGITAL                [50140010][              1]
MASSMKT1                   [      FF][              1]
MASSMKT2                   [     FEF][              1]
MGR-NY-STOREEXPRESS        [   81B27][              1]
MIS-PHCP1                  [ 501400E][              1]
MKT1                       [5026301D][              1]
MP-CONNECT1                [ 5014008][              1]
MP-MAIL1                   [ 5014007][              1]
MP-MAIL2                   [ 5014000][              1]Attached
MP-MAIL3                   [50140011][              1]
MP-MARKETING               [ 5014003][              1]
MP-PROD4                   [ 501400F][              1]
MP-QUADS                   [50140012][              1]
NETSAA                     [5029201B][              1]
NEWMEDIA1                  [ FACE0FF][              1]
NRP                        [ 5014004][              1]Default
NYAPP1                     [     ABC][              1]
NYDEV1                     [     ACF][              1]
NYETM1                     [ 6411112][              1]
NYETM2                     [   70693][              1]
NYIF1                      [  502109][              1]
OT-CREDIT-EXPRESS          [ 6666665][              1]
PHD01                      [  50269A][              1]
PHNDP                      [  50839A][              1]
PHSCUSR1                   [ 5551212][              1]
PPCHUB                     [FF000001][              1]
PRODUCTION1                [ 501400A][              1]
PRODUCTION2                [ 501400B][              1]
PRODUCTION3                [50140020][              1]
PTI-LAB                    [   35432][              1]
```

```
PTR1                        [5026609A][           1]
PURCHASING-1                [5026509D][           1]
QUE_02                      [ 5014002][           1]
REENGINEERING               [   10795][           1]
RIVERSIDE2                  [ 502909A][           1]
RIVFS1                      [5029201A][           1]
ROYALTY2                    [5026819B][           1]
SAMS                        [ 5014009][           1]
SBG_SC1                     [ 501609A][           1]
SFA_1                       [5027309A][           1]
SFELM1                      [5026321C][           1]
SFHED1                      [5026321A][           1]
SFSEC1                      [5026321B][           1]
SG_INVENTORY                [5027309B][           1]
SSCPNEED                    [   7777B][           1]
SS_TRADE                    [FACE0FF2][           1]
SYSBACK                     [12345678][           1]
SYSED1                      [    211D][           1]
SYSTECH1                    [5026509C][           1]
SYSTECH2                    [    211C][           1]
SYSTECH3                    [5026509A][           1]
SYSTECH4                    [5026509B][           1]
TELECOMM1                   [  512019][           1]
TRADEART1                   [FACE0FF5][           1]
USR-IST-EXPRESS             [  FADDEE][           1]
USR-SEG-EXPRESS             [  FADDED][           1]
WAREHOUSE1                  [ 5014006][           1]
WDC1                        [ 503209A][           1]
WNYACK1                     [ 502209A][           1]
WN_AS400                    [ 502209B][           1]
Total of 101 file servers found
```

Here's a piece of trivia: when the workstation first initializes the NetWare shell, you can only run two NetWare utilities before you log in. The first is LOGIN; the second is SLIST.

# Using USERLIST

The *USERLIST* utility shows a list of logged-in users and status information. The parameters you can use with it include the following:

◆ **/A.** Shows network address information with the user list display.

◆ **/O.** Shows object type information with the user list display.

◆ **/C.** Shows a continuous list without pausing at the end of each screen page.

◆ **username.** An optional file server specification followed by a user name for which you're requesting status.

 **Note** The asterisk (*) wild card character can be used when you're using the username specification.

Some examples are shown in the following listing:

```
P:\>USERLIST
User Information for Server PRIMER
Connection  User Name       Login Time
----------  --------------  ------------------
        1   SB              7-12-1995  8:02 am
        2   DD              7-12-1995 11:44 am
        3   KYO_160393      7-03-1995  1:21 pm
        4   AB              7-12-1995  8:12 am
        5   KYO_160203      7-03-1995  1:27 pm
        6   JK              7-12-1995  7:30 am
        7   IS              7-12-1995  7:23 am
        9   TA              7-12-1995  7:10 am
       10   DF              7-12-1995  7:26 am
       11   TT              7-12-1995  9:42 am
       12   SM              7-12-1995  9:33 am
       13 * WSTEEN          7-12-1995  8:09 am
       14   LW              7-12-1995  9:06 am
       15   JL              7-12-1995 11:23 am
       16   RL              7-12-1995  7:31 am
       17   AB              7-12-1995  8:19 am
       18   SS              7-12-1995  8:20 am
       19   LY              7-12-1995  8:04 am
       20   TR              7-12-1995  8:30 am
       21   AH              7-12-1995 11:52 am
       23   LF              7-12-1995 11:41 am
       24   RR              7-12-1995  8:33 am
       25   JS              7-12-1995  8:39 am
```

**265**

```
       26       SK           7-12-1995   8:35 am
       27       TH           7-12-1995   9:17 am
       28       CS           7-12-1995   8:24 am
       29       SW           7-12-1995   8:22 am
       30       LW           7-12-1995  12:12 am
```

```
P:\>USERLIST /A
User Information for Server PRIMER
Connection  User Name  Network     Node Address    Login Time
----------  ---------  --------    ------------    -----------------
         1  SB          [  B0FF0] [  608C84A8DA]   7-12-1995   8:02 am
         2  DD          [  B0FF0] [  608C85C72F]   7-12-1995  11:44 am
         3  KYO_160393  [ 501429] [  40AF139448]   7-03-1995   1:21 pm
         4  AB          [  B0FF0] [  20AF07CC4E]   7-12-1995   8:12 am
         5  KYO_160203  [ 501429] [  40AF138E58]   7-03-1995   1:27 pm
         6  JK          [  B0FF0] [  608C84A8D9]   7-12-1995   7:30 am
         7  IS          [  B0FF0] [  608C85C716]   7-12-1995   7:23 am
         9  TA          [ 501429] [  608C84A8E1]   7-12-1995   7:10 am
        10  DF          [ 501429] [  20AF127552]   7-12-1995   7:26 am
        11  TT          [  B0FF0] [  608C85C71B]   7-12-1995   9:42 am
        12  SM          [  B0FF0] [  608C84A8DE]   7-12-1995   9:33 am
        13  * WSTEEN    [  B0FF0] [  608C84A8DD]   7-12-1995   8:09 am
        14  LW          [  B0FF0] [  608C84A8D7]   7-12-1995   9:06 am
        15  JL          [  B0FF0] [  608C39BF47]   7-12-1995  11:23 am
        16  RL          [ 501429] [  20AF1C9680]   7-12-1995   7:31 am
        17  AB          [  B0FF0] [  608C84A8E9]   7-12-1995   8:19 am
        18  SS          [  B0FF0] [  20AF083344]   7-12-1995   8:20 am
        19  LY          [  B0FF0] [  608C84A8D2]   7-12-1995   8:04 am
        20  TR          [  B0FF0] [  608C85C711]   7-12-1995   8:30 am
        21  AH          [  B0FF0] [  608C84A8C9]   7-12-1995  11:52 am
        23  LF          [  B0FF0] [  608C84A8E4]   7-12-1995  11:41 am
        24  RR          [  B0FF0] [  20AF255CDB]   7-12-1995   8:33 am
        25  JS          [  B0FF0] [  608C84A8E5]   7-12-1995   8:39 am
        26  SK          [  B0FF0] [  608C85B77C]   7-12-1995   8:35 am
        27  TH          [ 501429] [  20AFD3A2A1]   7-12-1995   9:17 am
        28  CS          [  B0FF0] [  608CCBF6AF]   7-12-1995   8:24 am
        29  SW          [ 501429] [  608C84A8E3]   7-12-1995   8:22 am
        30  LW          [ 501400] [  608C85C722]   7-12-1995  12:12 am
```

```
P:\>USERLIST /O
User Information for Server PRIMER
Connection  User Name        Login Time            Object Type
----------  -------------    ------------------    ------------------
        1   SB               7-12-1995  8:02 am    User
        2   DD               7-12-1995 11:44 am    User
        3   KYO_160393       7-03-1995  1:21 pm    PrOnt Server
        4   AB               7-12-1995  8:12 am    User
        5   KYO_160203       7-03-1995  1:27 pm    PrOnt Server
        6   JK               7-12-1995  7:30 am    User
        7   IS               7-12-1995  7:23 am    User
        9   TA               7-12-1995  7:10 am    User
       10   DF               7-12-1995  7:26 am    User
       11   TT               7-12-1995  9:42 am    User
       12   SM               7-12-1995  9:33 am    User
       13 * WSTEEN           7-12-1995  8:09 am    User
       14   LW               7-12-1995  9:06 am    User
       15   JL               7-12-1995 11:23 am    User
       16   RL               7-12-1995  7:31 am    User
       17   AB               7-12-1995  8:19 am    User
       18   SS               7-12-1995  8:20 am    User
       19   LY               7-12-1995  8:04 am    User
       20   TR               7-12-1995  8:30 am    User
       21   AH               7-12-1995 11:52 am    User
       23   LF               7-12-1995 11:41 am    User
       24   RR               7-12-1995  8:33 am    User
       25   JS               7-12-1995  8:39 am    User
       26   SK               7-12-1995  8:35 am    User
       27   TH               7-12-1995  9:17 am    User
       28   CS               7-12-1995  8:24 am    User
       29   SW               7-12-1995  8:22 am    User
       30   LW               7-12-1995 12:12 am    User
```

The USERLIST command is the most useful utility of all for ascertaining who is currently on and utilizing your network. The options it includes determine how much information you see, and there are enough of them that you can get exactly what you are looking for, regardless of what that might be.

# Using WHOAMI

The *WHOAMI* utility shows virtually everything you ever wanted to know about yourself. It shows connection, identification, and security information, and can be used with a number of options, including the following:

◆ **/ALL.** Shows group membership and security equivalence.

◆ **/G.** Shows group information.

◆ **/O.** Shows object supervisor information.

◆ **/R.** Shows effective rights for each attached volume.

◆ **/S.** Shows security equivalencies.

◆ **/SY.** Shows general system information.

◆ **/W.** Shows workgroup manager information.

Only one option at a time can be entered with the WHOAMI utility. Some examples of its operation are shown in the following code listing:

```
P:\>WHOAMI
You are user WSTEEN attached to server PRIMER, connection 13.
Server PRIMER is running NetWare v3.11 (50 user).
Login time: Wednesday  July  12, 1995  8:09 am

You are user WSTEEN attached to server MP-MAIL2, connection 78.
Server MP-MAIL2 is running NetWare v3.12 (250 user).
Login time: Wednesday  July  12, 1995  8:17 am

P:\>WHOAMI /G
You are user WSTEEN attached to server PRIMER, connection 13.
Server PRIMER is running NetWare v3.11 (50 user).
Login time: Wednesday  July  12, 1995  8:09 am
You are a member of the following groups:
    EVERYONE
    PRIMER
    PLD
    DAY_TIMER
```

```
You are user WSTEEN attached to server MP-MAIL2, connection 78.
Server MP-MAIL2 is running NetWare v3.12 (250 user).
Login time: Wednesday  July  12, 1995  8:17 am
You are a member of the following groups:
     EVERYONE
     POST3

P:\>WHOAMI /O
You are user WSTEEN attached to server PRIMER, connection 13.
Server PRIMER is running NetWare v3.11 (50 user).
Login time: Wednesday  July  12, 1995  8:09 am

You are user WSTEEN attached to server MP-MAIL2, connection 78.
Server MP-MAIL2 is running NetWare v3.12 (250 user).
Login time: Wednesday  July  12, 1995  8:17 am

P:\>WHOAMI /S
You are user WSTEEN attached to server PRIMER, connection 13.
Server PRIMER is running NetWare v3.11 (50 user).
Login time: Wednesday  July  12, 1995  8:09 am
You are security equivalent to the following:
     EVERYONE (Group)
     PRIMER (Group)
     PLD (Group)
     SUPERVISOR (user)
     DAY_TIMER (Group)

You are user WSTEEN attached to server MP-MAIL2, connection 78.
Server MP-MAIL2 is running NetWare v3.12 (250 user).
Login time: Wednesday  July  12, 1995  8:17 am
You are security equivalent to the following:
     EVERYONE (Group)
     POST3 (Group)
```

The WHOAMI utility shows information about you and how you are interacting with the operating system. It shows what rights you have, where you are a trustee, and what other restrictions apply to your interaction.

*PRACTICE EXERCISE*

Using the software that comes with this book, you can emulate a running network without needing access to it. Because the executable file is called PRIMER, you can execute any command by preceding it with that call. If there's a command called XYZ, for example, the command is PRIMER XYZ.

Using this software, examine three of the utilities discussed in this chapter using the following steps:

1. Type **PRIMER SLIST**

2. Note that your current server is the only one seen.

3. Type **PRIMER USERLIST**

4. Note the information presented and what it is indicating. Who is logged in and where are they logged in?

5. Type **PRIMER WHOAMI**

6. Pay attention to the three lines of information given. These same three lines are carried over into any other WHOAMI request, regardless of any other parameters given.

7. Type **PRIMER WHOAMI /A**

8. Note the new information that was added by this parameter. You now can see the groups you belong to and security equivalencies.

# Real World

Be familiar with all these utilities and know their use very well. If you had to choose one chapter to memorize, this should be the one.

# Summary

This chapter looks at several miscellaneous command-line utilities that don't fit well into any other chapter. The fact that they do not fit does not, however, diminish their importance. These are some of the most important utilities to know and use on a regular basis. Chapter 19, "Supporting Workstations," explores the workstation—a component perhaps overlooked in other discussions in this book.

**19**
**CHAPTER**

# Supporting Workstations

The server is the most important part of the network and controls all functions therein. The server, however, is of little use without workstations.

This chapter examines networking from the perspective of the workstation, and looks at the technology in use and some of the major utilities.

## Understanding the DOS Requester

The DOS Requester is used on most workstations today. It replaces NETX and all the variants that Novell traditionally shipped with successive versions of NetWare. Providing complete backward compatibility, the DOS Requester uses a modular approach to anticipate future enhancements.

The COMMAND.COM file, in the DOS world, is what interprets user requests; it serves as the *shell*. COMMAND.COM accepts commands and determines whether the request can be handled internally, or whether to do a search of the PATH statement directories to find an executable file to carry out the command.

 **Note** A shell is an interpreter that takes what you enter and translates it for the machine to understand. The shell then takes what the machine says and translates it so that you can understand it.

When NetWare is installed, the DOS Requester encompasses the DOS shell and intercepts commands before they get to the shell. The DOS Requester then decides whether the command entered is a NetWare command (in which case, it directs it appropriately) or a DOS command (in which case, it passes it through to the DOS shell for regular processing). Figure 19.1 symbolizes the relationship between these two shells.

**Figure 19.1**

The relationship between the DOS Requester and the DOS shell.

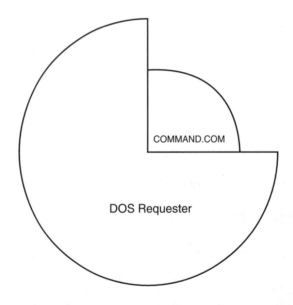

COMMAND.COM

DOS Requester

The Requester is actually more than one entity; it is composed of a number of .VLM files. Each .VLM (virtual loadable module) is a

TSR program that can be loaded and unloaded as needed. These are stored, by default, in the NWCLIENT subdirectory on the workstation, and are loaded and unloaded by the manager (VLM.EXE). If the .VLMs are in another directory, there must be a VLM= line in NET.CFG to point to the appropriate path.

# Installing the DOS Requester

To install on a client machine, perform the following steps:

1. Run INSTALL.EXE. The NWCLIENT directories and copies in the .VLMs are created.

2. Provide the Windows path when prompted, if you're using Windows.

3. Provide the configuration information when prompted—this will be used to build the NET.CFG file.

The files you should see are listed here:

| | |
|---|---|
| AUTO.VLM | Automatic reconnect |
| BIND.VLM | Protocol bindery service |
| CONN.VLM | Connection table manager |
| FIO.VLM | File input\output |
| GENERAL.VLM | Miscellaneous NETX functions |
| IPXNCP.VLM | Transport protocol using IPX |
| NETX.VLM | Shell compatibility |
| NWP.VLM | Protocol multiplexer |
| PRINT.VLM | Print redirector |
| REDIR.VLM | DOS redirector |
| RSA.VLM | Encryption |
| TRAN.VLM | Transport protocol multiplexer |

The VLMs load and unload on the workstation as needed.

# Working with IPX/NETX

Figure 19.2 depicts the IPX architecture and shows how the components work together. NCP is the *NetWare Core Protocol* that goes to the server; the *NetWare shell* goes to the workstation. The LAN driver can be Ethernet, ARCnet, Token Ring, or any other.

**Figure 19.2**

The IPX architecture for a DOS workstation.

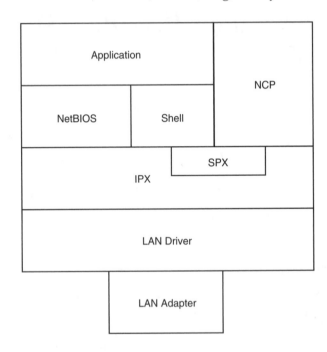

With NetWare, as with any client/server system, one station interacts with another as the client makes requests of the server. The IPX.COM and the NetWare shell carry out this interaction between the two components.

 **Note** The command IPX I shows information about the version of IPX running on your workstation.

**276**

The purpose of *Internetwork Packet Exchange* (IPX) is to function as a go-between for the NIC card and communication link. Suffice it to say that IPX is responsible for communication functions and management of the sockets used in the workstation. IPX is also responsible for ascertaining the address of the network segment that the workstation is connected to, the network number, and node address.

The NetWare Core Protocol regulates how connection control information is passed. Every server packet must have the connection number and a sequence number assigned to it. The only purpose for the sequence number is to ascertain when a packet is lost.

# What if You Cannot Connect to the Server?

Use the following steps if you find that a workstation cannot connect to the server:

1. Verify proper seating of the NIC, and connection of the cables.

2. Verify that the NIC is set to IPX configuration.

3. Look for conflicts.

4. Verify that the server LAN driver is bound to IPX.

These steps, taken in order, will help you track down the problem and solve it in an orderly fashion.

# The Watchdog

When users leave a workstation, they should log out from the server. Logging out clears their connection and frees up resources. The *Watchdog* process, running at the server, routinely sends a poll to workstations to verify activity. If a workstation is not active for a specified period of time, it is automatically cleared.

# Working with ODI

*ODI* is nothing more than a specification of how the data link layer works in the OSI model. Developed by Novell and Apple in 1989, ODI provides support for multiple protocols on the same network with one driver. Up to four network cards can be active in the same machine, and drivers can be unloaded as easily as they're loaded; meaning, IPX and TCP/IP can live in network harmony. ODI drivers have replaced IPX.COM in the workplace.

The components of ODI, include the following:

- LSL.COM
- The LAN driver
- IPXODI.COM (which includes SPX)

The Multiple Link Interface Driver (MLID) is a part of the LAN driver specification, which controls communication between the board and the LSL. Figure 19.3 illustrates the interaction between the components.

**Figure 19.3**

The ODI architecture.

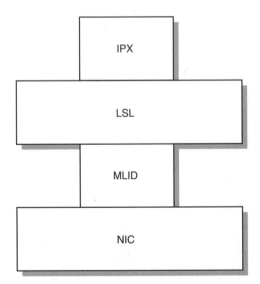

Protocol stacks figure into the equation as they receive packets from the LSL. They operate independently of the board type and remove the header information that's pertinent only to them. Protocol stacks include TCP/IP, AppleTalk, OSI, and IPX/SPX.

# Troubleshooting ODI

The first step when trying to diagnose ODI workstations is to check the board and cabling to make certain there are no obvious physical problems. Next, check that you have an ODI LAN driver for the board. Then, boot with a bare bones AUTOEXEC.BAT and CONFIG.SYS (loading no drivers of any kind). When booted, load LSL, the LAN driver, IPXODI, and the NETX.

 Any of the four networking components can be unloaded in the opposite order they were loaded by following their command with a U. An example follows:

```
NETX U
IPXODI U
{LAN driver} U
LSL U
```

If problems persist, turn your attention to the NET.CFG file. Within that file, main headings must be left-justified, with other entries indented by a tab or space. Headings must precede each section and end with a carriage return, while case sensitivity does not apply. Following is an example of a NET.CFG file:

```
Link Driver NE2000
     INT 5
     PORT 340
     MEM D0000
     FRAME ETHERNET 802.2
NETWARE DOS REQUESTER
     FIRST NETWORK DRIVE=F
```

INT must match the IRQ set on the board; PORT gives the I/O address. MEM shows the memory range used by the board, and FRAME is used with boards that support multiple types. Other entries that can be present, or needed, include the following:

◆ **DMA.** Enables the DMA channels to be configured.

◆ **NODE ADDRESS.** Overrides hard coded board addresses.

◆ **SLOT.** Makes the driver see a specific board first.

◆ **PROTOCOL.** Signifies that existing LAN drivers can handle new protocols.

# Troubleshooting with TRACK

*TRACK* is a console command that diagnoses router and server problems. It shows the network, server, and connection request information on a router-tracking screen. Information is depicted as it comes in, and goes out. TRACK ON turns the monitor screen on; TRACK OFF removes it.

Two requests to keep in mind are RIPs (router information protocols) and SAPs (service advertising protocols). RIPs are transmitted from routers to servers to advertise their presence; SAPs are sent by print servers, gateways, and all servers to denote their presence.

A file server is seen by a workstation when it is SAPing. Thus, the workstation knows it is there and attempts to connect to it— preferably the one within the nearest proximity. If a file server is not SAPing, there can be a problem with IPX not being bound to the card, or volumes not mounted.

When a workstation shell loads, TRACK should report three things on the console if all is working as it should:

1. `Get Nearest Server`

2. `Give Nearest Server server_name`

3. `Route Request`

SLIST can be detrimental in isolating problems if a message of Unknown file server appears when the user tries to log in at the workstation.

# Diagnosing Conflicts

Interrupt request channel (IRQ) conflicts can take a long time to diagnose, because the connection can work properly for a considerable amount of time, then die off at unexpected moments. IRQ conflicts don't happen until two devices attempt to access the same IRQ at the same time.

IRQs are directly tied to hardware components, such as modems and printers. When a call is made to their device, the CPU puts other jobs on a wait status and processes the request made of that interrupt (in essence, they're interrupting other processing). There are a number of utilities that can be used to diagnose IRQ problems, and Check It PRO is one worth noting. On DOS machines running version 6.x, MSD is a standard utility that offers similar information. The following listing depicts an example of an MSD report:

```
-------------------------- IRQ Status --------------------------
  IRQ   Address    Description      Detected            Handled By

 ------  --------  -------------    ----------          ----------
    0   2AB6:0000  Timer Click      Yes                 win386.exe
    1   0A79:1923  Keyboard         Yes                 Block Device
    2   08B4:0057  Second 8259A     Yes                 Default Handlers
    3   08B4:006F  COM2: COM4:      COM2:               Default Handlers
    4   0364:02C2  COM1: COM3:      COM1: Serial Mouse  MS$MOUSE
    5   08B4:009F  LPT2:            Yes                 Default Handlers
    6   08B4:00B7  Floppy Disk      Yes                 Default Handlers
    7   0070:06F4  LPT1:            Yes                 System Area
    8   08B4:0052  Real-Time Clock  Yes                 Default Handlers
    9   F000:9C54  Redirected IRQ2  Yes                 BIOS
   10   166A:01D4  (Reserved)                           3C509
   11   08B4:00E7  (Reserved)                           Default Handlers
   12   08B4:00FF  (Reserved)                           Default Handlers
   13   F000:9C45  Math Coprocessor Yes                 BIOS
   14   08B4:0117  Fixed Disk       Yes                 Default Handlers
   15   F000:FF53  (Reserved)                           BIOS
```

Normally, COM1 and COM3 use IRQ4, and COM2 and COM4 use IRQ3. It's also worth noting that early machines (XTs) have only eight interrupts; new ones have 16 (numbered 0–15).

The I/O address gives the memory range reserved by the CPU. These are areas set aside specifically for each interrupt. If more than one device is using the same address, conflicts occur. The range of CA000 to DFFFF is safe for network adapter configurations.

# Understanding Conflict Resolution

System configuration, once the domain of dip switches, now resides in *CMOS* memory. Usually, you can access CMOS during bootup by pressing a key sequence, which can be anything from the Esc key to Ctrl+Alt+Insert. The necessary key sequence is determined by the hardware manufacturer; there's no standard throughout the industry.

The EISA Configuration Utility is a menu-driven approach to configuring EISA boards and solving conflicts. It reads the .CFG file that comes with the board, and Verification Mode can be used to automatically check to see if conflicts can occur with other devices.

# Working with PC Memory

The following list shows the memory detail displayed with DOS 6's MSD utility:

```
------------------------------ Memory ------------------------------

   Legend:  Available " "  RAM "##"  ROM "RR"  Possibly Available ".."
       EMS Page Frame "PP"  Used UMBs "UU"  Free UMBs "FF"
   1024K FC00 RRRRRRRRRRRRRRRR FFFF  Conventional Memory
         F800 RRRRRRRRRRRRRRRR FBFF               Total: 640K
         F400 RRRRRRRRRRRRRRRR F7FF           Available: 442K
```

```
960K F000 RRRRRRRRRRRRRRRR F3FF                        452976 bytes
     EC00                  EFFF
     E800                  EBFF   Extended Memory
     E400                  E7FF                 Total: 15104K
896K E000                  E3FF
     DC00 PPPPPPPPPPPPPPPP DFFF   MS-DOS Upper Memory Blocks
     D800 PPPPPPPPPPPPPPPP DBFF           Total UMBs: 28K
     D400 PPPPPPPPPPPPPPPP D7FF      Total Free UMBs: 0K
832K D000 PPPPPPPPPPPPPPPP D3FF    Largest Free Block: 0K
     CC00 UUUUUUUUUUUUUUUU CFFF
     C800 ...UUUUUUUUUUUUU CBFF   Expanded Memory (EMS)
     C400 RRRRRRRRRRRRRRRR C7FF          LIM Version: 4.00
768K C000 RRRRRRRRRRRRRRRR C3FF   Page Frame Address: D000H
     BC00 ................ BFFF                Total: 1024K
     B800 ................ BBFF            Available: 1024K
     B400 ................ B7FF
704K B000 ................ B3FF   XMS Information
     AC00 ................ AFFF           XMS Version: 2.00
     A800 ................ ABFF        Driver Version: 2.05
     A400 ................ A7FF     A20 Address Line: Enabled
640K A000 ................ A3FF     High Memory Area: In use
                                           Available: 1024K
                                  Largest Free Block: 1024K
```

When the 8088 CPU was first designed, it divided the 1 MB address space into several areas, including 640 KB for application usage. To maintain compatibility, subsequent CPUs have kept the same scheme. Memory optimizers, such as MEMMAKER (MS-DOS) and OPTIMIZE (QEMM) enable you to avoid manual memory tuning, and automatically configure your system for optimal memory performance.

*Real mode* is the term used to indicate the backward compatibility between subsequent models of CPU boards and the 8088. All x86 machines, when running in real mode, act as if they were running an 8086 chip.

*Protected mode* is the native mode for all CPUs from 80286 on up. Protected mode signifies that memory is not used without first requesting it from the operating system.

# Memory Types

*Conventional memory*, also known as *base memory*, is everything within the first 640 KB that's available to DOS applications. The following 384 KB is known as *upper memory*, and is used by adapter cards, video, and serial ports. Together, this completes the first 1 MB, or 1,024 KB of memory. *Expanded memory* is nothing more than pages of memory that can be swapped in and out of the upper memory space.

*Extended memory* comes next, and is everything above the 1 MB space. *High memory* is a subset of extended memory, and comprises the first 64 KB of extended memory. Within the range of 1,024 KB to 1,088 KB, it is available to DOS applications with an XMS memory manager.

Figure 19.4 illustrates the memory concept.

**Figure 19.4**

The memory model.

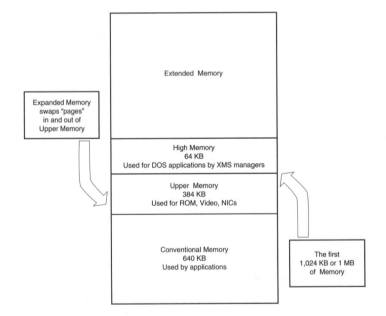

Loading LAN drivers into high memory can free up more of the lower 640 KB for applications. You load LAN drivers by placing lines in CONFIG.SYS similar to the following:

```
DEVICE=C:\DOS\HIMEM.SYS
DEVICE=C:\DOS\EMM386.SYS NOEMS
DOS=HIGH,UMB
```

This task is followed up in the AUTOEXEC.BAT file with the following:

```
LH LSL
LH 3C509 (or your card type)
LH IPXODI
LH NETX
```

# Understanding DR DOS

DR (Digital Research) DOS, from Novell, is a workstation operating system fully compatible with Microsoft's DOS. It features data compression, disk defragmentation utilities, a read/write cache, task switching, and enhanced memory management.

Enhancements have been made to the following external DOS commands:

- ◆ CHKDSK
- ◆ DISKCOPY
- ◆ HELP
- ◆ MEM
- ◆ REPLACE
- ◆ TREE
- ◆ UNDELETE
- ◆ XCOPY

Typing any command and following it with /H or /? displays all the options available. The following are additional features DR DOS offers over other products:

**285**

◆ **DISKMAX.** The set of compression utilities.

◆ **DOSBOOK.** Offers online documentation of the available commands.

◆ **HIDOS.SYS.** A driver for configuring memory on 80286 and earlier machines.

◆ **HIDOS=ON** and **HIBUFFERS=xx.** Used in conjunction to move the operating system out of base memory.

◆ **LOCK.** Used to lock the keyboard—no one can use it without first entering the password. This feature provides additional security at the workstation level.

◆ **SETUP.** A full-screen menu used to configure any of the DOS features, including TASKMAX, MEMMAX, and DISKMAX.

◆ **TASKMAX.** The task switcher, enabling you to move between DOS programs in much the same manner as Windows does.

# Understanding DOSGEN and Diskless Workstations

The *DOSGEN* utility is used to enable diskless workstations to log in to the network. It creates a boot image file named NET$DOS.SYS—which is a copy of the files on the system's book disk—in the SYS:LOGIN directory.

 To run, DOSGEN needs two drives mapped:

```
MAP F:=SYS:SYSTEMMAP G:=SYS:LOGIN
```

To use this command to create a remote boot image file, complete the following steps:

1. Log in as supervisor.

2. Insert a configured boot disk for the remote boot workstation into drive A.

3. Map drive F to SYS:SYSTEM.

4. Map drive G to SYS:LOGIN.

5. Change to SYS:LOGIN.

6. Type **F:DOSGEN A:**

7. Make or copy an AUTOEXEC.BAT file into the SYS:LOGIN subdirectory, and then into the default directory specified in the user's login script.

8. Flag NET$DOS.SYS as being Shareable and Read/Write:

```
FLAG NET$DOS.SYS SRW
```

# Updating Workstation Files

The WSUPDATE utility enables you to update workstation files with newer versions located on the server.

To copy a new AUTOEXEC.BAT file, which is located on the server, to a workstation, for example, the command would be

```
WSUPDATE F:\PUBLIC\AUTOEXEC.BAT C:\AUTOEXEC.BAT
```

This routine can be added to the user(s)' login scripts to automatically perform the copy without any interaction required on your part.

If WSUPDATE is run from a batch file, several new options become available:

| | |
|---|---|
| /ALL | Searches all mapped drives. |
| /C | Copies new over old file without creating a backup. |
| /CON | Scrolls output. |
| /E | Erases any existing log file. Also uses /L option. |
| /L=pathfile | Creates a log file. Specifies the path. |

**287**

| | |
|---|---|
| /F=pathfile | Specifies the path (location) and name of a file containing workstation update commands. |
| /LOCAL | Searches any local drives. |
| /N | Creates specified directory. |
| /P | Requires a prompt before proceeding. |
| /O | Updates even the Read-Only files. |
| /R | Saves old file with a .OLD extension. |
| /S | Searches for outdated files. |
| /V | Updates CONFIG.SYS and renames old one to CONFIG.VLM. |

The WSUPDATE utility can check the date and time on workstation files and update them from the server. These tasks can be done automatically for all workstations across the network, and are extremely useful for large sites.

# Using SYSTIME

The *SYSTIME* utility is a miscellaneous one that you should keep in mind. It enables you to view and change the date and time on your workstation to that of the file server.

When you log in to a server, the date and time on the workstation are automatically set to that of the server. If you change the time on the server, the workstation time does not change unless you log out and back in again, or run the SYSTIME utility to match it up.

You also can specify a server name after the utility to set your workstation time to that of a server other than your primary one.

# Summary

This chapter looks at networking from the standpoint of the workstation, and discusses what must transpire there. Additionally, three utilities are explored: DOSGEN, WSUPDATE, and SYSTIME.

# Troubleshooting

Troubleshooting is an art—and an eventuality. There's no way you can administer a sizable network without knowing how to troubleshoot it. Unfortunately, there's no good way to teach the art in a short period of time—just as there's no way to teach painting without devoting a great deal of time to it.

This chapter covers as many bases as possible, and focuses on two key components of network management:

◆ Problem Prevention

◆ Troubleshooting

These will be discussed in order, including the utilities that you use.

## Preventing Problems

Preventing problems after a network is running is one of the administrator's primary jobs. So many types of problems can occur that you can't possibly plan for all of them. The possibilities, however, can be divided into four main categories:

◆ Physical

◆ Electrical

◆ Security

◆ Viruses

Each of these trouble areas is discussed in the following sections.

## Physical Problems

Temperature is one of the most critical environmental components of a computer's operation—for a server or workstation. Ambient temperature is important, but what's more important is the temperature inside the computer. The temperature can vary as much as 40 degrees between the inside and outside of a computer, due to the heat generated by the components. (Some users leave their computers turned on all the time to prevent the internal temperature from fluctuating too greatly.)

 When new equipment arrives, let it adjust to room temperature before using it. Doing so ensures that no undue thermal strain is placed on the components. (After all, the equipment might have been bouncing around in a frozen transport truck for three days.)

A server must have adequate ventilation to keep it from overheating. Otherwise, *chip creep* can occur. Chip creep happens when integrated circuits lose their seating and make contact with the socket. It's equally important that ambient air, which is sucked into the machine, be filtered and of as high a quality as possible. A consistent temperature in the room should be maintained, and particles such as smoke and dust should be filtered out.

# Electrical Problems

Physical problems slowly deteriorate a server or other equipment, but electrical problems tend to deteriorate equipment immediately. Such problems can destroy components, trash data, and make you wonder why you didn't keep the job at ChemLawn. The four types of electrical problems are as follows:

◆ **Crosstalk.** When two wires interfere with the magnetic fields of each other. The best solution is to use proper cable shielding and avoid physical proximity between cables.

◆ **Static.** It's not static buildup that wreaks damage; it's the sudden discharge. What makes static dangerous is that it can build to phenomenal levels before discharging all at once. Also known as ESD (Electro-Static Discharge), static must be beyond 3,000 volts for you to even feel it, but charges of 20 and 30 volts can damage equipment. The best solution to avoiding ESD is to use static discharge equipment and ground cords.

You should always ground yourself, and any equipment that you will be working on. Never directly touch any electrical leads, and always use anti-static bags to store components. Static also can be controlled by keeping ambient humidity low.

◆ **Transients.** Sudden, high-voltage bursts of current. Also known as *spikes*, they usually occur randomly and last for less than a second. The randomness makes them hard to isolate, and they can often be associated with trouble farther down a power line, such as a blackout or lightning strike. Suppresser Diodes are the best line of defense, as well as putting computers on their own circuit with isolated grounds.

◆ **Line noise.** Low voltage, and low in current, *noise* usually occurs in an observable pattern. Most of the time, the culprit is another electrical device such as a microwave oven, a motor, or even the ballast in fluorescent lighting. The best solution is to properly ground equipment and avoid running cable near other sources of interference.

When discussing noise, two acronyms are important to note. Radio frequency interference (RFI) is caused by microwaves, ovens, and appliances. Electromagnetic interference (EMI) is caused by lights, radar, and industrial tools.

## Security Issues

Network security—and the implementation thereof—is the responsibility of the system administrator. Electronic data processing (EDP) environmental security involves thoroughly thinking through all the risks in your installation, and creating a plan for dealing with them. The four types of threats follow:

- ◆ Destruction
- ◆ Corruption
- ◆ Disclosure
- ◆ Interruption

To deal with these threats, the administrator needs to think about each network segment and evaluate any potential risks. Next, the administrator should evaluate steps that can be taken to minimize those risks, and to implement those steps. Some examples of security implementation include the following:

- ◆ Restricting login times to business hours.
- ◆ Requiring regular password changes.
- ◆ Requiring unique passwords.
- ◆ Turning off modems after working hours.
- ◆ Building RAID and redundancy into the server.

Encryption also can keep an intruder from understanding any intercepted data. Beginning with NetWare 3.11, password encryption is now standard—providing the SET command has ALLOW UNENCRYPTED PASSWORDS set to OFF.

# Viruses

*Viruses* are programs that interfere with the normal flow of processing. They can interfere by changing files and configurations, or by attaching themselves to everything they come in contact with and growing exponentially.

Viruses, by nature, require an action to become activated, and thus they attach themselves to executable files. Those files are usually denoted by their extension, which can be .BAT, .EXE, or .COM. *Overlays* (.OVL) provide other opportunities, however, as do *FAT tables* and *boot sectors*.

Viruses are rare in retail software. Viruses usually enter a computer or network through pirated software, downloaded shareware, or other suspect software. The best solution (in a perfect world) is to prevent anyone other than the system administrator from installing software on the network. By network, in this sense, the reference is to all things physically attached—so not only would that be the server, but all workstations, too.

Because it isn't a perfect world and you often can't prevent installation of software on an individual's workstation, you must contend with the possibility of a virus attack. To do so, make sure you do the following:

◆ Regularly back up the server and workstations.

◆ Routinely scan for viruses with third-party software.

◆ Flag .EXE and .COM files as Read-Only and Execute-Only.

◆ In the PUBLIC and LOGIN directories, grant Read and File Scan rights only.

◆ Scan every floppy disk for viruses before you install.

◆ Discourage downloading of BBS software.

◆ Be prepared for action.

NetWare does include some safeguards against virus attacks. The FAT table, for example, is different from that of workstations and cannot be attacked. For this reason, NetWare viruses aren't as common as DOS viruses. Most virus attacks occur on work-stations.

# Troubleshooting

After a problem occurs, prevention is a meaningless word and troubleshooting comes into play. The goal of troubleshooting is to restore service in a timely manner. The basic troubleshooting model has four steps:

1. Gather information.

2. Develop an attack plan.

3. Isolate the problem, and execute the plan.

4. Document what was done.

If you follow these four steps, you can successfully restore a network to its fully operational state—in the most efficient time possible. The importance of the fourth step cannot be overstated; thus, it's easy to see where an experienced administrator has an advantage over an inexperienced one.

 You should ask several questions when someone you know or work with first reports a problem—before you undertake any troubleshooting measures—including the following:

◆ **Has it ever worked?** Quite often, when a user calls to complain about something that doesn't work, it's because they just installed it or made some other major change that they don't want to mention without prodding.

◆ **When did it work last?** If the accounting clerk calls to complain about a printer that's not printing checks, it's helpful to know that the printer has been offline for the last year and a half.

◆ **What has changed since then?** Such as did you move from one building to another, or rearrange your offices? Did you pull your own cable through the ceiling?

The four-step troubleshooting model discussed previously suggests the following steps to solving workstation problems:

1. Rule out any possibility of user error.

2. Check the physical site to verify all is as it should be. Make certain an electrical cord didn't come unplugged, or a printer cable.

3. Power everything down and reboot.

4. Back up data if there's a question of storage media (a hard drive or drives).

5. Eliminate as much overhead as you can. If the problem is the workstation, reduce the CONFIG.SYS and AUTOEXEC.BAT to the bare minimum and try the process again. Make sure all terminate-and-stay-resident (TSR) programs that don't need to boot are commented out of the AUTOEXEC.BAT file.

Whether you're solving problems on a workstation or server, you should always think in terms of dollars. During the hypothesis stage, consider all the possibilities and try those that cost the least first. Keep in mind that dollars are associated not only with any components that might need to be replaced, but also with downtime and the time of the administrator.

## Know the Files You're Dealing With

There's a method to the madness of file-name extensions. For the most part, NetWare tries to emulate the extensions used in DOS; the list that follows is reflective of that.

| | |
|---|---|
| BAT | Executable batch file |
| COM | Executable command file |
| DAT | ASCII text file |
| ERR | Error log file |
| EXE | Executable file |
| GRP | Windows program group file |
| INI | Windows Initialization file |
| HLP | Help screens |
| MSG | Message file |
| OVL | Graphical overlay |
| PIF | Windows file for running non-Windows (DOS) applications |
| SWP | Windows Swap file |
| SYS | System operating file |

The extensions in this next list have no equal in DOS and are specific to NetWare.

| | |
|---|---|
| DSK | Server disk driver |
| LAN | Server LAN driver |
| NAM | NetWare name space support |
| NCF | NetWare server executable batch file |
| NDS | NetWare Directory Services file |
| NLM | NetWare Loadable Module |
| PDF | Printer definition file |
| Q | Print job file |
| QDR | Print queue definition directory |

Knowing what type of file you are dealing with is often the first step in ascertaining what types of problems you are faced with.

# Documents and Records

As mentioned previously, the importance of documentation cannot be overstated. The importance of good documentation can never be surpassed by any other tool. Even on the smallest network, time and money can be saved by documenting problems and keeping good records.

Three types of records should be maintained: records relating to the LAN system, the history surrounding it, and the resources available.

For the LAN system, there should be a detailed map identifying the location of users, and all tangible components (printers, routers, bridges, and so on). You also should keep an inventory of the components and documentation on cabling and the workstations.

The history of the LAN should include the following:

◆ User profiles

◆ The purpose of the LAN

◆ A log of past problems

◆ Usage information

Not only can these come in handy when an administrator is trying to diagnose a problem, but also when the administrator meets a bus somewhere other than the bus stop. Should a change occur in administrators, there's no better way to keep a business afloat than to make sure the network is thoroughly documented.

The documentation regarding available resources should include information about the protocols and routing in use as well as the LAN architecture. The most important resource of all, however, is people. A chart of people and phone numbers should be readily available when problems become too difficult for the administrator to handle. VAR or retailer phone numbers, manager numbers, and any other emergency personnel numbers should be kept in an easy-to-find location.

# Diagnostic Software

Diagnostic (third-party) software provides information about hardware. That hardware can be virtually anything from the server to a workstation or a cable. A considerable number of packages are available at a variety of prices, and the most important consideration should be that they offer information useful to you.

Check It Pro is one program that can provide quick facts about your hardware and operating system. It also can benchmark the components and show information about the interrupts.

There are a variety of programs with similar features, and the following listing shows an example of output generated at a workstation using System Information—one of the tools available in Nortons Utilities:

```
        Computer Name: IBM AT
      Operating System: DOS 6.20
   Built-in BIOS dated: Friday, January 15, 1988
        Main Processor: Intel 80386           Serial Ports: 2
          Co-Processor: Intel 80387         Parallel Ports: 3
 Video Display Adapter: Video Graphics Array (VGA)
    Current Video Mode: Text, 80 x 25 Color
 Available Disk Drives: 13, A: - C:, F: - I:, P:, S:, V:, X: - Z:
DOS reports 639 K-bytes of memory:
   254 K-bytes used by DOS and resident programs
   385 K-bytes available for application programs
A search for active memory finds:
   640 K-bytes main memory     (at hex 0000-A000)
   128 K-bytes display memory  (at hex A000-C000)
   128 K-bytes extra memory    (at hex C000-E000)
 1,024 K-bytes expanded memory
ROM-BIOS Extensions are found at hex paragraphs: C000
   Computing Index (CI), relative to IBM/XT: Testing..._ __ __ __ __
➡_ __ __ __ __ _73.0
        Disk Index (DI), relative to IBM/XT: Not computed. No drive
➡specified.
Performance Index (PI), relative to IBM/XT: Not computed.
```

Much of the same workstation information can be achieved with newer versions of DOS and MSD utility. Following is an excerpt from the first pages of a report run on the same machine with this utility:

```
Microsoft Diagnostics version 2.01    9/24/95    7:44pm    Page  1
===========================================================================

----------------- Summary Information ---------------------

          Computer: Gateway/Phoenix, 486DX
            Memory: 640K, 15104K Ext, 1024K EMS, 1024K XMS
             Video: VGA, ATI , Ultra
           Network: Novell, Shell 4.10.00
        OS Version: MS-DOS Version 6.20, Windows 3.10
             Mouse: Serial Mouse 7.05
    Other Adapters: Game Adapter
       Disk Drives: A: B: C: F: G: H: I: P:
         LPT Ports: 3
         COM Ports: 2

--------------------- Computer ----------------------------

     Computer Name: Gateway
 BIOS Manufacturer: Phoenix
      BIOS Version: 680486 ROM BIOS PLUS Version 0.10 G21-2
     BIOS Category: Phoenix PC/AT Compatible BIOS
     BIOS ID Bytes: FC 81 00
         BIOS Date: 01/15/88
         Processor: 486DX
   Math Coprocessor: Internal
          Keyboard: Enhanced
          Bus Type: ISA/AT/Classic Bus
    DMA Controller: Yes
     Cascaded IRQ2: Yes
 BIOS Data Segment: None

--------------------- Network -----------------------------

            Network Detected: Yes
                Network Name: Novell
     MS-DOS Network Functions: Not Supported
             NetBIOS Present: No
               Shell Version: 4.10.00
                    Shell OS: MS-DOS
            Shell OS Version: V6.20
               Hardware Type: IBM_PC
              Station Number: 3
     Physical Station Number: 0060:8C84:A8DD
               IPX Installed: Yes
               SPX Installed: Yes
           ODI/LSL Installed: Yes
```

Regardless of which utility you use, you should run reports regularly and store them in a place where they are accessible. When problems arise, you should immediately run the utility again and look for any discrepancies that might signal a problem.

# Troubleshooting Utilities

There are three utilities used to solve problems on the file server:

◆ BINDFIX

◆ BINDREST

◆ VREPAIR

BINDFIX takes the existing bindery and saves the three files with a new extension (.OLD). It then rebuilds three new files using the information it can pull from the .OLD files. Thus, rebuilding the bindery and removing any garbage that might be within it. This step should be used if you cannot add more users, or if users are having trouble logging in when no other reason for the problem exists.

BINDREST is used to restore the .OLD files to their original extension should there be a problem with BINDFIX.

VREPAIR is used to repair volumes in case they become degradated. The most common use for it is when mirroring or duplexing suddenly fails. If you cannot mount a volume, then use VREPAIR to examine it for problems and make necessary changes.

# Understanding Common Error Messages

The following sections describe common network-related errors, and when possible, what caused them and how the situation can be rectified. Each section opens with the error message(s) itself, followed by a brief explanation.

# FILER

`Access has been denied`

You don't have the rights to perform the operation you're attempting. Verify rights, and grant them where necessary.

`The first extended attribute could not be found`

A file being copied has extended attributes that cannot be identified. Try the operation again.

# FLAG

`Access is denied`

The file is in use, or you're attempting to change rights to a directory that another user is in. Try again later.

`The Search mode is not supported for local files`

You can only use Search on network drives and not those on workstations.

`This utility was unable to parse the specified path`

The directory path you provided is invalid. Verify and try again, or use MAP if necessary.

# LOGIN

`Access to the server has been denied`

You don't have an account, or it has been disabled. Try again, verifying the correct LOGIN and password.

`Access to the server has been denied and you have been logged out`

You were already logged in and trying to do so again. Log in once more.

`All drives are in use`

All drives from A to Z are accounted for, and no more can be added. Check where they're being mapped to and remove any that are not appropriate.

`Insufficient memory is available to add the variable to the path`

There's not enough room in the workstation's environment. Create more room by restarting COMMAND.COM with the /E option and specifying more bytes.

`Intruder detection lockout has disabled this account`

You successfully logged in but only after exceeding the number of times you could fail. The system administrator must re-enable the login.

`The line contains no end quote`

A text message has a quotation mark at the beginning of the text, but not at the end. Edit the login script, and correct the problem.

`The line is too long`

A line within your login script is exceeding the 254-character limit. Shorten the line.

`The NetWare shell is not loaded`

Reboot the workstation and try to log in again.

`The server does not respond`

Power was lost while files were still open, or the cable has become improperly terminated. The first step should be an effort to isolate the problem.

`This utility could not get your connection status`

LOGIN was unable to see if you were already logged in or not. Reboot the workstation and try to log in again. If it persists, down the server and restart.

`This utility was unable to map ...`

The limit of 16 search drives was reached and exceeded. Reduce the number of search drives.

```
You could not be authenticated to server
```

The server does not find the login and password you provided.
Try again.

# MAP

```
Access to the server was denied
```

The password or login name provided is wrong. Try logging in
again.

```
All drives are in use
```

There are no free drives to map. Check the last drive variable to
see if it's as low as it can go. If so, begin deleting drives that you
don't use regularly.

```
The server did not respond
```

The server is not running, and a DOWN command was not issued, or there's a faulty connection. Check the status of the server.

```
The specified server is unknown
```

The name of the server was mistyped or it isn't up and running.
Type **SLIST** to see a list of valid servers in operation.

# NCOPY

```
Internal error ...
```

Try the operation again, verifying syntax. If it happens again, exit
from the subdirectory and try the operation from one level back.

```
Multiple files cannot be copied to a single file
```

If you're trying to copy (and not concatenate), reissue the command and be more specific. If you, indeed, are trying to concatenate, use the COPY command from DOS, which does allow
multiple files to be copied into one.

`The file cannot be copied`

You have insufficient rights to the file, or it's locked by another user accessing it. Check your rights and try the operation again when you are certain the file is not in use.

`The maximum number of directory levels ...`

NCOPY only supports 25 levels. Use another copy routine, or rearrange the directory so that there are not so many levels.

`The server has run out of dynamic memory`

Dynamic memory and RAM are one and the same. The ideal solution is to add more RAM, but for now, reboot the server to clear the memory and try the copy again.

`The server is out of directory entries`

Each volume can hold a specific number of files based on the size of the volume. The best solution is to purge deleted files and retry the operation. If it persists, archive files no longer needed from the volume and try once more.

`The source file cannot be opened`

The file you are trying to copy is Read-Only, or in use by another user. Check the rights and try to copy again.

`Volume does not exist`

Verify that there aren't errors in the command you've given. If there are not, use FILER to verify that the volume does exist.

# RIGHTS

`An error occurred while ...`

Try the operation again.

`Open is invalid with 386 server`

You can't use the Open right on any server running NetWare 3.x.

`The message file for this utility cannot be found`

The file RIGHTS.MSG is missing, or not in the search paths. Find it and copy it over, or add to the search paths.

## SETPASS

`Account for {server} is restricted. Your password was not changed`

The number of grace logins has expired, and now the password cannot be changed. The system administrator can still change with FILER.

`An unexpected error occurred ...`

Try the operation again after verifying the server is still up and the workstation connected. Reboot the workstation, if necessary.

`The message file for this utility cannot be found`

SETPASS.MSG is missing or not in the search path. Locate it and map a drive over.

## WHOAMI

`An error occurred during ...`

Try again.

`The message file for this utility cannot be found`

WHOAMI.MSG is missing or not in the search path. Locate it and map a drive.

`This utility was unable to allocate sufficient memory for the Directory Services attribute buffer`

The workstation lacks sufficient RAM. Reboot, and if that doesn't work, add more memory to the workstation.

# Summary

This chapter examines troubleshooting and the basics therein. This chapter concludes the concepts of *Managing the NetWare 3.x Server*. The appendixes and glossary that follow offer additional information and resources.

**APPENDIX**

# The CNA Title

Since Novell created the CNE (Certified NetWare Engineer) certification years ago, it has become the method by which professionals prove their knowledge in the marketplace. The reasons for its mass acceptance as a means by which to judge someone's wisdom can be explained. First, and foremost, half of the tests focus on non–product-specific topics—Networking Technologies, for example, asks questions about protocols and layers, and not about NetWare. Second, Human Resources professionals, the first ones you see when applying for a job, usually have no knowledge whatsoever of networking, and need some way to determine whether a candidate knows what he or she is talking about—Novell certification provides that.

In 1993, Novell realized that there was merit in creating a certification beneath that of CNE. The CNE certification requires passing seven tests and knowing about much more than just NetWare. For those wanting to prove their knowledge with the product, however, they created the CNA—Certified NetWare Administrator—certification.

The tests are proctored, given electronically and administered by Drake Prometric. Adaptive in nature, they ask only a few questions (15 minimum). After you complete those questions, if you have scored high enough to pass, they stop. If you are failing after the first 15 questions, more will be asked on subjects that you initially missed the questions on, making the test adaptive. Up to 25 questions might be asked. The tests are generally multiple choice, though there are some fill-in-the-blanks. Of the multiple choice questions, there can be multiple correct answers.

To become a CNA, the candidate needs to take only one test, NetWare 3.12 Administration.

Passing this one test not only makes the person a CNA, but also qualifies as one of the seven tests necessary to become a CNE should the individual decide to go on with the testing procedure.

Because the test only requires the answering of 15 questions correctly for certification, many of the questions are tricky in nature, and require rote memorization of facts. The following sections assume that you have been using NetWare 3.12 and are familiar with its basic functions. They provide you with many of the facts and incidental test fodder items that you need to know in order to pass the test.

# Generally Speaking

Access to NetWare resources is available through three types of utilities: DOS text-based menus (such as SYSCON), command line (such as PSC), and graphical through Windows (such as NetUser). NetUser, incidentally, is nothing more than a graphical representation of SESSION. Within the DOS text utilities, the following are hot keys:

- ◆ **F1.** Opens the .HLP file.

- ◆ **F1-F1.** Provides help on the function keys.

- ◆ **F3.** Enables you to choose an option and modify it.

- ◆ **F5.** Marks multiple items.

- **Alt+F10.** Gives a quick exit regardless of how many layers deep you are in the menu structure.

- **Insert.** Enables you to add an entry.

- **Delete.** Removes the current entry.

The basic function of a network is to allow for the accessing of shared resources. Those shared resources include the following:

- File storage and retrieval

- Distributed and centralized processing security

- Printing

- Backup and protection of network data

- Network connectivity

The core NetWare operating system, SERVER.EXE, provides three basic services: file storage, security, and routing. The NetWare Loadable Modules (NLMs) provide printing services, server management and monitoring, remote console access, UPS protection, and network communication services.

A server running 3.12 must have a minimum of 4 MB of RAM memory; NetWare sees up to 4 GB of RAM. Memory above that needed by the NetWare operating system is used for file caching.

Users can be created using SYSCON, MAKEUSER, or USERDEF. Files loaded at the file server can end with extensions of .DSK, .LAN, .NAM, or .NLM.

# Commands

The ATTACH command enables you to log in to more than one server. The difference between ATTACH and LOGIN is that the former does not execute the login script. SYSCON also enables you to attach to a file server other than the one you are currently connected to. SLIST is used to see a list of the file servers that are up and running.

Messages can be sent with both BROADCAST and SEND, and CASTOFF keeps messages from coming in to a workstation. CASTOFF ALL prevents even messages from the console from getting through. CASTOFF is reversed with CASTON.

The MAP command is equivalent to the PATH command in DOS. There are two types of MAP—regular and search. Search acts exactly like a DOS PATH drive.

The correct syntax is as follows:

```
MAP [option] drive_letter:=directory_path
```

The options you can use—as well as what those options are actually saying when used—are examined in the following list:

- ◆ **root.** Make this drive appear to the user as if it were the root directory.

- ◆ **N.** Use the next available drive letter.

- ◆ **DEL.** Remove an existing map.

- ◆ **INS.** Add a new map.

- ◆ **INS S1.** Make this drive the first search drive.

If you are not mapping to the current default server, you must give the exact path of the other server, followed by a slash, then the volume name (which ends in a colon), and the appropriate directory, and subdirectory.

NCOPY has several advantages over the COPY command in DOS. It can copy extended file attributes, and verify that the copy was successfully created. The parameters that can be used with it—as well as what those parameters are actually saying when used—are examined in the following list:

- ◆ **/A.** Copy only files with the archive bit set and let it set.

- ◆ **/C.** Only copy DOS files.

- ◆ **/F.** Sparse files.

- ◆ **/I.** Notify if the file will lose something in the copy (non-DOS file).

- ◆ **/M.** Copy only files with the archive bit set, then turn it off.

- ◆ **/R.** Keep compression.

- ◆ **/S.** Include subdirectories.

- ◆ **/SE.** Include subdirectories, including empty ones.

- ◆ **/V.** Verify the copy of local DOS files.

SETPASS is the utility users use to change their own password from the command line (or they can do so from the SYSCON utility).

TLIST shows all the users and groups that have rights to a directory; LISTDIR offers a great deal of flexibility in what it reports, based on the parameters you give:

- ◆ **/D.** Shows the date a subdirectory was created.

- ◆ **/E.** Shows the effective rights for all subdirectories of the specified directory.

- ◆ **/R.** Shows the Inherited Rights Masks (IRM) of all subdirectories in a specific directory.

- ◆ **/S.** Includes all subdirectories.

- ◆ **/T.** Shows the time a subdirectory was created.

- ◆ **/A.** Gives all information.

The WHOAMI utility shows the server you are logged in to, as well as the time you logged in (including date), and user name.

In order to recover files with SALVAGE, you must have Read, File Scan, and Create rights in the directory. The minimum rights necessary to change file or directory attributes are simply Modify.

You can view and manage file system information with four utilities: CHKVOL, FILER, SLIST, and VOLINFO. To obtain information about NetWare directories, use LISTDIR (mentioned previously) or NDIR.

**311**

# Login Scripts

There are three types of login scripts: System, User, and Default. The Default login script is a part of the LOGIN.EXE file. The two specific rules governing these scripts are that each line can contain only one executable command, and no line can be longer than 150 characters. The network supervisor can change any and all scripts; individual users can change only their own.

Commands that you can use are included in the next several paragraphs.

**#** executes a command outside the login script—an external .COM or .EXE file. You cannot run programs that terminate and stay resident in memory.

**BREAK ON** provides a method to terminate the login process by enabling the Ctrl+C key combination. This command is useful in the event that something goes awry and you don't want to complete the execution of the login script. **BREAK OFF** is the exact opposite in that it disables the ability to break from the routine.

**DOS SET** appoints local PC variables in the same way that the DOS command SET does. In this manner, it is possible to pass variables from the network to an individual PC. One word of caution: the amount of space that you have available for local variables is controlled by the COMMAND.COM file. If you find that you cannot load all variables into memory, then you must increase the local PC environment size.

**FDISPLAY** works in the same manner as the TYPE command in DOS in that it displays the contents of an ASCII file to the screen. One major difference, however, is that if a file is specified and none exists, no error message is generated.

**EXIT** "specifications" ceases the processing and executes whatever commands are within the quotation marks. Specifications can be for DOS internal commands, .BAT, .COM, or .EXE files. The only restrictions are that the specifications cannot be more than fourteen characters long, and cannot load programs that terminate and stay resident in memory.

**INCLUDE** enables you to include commands contained in locations other than the login script. One of the major benefits of this command is that it permits you to shorten restrictions in the Login script by placing them in subscripts. The subscripts can be changed as frequently as needed to meet specifications present at the moment.

**PAUSE** causes the implementation to hesitate and wait for the user to strike a key before continuing. This command is predominantly used when displaying the contents of a file that must be read before proceeding to the next command.

**WRITE** works in the same manner as the ECHO command for DOS. Novell variables can be used, as long as they are preceded by a percent sign, and typed in capital letters. GREETING_TIME, for example, becomes Morning, Afternoon, or Evening depending on the actual time. You also can include commands such as \n for a new line, or \7 for the computer to emit a beep.

# Menus That You Create

You can create menus for your use, or the use of users, similar to the DOS-based ones used for most of 3.12 administration with the NMENU utility. NMENU files consist of several components, each extremely important to the operation of the finished product:

- ◆ Titles
- ◆ Options
- ◆ Submenus
- ◆ Commands
- ◆ Prompts

Titles are simply text that appear at the top of the menu. There is a limit of 40 characters, but no other restrictions on content. Options are placed within curly braces ({}) and denote actions to take place. Titles of options appearing on the menu itself cannot exceed 60 characters in length. Executable options include the following:

- **BATCH.** Removes the program from memory before executing the item—freeing up 32 KB.

- **CHDIR.** Changes to a specified drive\directory before executing the next command.

- **NOCLEAR.** Leaves the present screen display exactly the way it is.

- **NOECHO.** Does not echo commands it executes.

- **PAUSE.** Stops the display and waits for an acknowledgment.

- **SHOW.** The opposite of NOECHO; it shows the commands being executed.

Submenus are further branches of this menu. One choice on a main menu, for example, might be Word Processors. Upon selecting that option, a submenu might open offering choices between Word, WordPerfect, or Lazy Write. The only restriction here is that submenus can go only 10 layers deep.

Commands are the heart of the operation and include, in order of importance, the following:

- **MENU.** Marks the beginning of a new menu or submenu.

- **ITEM.** Signifies a menu choice and the title it is to use.

- **EXEC.** Tells DOS to run an item.

- **LOAD.** Summons a submenu from a separate .DAT file.

- **SHOW.** Shows a submenu from the same .DAT file.

Last, prompts request additional information from the user, which is then used within the operation. There are three types of prompts:

- **GETO.** Requests optional information before executing the item. If the user presses Enter without giving a value, no harm is done.

- **GETR.** Requests required information. A value *must* be given before processing continues.

◆ **GETP.** Converts the input into a parameter and saves the value.

Menus created prior to 3.12 were done with a similar utility called MENU. Older files for MENU can be converted to .DAT format through the MENUCNVT program. The executable file creates a .SRC file from the original that then can be run through MENUMAKE.

# Printing and Its Components

The five components to printing are: clients, printers, print queues, print servers, and file servers. There are four basic steps to setup: configuring printing, initializing servers, connecting printers, and customizing. Additionally, there are three ways to connect a printer: connect directly to the printer server (called a local printer), connect to a workstation (called a remote printer), or connect directly to the cabling.

You can have a maximum of 16 printers to each print server and eight file servers for each print server. PSERVER is the utility used to handle printing functions. If the printer is connected to a server, then use PSERVER.NLM (with the LOAD command); if it is connected to a workstation, you use PSERVER.EXE. Redirection is then accomplished with either the CAPTURE or NPRINT commands. If you want to automatically load PSERVER on the server with each boot, the LOAD command should be placed in the AUTOEXEC.NCF file.

The three major printing utilities are PCONSOLE, PRINTCON, and PRINTDEF. PCONSOLE is used to perform the following tasks:

◆ Create and configure print servers

◆ Create and configure print queues

◆ Define types of printers being used

◆ Establish a logical connection

PRINTCON is used to create print queues, copy one user's print job information to another user, and customize print jobs. PRINTDEF can be used to perform the following tasks:

◆ Edit printer names and definitions

◆ Create printer names and definitions

◆ Import a printer name and definition

Only a supervisor, or equivalent, can create print job configurations.

Printer devices are included in the .PDF files within the PUBLIC directory, and you can have more than one identical printer servicing the same print queue. Print queues are stored in SYS:SYSTEM, and have an extension of .QDR.

PSC is the command-line utility that enables you to change the mounted form on a printer. CAPTURE is used to redirect printed output from the local printer to a network printer, and the options that can be used with it are the following:

◆ **/AU.** Short for autoendcap; it ends the redirection.

◆ **/B{anner}=bannername.** Enables you to specify a 12-character banner.

◆ **/C{opies}=n (1-999)**

◆ **/CR{eate}=path.** Enables you to use a file storage area other than the print queue.

◆ **/F{orm}=form or n.** The name of the form you want to use, or the form number.

◆ **/FF.** Sends a FormFeed at the end of each print job.

◆ **/J{ob}=jobname**

◆ **/K{eep}.** Enables CAPTURE to keep all the data it grabs during a print capture in case there is a lockup.

◆ **/L{ocal}=n.** The LPT port you want to capture.

◆ **/NAM{e}=name.** The 12 characters to appear on a banner in the name space area.

- ◆ **/NB.** No Banner.

- ◆ **/NFF.** No FormFeed.

- ◆ **/NNOTI.** No Notify.

- ◆ **/NT.** No Tabs.

- ◆ **/NOTI.** Notify when the print job has cleared the queue.

- ◆ **/Q{ueue}=queuename.** The file server queue to which the print job is to be sent.

- ◆ **/S{erver}=fileserver.** The name of the file server you are sending the job to.

- ◆ **/SH.** Shows the status of the current redirection (or lack thereof).

- ◆ **/T{abs}=n (1-18)**

- ◆ **/TI{meout}=n.** The number of seconds to wait without further data being sent before assuming there is no more data and the job has been completely sent.

# How to Keep the System Secure

NetWare offers four levels of security: Login, Rights, Attributes, and File Server. Login validation entails checking for password requirements, matching the given id and password, and checking for user account restrictions. The restrictions can be based on time, passwords, and stations. The available rights are supervisor, supervisor equivalent, workgroup manager, account manager, PCONSOLE operator, FCONSOLE operator, and user.

File System security is divided into trustees, directory and file rights, inheritance, Inherited Rights Mask (IRM), and effective rights. The eight rights are Access Control (ability to modify trustee assignments and IRMs), Create, Erase, File Scan, Modify, Read, Supervisory, and Write. IRMs cannot filter out supervisory rights, and user effective rights are determined by looking at the user's inherited rights, the IRM, and any group affiliations or

**317**

equivalencies the user might have. Rights that can be included in an IRM are [SRWCEMFA]. Users can receive rights from their user account, from belonging to a group (including EVERYONE), or receiving the security equivalence of another user. The default rights to EVERYONE include Read and File Scan in the PUBLIC directory. These are also the rights you have when you change to the first network drive without yet logging in.

Attributes consist of Read-Only, Read-Write, Sharable, Hidden, System, Transactional, Purge, Archive Needed, Read Audit, Write Audit, Copy Inhibit, Execute Only, Delete Inhibit, and Rename Inhibit. Attributes are set using FILER, FLAG, and FLAGDIR.

As for the file server, you can change the console password using the Lock File Server Console option from MONITOR.NLM. This utility also can be used to display statistics on how efficiently the network is running.

A packet signature prevents forging packets to gain greater access to the network than was originally granted. It is defined at both the server and the client, and is set by adding the following line at the console or in the AUTOEXEC.NCF file:

```
SET NCP PACKET SIGNATURE OPTION = {number}
```

The number ranges from 0 to 3, with 3 providing the greatest amount of security.

Related security commands are ALLOW (which changes IRMs), RIGHTS, TLIST, GRANT, REVOKE, and REMOVE. The SECURITY command is also useful because it evaluates the bindery for possible security violations.

# Rights

An *inherited right* is a right received at all subdirectories or files below the level at which the right was granted. Once granted, rights flow through the directory structure until either another set of rights is granted, or the IRM prevents you from inheriting those rights. If, for example, a subdirectory of GCS is created, and you have Read, File Scan, and Create rights to that subdirectory, then, barring any extraneous factors, those rights also apply to you in the subdirectory GCS\STEEN.

An IRM is automatically created on every file and directory when that file or directory is created, granting all rights to the file or directory, by default. You can, however, modify any IRM to filter out rights you do not want users to have for a particular file or directory. Changing the IRM for a given directory to remove a right removes it from any user who would have inherited that right. The IRM takes effect from the point in the directory at which the IRM is modified on down through the balance of that portion of the directory structure.

IRMs cannot, however, filter out the Supervisory right. If you give the Supervisory right to an individual, you cannot prevent that user from having full access to all files and directories from there on, without removing the Supervisory right.

Effective rights are determined by looking at all the pieces of the puzzle: the user's inherited rights, the IRM, and any group affiliations or equivalencies the user has. Usually, explicit rights granted to a user are the same as his or her effective rights. Should the user have additional rights granted because that user is a member of a group, those additional rights are added to the explicit rights granted to the user at that level in the directory structure. The sum of those two now equals the user's effective rights.

If, in the directory, no rights are explicitly granted to the user, and no rights are granted based on the user's association with a group, the user's effective rights are those that have been granted elsewhere at a higher level in the directory structure—with the exception of an IRM. If an IRM has been applied, then the rights the IRM filters out are taken away from that user. Bear in mind the one exception is the Supervisory right, which cannot be removed with an IRM.

# Your Server

The hard disk is divided into logical structures consisting of volumes and directories, and the root volume is the highest you can go. Volume names must be 2 to 15 characters in length, and are identified, when written, by a colon immediately following the name. Volume names must be unique on a file server, and can be as large as 32 TB and span as many as 32 hard disks. The maximum number of volumes on a file server is 64, and the size of all of them added together must be equal to, or less than, the 32 TB. There is only one volume that is required by NetWare, and that is SYS.

You can navigate volumes and directories with the CD command in DOS, as well as the CHDIR command, by creating a map and using that as a pointer, or with any Windows application that changes directories. The recommended length of a directory user name is eight or fewer characters.

The directories that are created when the operating system is first installed are as follows:

- ◆ DELETED.SAV
- ◆ DOC
- ◆ LOGIN
- ◆ MAIL
- ◆ PUBLIC
- ◆ SYSTEM

The SYSTEM directory houses the NLMs, the bindery, and supervisory utilities.

There are five types of console commands: configuration, installation, maintenance, screen display, and other. Configuration commands include CONFIG (which shows details of current server configuration), NAME, TIME, UPS STATUS, and VOLUMES.

Installation commands are BIND (which links the LAN Driver to the communication protocol), LOAD, and MOUNT. Maintenance commands are CLEAR STATION, DISABLE LOGIN, DOWN, ENABLE LOGIN, REMOVE DOS, UNBIND, and UNLOAD.

Screen Display commands are BROADCAST, CLS, EXIT, and SEND. Other commands are ADD NAME SPACE, DISPLAY SERVERS, MODULES, NAME (shows the name of the file server), SECURE CONSOLE (which unloads DOS from memory and requires a warm boot), SET, TIME, and UPS TIME. SECURE CONSOLE not only removes DOS from memory, but also allows only those NLMs that reside in SYS:SYSTEM to be loaded. Incidentally, all name space modules end with the extension .NAM.

File storage space on the server can be limited by user or by directory. DSPACE is the utility used for space limitations, and default restrictions based on time, workstation, or other variables are established using the SYSCON utility.

# The Workstations

There are four files loaded for workstation communications with the server, and they are loaded in the following order:

◆ LSL.COM

◆ LAN Driver

◆ IPXODI.COM

◆ VLM.EXE

LSL is the Link Support Layer. It adheres to and implements ODI specifications, while routing network information between the LAN Driver and the communications software. ODI is Open Data-link Interface and it is a set of rules for communicating that are loaded by IPXODI.COM. VLM is the Virtual Loadable Modules, also known as the DOS Requester; it is the connection point between DOS and the network.

Client software is loaded on the workstation using the WSDOS_1 disk. Type **INSTALL** to start the process in motion. Old configuration files stored with a .BNW extension.

NET.CFG is not a standard computer configuration file. It provides the configuration parameters for the correct operation of the network drivers; that is, LSL.COM, Lan Driver, IPXODI.COM, and VLM.EXE. An example follows:

```
Link Driver NE2000
       INT 5
       PORT 340
       MEM D0000
       FRAME ETHERNET 802.2
NETWARE DOS REQUESTER
       FIRST NETWORK DRIVE=F
```

AUTOEXEC.BAT and STARTNET.BAT are two local files that work with NET.CFG. An example of the STARTNET.BAT file follows:

```
SET NWLANGUAGE=ENGLISH
cd\
LSL
:DRIVER1
3C509.COM
IPXODI
VLM
```

# Miscellaneous Items

NetWare 3.12 includes Electro Text. Electro Text is a version of the product documentation on CD that can only run from Windows. To install it, you need 30 MB of free hard drive space, a copy of the program software (ET.EXE), and a copy of the 3.12 electronic book set. The CD can be accessed from a Windows client, a 3.12 file server, or a CD-ROM drive. It enables you to choose a manual, browse its contents, search for topics, and print your findings. The three major components of Electro Text follow:

◆ Search engine

◆ A bookshelf of electronic manuals

◆ A viewer

SBACKUP is the utility provided by NetWare for backing up servers and workstations. Not only can it be used on DOS files, but it works equally well backing up OS/2 and Unix files. A differential backup gets only the files that have changed since the last backup. TSA_DOS.COM (on the workstation) is the file used to back up a DOS client. Three files are automatically loaded when you load DOS_TSA.NLM (on the server):

◆ STREAMS.NLM

◆ SMDR31X.NLM

◆ TLI.NLM

When you run RCONSOLE, you are prompted for a password. RCONSOLE is interchangeable with ACONSOLE, depending on whether you are remotely accessing the server from the LAN or from a modem. Related NLMs are REMOTE and RSPX—they must always be loaded on the server regardless of whether ACONSOLE or RCONSOLE is to be used.

The two mail packages that come with 3.12 are Basic MHS and First Mail.

Deleted files that are not marked for purge upon deletion are maintained on the server until they are purged, or the server runs out of disk space. In the event that the server does run out of disk space, the deleted files are purged on a first-in, first-purged basis.

# Sample Questions

1. What is VLM?

   A. Virtual Load Mode

   B. Virtual Load Module

   C. Virtual Loadable Module

   D. Virtual NetWare Module

2. File system security utilities include (select two):

   A. FILER

   B. MAKEUSER

   C. BINDREST

   D. SYSCON

3. The correct loading of the DOS Requester is:

   A. LSL, IPXODI, (board driver), VLM

   B. VLM, LSL, (board driver), IPXODI

   C. LSL, (board driver), IPXODI, VLM

   D. IPXODI, LSL, (board driver), VLM

4. What is the command used to link the LAN Driver with the network?

   A. INSTALL

   B. SLIST

   C. VLM

   D. BIND

5. What is the maximum supported volume size:

   A. 4 GB

   B. 32 GB

   C. 4 TB

   D. 32 TB

6. What is the maximum number of file servers a print server can serve?

    A. 4

    B. 8

    C. 16

    D. 32

7. What is the command, and proper syntax, used to create a fake root drive?

    A. MAP G:=HOME\ROOT

    B. MAP ROOT

    C. MD ROOT ; MAP

    D. MAP ROOT G:

8. Which of the following are required NetWare volumes:

    A. PUBLIC

    B. LOGIN

    C. SYS

    D. SYSTEM

9. Print Queues:

    A. Only enable NLMs to be loaded

    B. Must not contain uppercase letters

    C. Have an extension of .QDR

    D. Reside in SYS:SYSTEM

10. Which rights can be included in an Inherited Rights Mask?

    A. SRWCEMFA

    B. RWCEMFA

    C. RWCEMA

    D. RWC

# Answers

1. C
2. A D
3. C
4. D
5. D
6. B
7. B
8. C
9. C D
10. A

# Server Speed and Criteria

Speed.

From zero to 60 in under five seconds. Able to throw a curve ball at 100 MPH. Processing on a 486DX2/50.

Whether the topic is how fast a car can accelerate, the velocity of a baseball, or the promptness of a processor within a computer, speed is important. In fact, speed is even more important when discussing your computer, because here it is directly linked to your livelihood. The problem, however, is that unlike the other two conversational topics, there are numerous components within a computer that relate to the speed at which you are able to do processing, and the processor itself is but one.

Functioning as a stand-alone machine, and ignoring external influences such as a network, the speed-related components within the computer can be broken down into six subcomponents:

◆ The processor

◆ The data bus

◆ RAM

◆ The hard disk

◆ Ports

◆ The CD-ROM

This appendix examines these six items in detail, showing how they interact with one another. Monitor and video resolutions are also discussed to round out the coverage.

Before examining the individual components, it is worthwhile to examine the minimum requirements established for most NetWare servers. The usual requirement is a 386 or greater processor using Industry Standard Architecture (ISA), Extended Industry Standard Architecture (EISA), or Micro Channel Architecture (MCA). Additionally, there must be a minimum of 4 MB RAM.

# The Processor

Eight major Intel chips have been released since the first one for the PC in 1978. The Intel chip revolutionized the computing world for several reasons: it used 20-bit memory addressing to enable it to read 1 MB of RAM, it had clock speeds of 4.77 to 10 MHz, and so on. One megahertz is equal to 1 million clock cycles per second.

The 80286 chip, of which Xenix requires a minimum of to run, was released in 1984. It became the standard AT chip and featured 16-bit architecture. It was the first chip to use *virtual memory*—disk space that appears as RAM—and was capable of creating up to a 1 GB virtual drive. It also had hardware multitasking, as well as real and protected modes. Real mode is nothing more than 8086/8088 emulation; protected mode enables multitasking and some minimal lockup protection. The 80286 supports a clock speed of up to 20 MHz.

The 80386 chip is the most popular in world. It enables switching between real and protected modes without the need to reboot, and has a virtual real mode, where multiple real-mode sessions can run simultaneously. Clock speeds of 16, 20, 25, 33, and 40 MHz are available. Up to 4 GB of RAM and 64 TB of virtual memory also are supported (1 TB is equal to 1,000 GB). The SX model uses a 32-bit bus to talk to the internal components and a 16-bit bus to communicate with external components. The DX, on the other hand, uses a 32-bit internal and external bus.

The 80486 chip features an internal CPU cache with 8 KB of internal processor caching. DX models have a math chip built directly in (it has always been available optionally with all other models). Clock doubling allows internal commands to process twice as fast, thus doubling throughput. When clock doubling is employed, a number 2 is placed after the two-letter acronym. Thus a 80486DX runs at 25 MHz without doubling, and a 80486DX2 runs at 50 MHz.

The newest entry, the Pentium chip, can execute up to two instructions per clock cycle. It features a separate data and code cache (8 KB each), whereas the 80486 uses a single cache for both data and code. A 32-bit address bus is retained, but the data bus width doubles to 64 bits, and over three million transistors are employed (no wonder the heat is a problem); meaning, speeds of over 120 MHz can be obtained. Ignoring all the jokes about mathematical errors, there is an FPU (Floating Point Unit) built in that enables the firmware to achieve a 300 percent increase in computations speeds.

As a point of reference, and to put some of this into perspective, the mainframe world has always measured speed in terms of *MIPS*—millions of instructions per second. Most mainframes run between 55 and 100 MIPS. The 80286 runs at 3 MIPS, and the 80386 operates at 11 MIPS. Likewise, the 80486 can achieve 41 MIPS, and the Pentium operates at approximately 100 MIPS.

# The Data Bus

The data bus, quite simply, is the communications path between the processor and the other components—internal and external. All system subcomponents are connected by the data bus. The XT bus was built around the 8088 processor, and it was only 8 bits wide. The larger the bus, the more data that can simultaneously transmit. A good analogy is lanes on a highway. The more lanes available, the faster the traffic can flow.

When the AT computer appeared on the scene in 1984, it used an 80286 processor and incorporated a 16-bit bus. The three main data buses currently in use are the following:

◆ ISA

◆ EISA

◆ MCA

*ISA*, or Industry Standard Architecture, came on the scene in 1979. It is a 16-bit data and expansion bus, and is the most common bus in use today. It is ideal for workstations and small servers. When getting into a heavy computing environment, however, better choices are available, primarily because ISA does not take advantage of any of the 32-bit processing that became available starting with the 80386. Regardless, it is the bus used in XTs, ATs, and most clones.

*EISA*, or Extended Industry Standard Architecture, is a 32-bit enhancement of the standard ISA. It was created by the so-called *Gang of Nine*—a group of vendors whose only commonality was that they did not like IBM. The important thing about EISA is that it does not replace ISA, it only expands on it. It is not at all uncommon today to buy a server with six ISA slots and two EISA slots. The two EISA slots are then used for a 32-bit network interface card and a 32-bit disk controller.

*MCA*, or Micro Channel Architecture, was developed by IBM, which did not take well to the Gang of Nine. It is a 32-bit proprietary alternative to ISA. Unlike EISA, it is not compatible with

ISA. Although MCA was intended to be the underlying basis of the PS/2, only models 70, 80, 90, and 95 use the 32-bit MCA. Models 50 and 60 use a 16-bit version of MCA, and Models 25 and 30 still use the old 16-bit ISA.

# RAM

Memory, as has been drilled into the heads of every administrator since day one, comes in two flavors—ROM (Read Only Memory) and RAM (Random Access Memory). Read Only Memory is built into the computer and contains such information as bootup parameters, the BIOS, and so forth. ROM is semi-permanent in that the data values stay if the power is turned off, but are lost if the battery maintaining them dies. Random Access Memory, on the other hand, is used for caching, buffering, and all other operations. In short, it is something that you can never have enough of.

With memory, measurements are done in nanoseconds; the smaller the number of nanoseconds, the faster the memory, or *SIMM*. Most memory access falls within the range of 70 to 90 nanoseconds, and as a rough approximation, RAM access is 100 times faster than from disk.

The two most popular types of RAM are *DRAM* (Dynamic) and *SRAM* (Static). DRAM is the most popular and consists of capacitors storing values of 0s and 1s. Being dynamic, it must be continually refreshed to hold its data. SRAM contains no capacitors and is mechanical in nature, consisting of a number of switches. The mechanical nature reduces the access time, as well as the need to refresh. With SRAM, access times drop to between 60 and 70 nanoseconds.

A typical motherboard has either four or eight SIMM slots. If there are eight, they consist of two banks of four, and provide for a maximum of 256 MB of DRAM.

# The Hard Disk

Hard drives are made from platters of aluminum and coated with magnetic recording media, as opposed to floppies that are made of mylar. Most hard disks are made of either one or more platters, each with two sides, and the platters revolve clockwise during disk access at speeds of 3,600 to 7,200 rpm. Hard disk performance is measured in random access time, with the majority of drives falling in the range of 7 to 20 milliseconds. Hard disk capacity is measured in terms of megabytes.

The first IBM PCs used an ST506 interface from Seagate Technology. For the most part, this technology is now obsolete and should not still be in use in any existing machines. It is important to know, however, that two data encoding techniques were employed:

1. *Modified Frequency Modulation* (MFM) enabled data transfer rates of up to 5 Mbps.

2. *Run Length Limited* (RLL) enabled data transfers at 7.5 Mbps and increased drive capacity by 50 percent.

Though ideal for small—20 MB and 40 MB—hard drives, it could not keep up with anything beyond that size with any reasonable amount of speed.

When the AT computer came out, it went away from ST506, and to ESDI, which is a standard of the American National Standards Institute (ANSI). Greatly improving on ground broken by ST506, ESDI can transfer data at rates from 10 to 15 Mbps. ESDI was excellent for 100 MB to 340 MB drives, but had difficulties keeping up with requests if that drive were placed under a high load.

The two most commonly used interfaces today, however, are IDE and SCSI. IDE employs a Western Digital drive controller that is closely matched to the hard drive. IDE uses RLL encoding to support high data transfer rates and dense disk storage. The access rate is from 1 to 5 Mbps, and it is a good choice for drives less than 340 MB in size.

*SCSI*, Small Computer System Interface, performs parallel, eight-bit file data transfers, and is the most common interface for high-performance computers and file servers. The other interfaces perform serial, one-bit-at-a-time transfers. Consequently, SCSI is ideal for servers, and the fact that it supports a variety of devices—besides hard drives, including CD-ROMs and tape drives—serves as a bonus. SCSI is configured as a bus that can support up to seven devices from a single controller card. Each device is identified by a number ranging from 0 through 6. SCSI is the ideal interface for drives greater than 340 MB in size.

The speed of a SCSI drive is dependent on the bus width and whether the drive is "standard SCSI" or "fast SCSI." With standard SCSI, transfer rate is 5 Mbps on an 8-bit bus, 10 Mbps on a 16-bit bus, and 20 Mbps on a 32-bit bus. Those numbers double with fast SCSI; it is 10 Mbps on an 8-bit bus, 20 Mbps on a 16-bit bus and 40 Mbps on a 32-bit bus.

# Ports

The two ports on a computer are *serial* and *parallel*. The parallel port provides one-way data transfer from the computer to another device. Because it transfers data in only one direction, it can use eight different lines and transfer eight bits at the same time. The most significant limitation of parallel ports is that cables have a limited length. Ten feet is the generally recommended maximum, but 50-foot cables can function reliably. When cables get too long, crosstalk and other distortion-causing effects can affect the integrity of the data signals.

Serial ports, on the other hand, can be considerably longer in length without data integrity problems. Serial communications also permit two-way data transfer, and thus they support the transfer of eight bits, one after another. The two methods of communication are *synchronous* (where both devices on each end of the cable are synchronized) and *asynchronous*. With asynchronous, neither data device cares where the other is and data frames are employed to send messages. Data frames are 11 bits in size, and constitute three components:

◆ 8 bits of data (byte)

◆ 1 bit on front (start bit)

◆ 2 bits on back (stop bits)

Serial rates are measured in terms of bits per second (bps). One important note: bits per second always refers to the amount of data transmitted; quite often serial devices, such as modems, are given in baud speeds. Baud rate is the number of frequency changes and not the amount of data. A 9,600 baud modem, therefore, can really be running at 2,400 bps—it is then said to be a quadbit modem. Most standard telephone lines only support low bps rates—from 300 to 9,600.

# The CD-ROM

A CD-ROM drive, attached to a server or workstation, is the slowest component of that computer. Drive access speeds vary from 200 milliseconds to 1,000 milliseconds, with the majority of them falling between 300 and 500 milliseconds. In addition to access time, there is also transfer time measured in terms of kilobytes per second. The ranges vary from nothing to 600 KB per second. A sustained data transfer rate of at least 150 KB per second is required to maintain a continuous flow of data through the buffers. At speeds any slower than that, motion video displays flicker and stutter.

It goes without saying that the lower the milliseconds and the higher the kilobytes per second, the better and more suitable the drive. Double-speed CD-ROMs simply spin the platter at twice their normal rotational speed; meaning, the access time is essentially cut in half, and the transfer rate is doubled—a winning combination. Some CD-ROM drives are also capable of decreasing access time and increasing transfer time by incorporating read ahead cache buffers, and it is not unusual to find cache buffers in the range of 128 KB or 256 KB.

# Monitor and Video

Technically, a discussion about video does not fit in with the other categories. The other components are centered on processing and input, and video is an output device. Nevertheless, there are five standards for video in use on servers and workstations today:

◆ **Monochrome**

◆ **RGB.** The original IBM color monitor with four colors.

◆ **CGA.** Sixteen real colors at $320 \times 200$ pixels.

◆ **EGA.** Sixty-four colors at $640 \times 350$ pixels.

◆ **VGA.** Can switch between high resolution/low color ($640 \times 480$ with 16 colors) and low resolution/high color ($320 \times 200$ with 256 colors).

The speed of a monitor is measured in terms of its refresh rate, or scanning frequency. Horizontal and vertical scan rates directly refer to the amount of time it takes for the screen to be refreshed from that direction.

# Tying It All Together

Because no two components are measured with the same scale, discussing component speeds can be quite difficult. The components most easily paired in terms of speed and performance are the hard drive with the CD-ROM and the data bus with computer ports. Megabits that can be transferred per second is a measurement used to determine the speed of a hard drive interface, and the number of milliseconds it takes to find the data is used to discuss the disk performance. The speed of the CD-ROM device is determined by similar standards. A data bus is measured in terms of how many pathways it has to transfer data. The more pathways, the more data that can simultaneously be transmitted, and the better the performance. Ports are similar to data buses in that their measurement is in terms of how many pathways are allowed

**335**

to communicate simultaneously. Processor performance, alone, is calculated in terms of megahertz—or how many million cycles per second. RAM runs at a consistent speed, and is limited only by its quantity and the amount that can be recognized and accessed.

Using those parameters, if the computer has a CD-ROM drive connected to it, that will be the slowest component of the machine. Barring that, the hard drive is the next slowest component. Anything that can be done to speed up the hard drive, or decrease dependence on it, greatly increases operating performance. Adding additional RAM, given the access time to retrieve data from it, is the best possible solution for an existing machine.

When purchasing a new machine, all the numbers should be considered together to get the most efficient system possible. At the present time, that would be a Pentium with an EISA bus, fast SCSI hard drive, and as much RAM as you can afford. If a CD-ROM is critical, purchase one running at double, or triple speed, with a low access time and high transfer rate.

# Command Reference

This appendix offers a listing of the most used NetWare commands, along with a reference to each command's correct syntax.

## ADD NAME SPACE

### Purpose
Enables the storing of non-DOS files on a NetWare volume.

### Syntax
```
ADD NAME SPACE name TO VOLUME volume
```

### Options

| | |
|---|---|
| Macintosh | Use for Macintosh files. |
| OS2 | Use for OS/2 files. |
| NFS | Use for Unix files. |
| FTAM | Use for Unix files. |

# ALLOW

## Purpose

Permits changing of the Inherited Rights Mask (IRM) of a file or directory.

## Syntax

```
ALLOW path\file rights
```

## Options

| | |
|---|---|
| ALL | Specifies all rights. |
| No Rights | Specifies no rights; does not remove Supervisory. |
| Read | Opens and reads files. |
| Write | Opens and writes to files. |
| Create | Creates and writes to files. |
| Erase | Deletes a file or directory. |
| Modify | Renames files or directories; modifies file or directory attributes. |
| File Scan | Views files and directories. |
| Access Control | Enables changes to security assignments. |

# ATTACH

## Purpose

Gives access to services on a file server other than the one you have logged in to.

## Syntax

```
ATTACH fileserver/username /P /G
```

## Options

| | |
|---|---|
| *fileserver* | The name of the file server to which you want to attach. |
| *fileserver\username* | The file server name and user name for the file server to which you are attaching. |
| *private* | For OS/2 sessions only; this option enables you to attach to a server in a single session. |
| *global* | For OS/2 sessions only; this option enables you to attach to a server in all sessions. |

## See Also

LOGIN

SLIST

# BIND

## Purpose

Ties the LAN drivers to a communication protocol and to a network board in the file server. Unless this task is performed, the communication protocol is unable to process packets.

## Syntax

```
BIND protocol to board_name protocol_parameter
```

## Options

| | |
|---|---|
| *protocol* | Normally, you would use IPX (Internet Packet Exchange) protocol. You may use other protocols such as IP. |
| *LAN_driver* | The name of the driver you loaded for the network board. |

| | |
|---|---|
| *board_name* | The board name you assigned when you loaded the driver. |
| DMA=*number* | The DMA channel the network board is configured to use (if any). |
| FRAME=*name* | Frame type the driver is to use for this network board. |
| INT=*number* | The hardware interrupt the network board is configured to use. |
| MEM=*number* | The shared memory address the network board is configured to use (if any). |
| PORT=*number* | The I/O port address (in hex) the network board is configured to use. |
| SLOT=*number* | The slot in which the network board is installed (valid only for EISA and IBM Micro Channel-equipped machines). |
| *driver_parameter* | Include a driver_parameter when you have more than one network board of the same type in the file server. |
| NET=*number* | The unique network address number for the cabling system that is attached to the board. |
| *protocol_parameter* | Use for the parameters unique to the selected communications protocol. IPX has only one: NET. |
| ADDR=*number* | The unique IP address for that machine. |

# BINDFIX

### Purpose

Rebuilds the NetWare bindery files (NET$OBJ.SYS, NET$PROP.SYS, and NET$VAL.SYS).

340

## See Also

BINDREST

BROADCAST

DISABLE LOGIN

MONITOR

# BINDREST

## Purpose

Restores the original bindery files as if BINDFIX had never been run. The backup bindery files that get restored are NET$OBJ.OLD, NET$PROP.OLD, and NET$VAL.OLD.

## Syntax

```
BINDREST
```

## See Also

BINDFIX

BROADCAST

DISABLE LOGIN

MONITOR

USERLIST

# BROADCAST

## Purpose

Sends one message to all users logged in to the file server.

## Syntax

```
BROADCAST "message" TO user
```

## Options

| | |
|---|---|
| *user* | The user's login name. |
| *connection number* | The connection number listed by the USERLIST command. |

## See Also

MONITOR

# CAPTURE

## Purpose

Redirects output meant to be printed from applications not designed to run on a network to a NetWare print queue.

## Syntax

```
CAPTURE options
```

## Options

The optional switches used by CAPTURE consist of one or more of the following:

| | |
|---|---|
| AU (AUtoendcap) | Automatically closes out a print job when you exit an application. AUtoendcap is enabled by default. |
| NA (NoAutoendcap) | Requires the use of the ENDCAP utility to terminate the effects of CAPTURE. Use NoAutoendcap to move in and out of your applications without prematurely closing the print queue file(s) you are creating. |
| B (Banner) | A banner name can be any word or phrase up to 12 characters in length that you want to appear on the lower part of the banner page. To |

|  |  |
|---|---|
|  | represent a space between words, use an underscore character; the underscore character will print (default is LST). |
| NB (NoBanner) | Tells NetWare not to print a banner page. |
| C (Copies=*n*) | Replace *n* with the number of copies you want to print (1 to 999). The default is 1 copy. |
| CR (CReate=*filespec*) | Creates a print file in which to store instead of sending the print job to a file server's print queue. *Filespec* can be any legal DOS file name and can include path information; you can create the print file, however, only on a network drive. |
| FF (FormFeed) | Sends a form-feed code to the printer at the end of each print job so that the next print job can start at the top of the next sheet of paper. If your application sends a form-feed code at the end of the print job, an extra page is fed through the printer, wasting paper. Form-feeding is enabled by default. |
| NFF (NoFormFeed) | Disables the sending of form-feed codes at the end of a print job. |
| F (Form=*formname* or *n*) | Replace *formname* with the name of the form on which you want your print job to print. Replace *n* with the form number onto which you want your print job to print. Use the PRINTDEF utility to define form names or numbers (or both) before using this option. |

J (Job=*jobconfig*)     Replace *jobconfig* with the name of a predefined print job configuration you want to use. You must use the PRINTCON utility to define print jobs before using this option.

K (Keep)     Tells CAPTURE to keep all data it receives during a print capture in case your workstation locks up or loses power while capturing data. This option is useful if you capture data over a period of several hours. If your workstation loses its connection to the file server, the server sends the data to the print queue after the server realizes your station is no longer connected to it.

L (Local=*n*)     Indicates which local LPT ports you want to capture. Valid choices are 1, 2, or 3. The default is 1. The local LPT ports defined here are "logical" connections, not "physical" ports. You can print to and capture from all three LPT ports, even though your workstation might have only one physical LPT port installed.

NAM (NAMe=*name*)     *name* can be any word or phrase, up to 12 characters in length, that you want printed on the upper part of the banner page. The default is the user's name used when you logged in to the file server. The NoBanner option defeats the purpose of using this switch, because no banner page is printed.

Q (Queue=*queuename*)     *queuename* is the file server queue name to which you want to send the print job. This option is useful if

| | |
|---|---|
| | multiple queues are mapped to one printer. If you fail to specify a queue name, CAPTURE defaults to the queue to which Spooler 0 has been assigned. |
| S (Server=*name*) | *name* is the name of the file server to which you are sending the print job and the server on which the print queue is located. The default is the default server you first logged in to. |
| SH (Show) | Displays a list of the currently captured LPT ports. SH does not affect the capture status of an LPT port. It merely returns the currently active CAPTURE options (if any). You cannot use SH with other CAPTURE options. |
| T (Tabs=*n*) | Use this option only if your application program does not support print formatting; most do. *n* is the number of characters in each tab stop, from 0 to 18. The default is 8. |
| NT (NoTabs) | Ensures that all tabs arrive at the printer unchanged. By default, this option also specifies the file to be a binary or "byte stream" file. Use this option only if your application program has its own print formatter. Most applications produce embedded printer-specific codes. This option ensures that those codes arrive at the printer intact. |
| TI (Timeout=*n*) | Enables you to print from an application without forcing you to exit it. It sends the print data to the print queue in a specified number of |

seconds after the application finishes writing to the file or after waiting the specified number of seconds for additional print output. After the specified amount of time, CAPTURE begins again. For best results, TI should not be set to less than 5 seconds or greater than 60.

$n$ = number of seconds, 1 to 1,000. Timeout is disabled by default.

### See Also

ENDCAP

PSC

## CASTOFF

### Purpose

Stops SEND and BROADCAST messages from appearing on the workstation.

### Syntax

```
CASTOFF
```

or

```
CASTOFF ALL
```

### Option

A or ALL              Blocks messages from both the file
                      server console and other worksta-
                      tions on the network.

### See Also

BROADCAST

CASTON

SEND

# CASTON

## Purpose

Enables the workstation to again receive messages after CASTOFF was used.

## Syntax

CASTON

## See Also

BROADCAST

CASTOFF

SEND

# CDROM

## Purpose

Enables management of CD-ROM volumes on the server.

## Syntax

LOAD CDROM

# CHKDIR

## Purpose

Shows information on directories and volumes.

## Syntax

CHKDIR *path*

## Option

*path*   The directory path leading to and including the path you want to check.

**347**

### See Also

CHKVOL

# CHKVOL

### Purpose

Shows space currently in use and available on the volume.

### Syntax

```
CHKVOL fileserver\volume
```

### Options

*fileserver*   The name of the file server's volume to view.

*volume*   The name of the volume to view.

*   Specifies all file servers you are attached to, or all volumes.

### See Also

CHKDIR

# CONFIG

### Purpose

Shows information about the file server, including the following:

◆ File server name

◆ Internal network number

◆ Loaded/Linked LAN drivers

◆ Hardware settings on network boards

◆ Node (station) addresses (ID) of network boards

◆ Communication protocol bound to the network board

- Network number of the cabling scheme for a network board
- Frame type assigned to the board
- Board name assigned

### Syntax

```
CONFIG
```

### See Also

MONITOR

# DISABLE LOGIN

### Purpose

Keeps users from logging in to the file server.

### Syntax

```
DISABLE LOGIN
```

### See Also

ENABLE LOGIN

LOGIN

# DISMOUNT

### Purpose

Dismounts a NetWare drive partition or disk for repair or maintenance.

### Syntax

```
DISMOUNT volume
```

### Option

*volume*  The name of the volume you want to take out of service.

**349**

**See Also**

MOUNT

# DISPLAY NETWORKS

## Purpose

Displays the following information:

◆ Network numbers, both cable and internal IPX

◆ The number of hops required to reach the network

◆ The estimated time in ticks required for a packet to reach the other network

◆ The total number of networks recognized by the internal router

## Syntax

DISPLAY NETWORKS

## See Also

DISPLAY SERVERS

# DISPLAY SERVERS

## Purpose

Displays the following information:

◆ The file servers recognized by the internal router

◆ The number of hops required to reach the server

## Syntax

DISPLAY SERVERS

## See Also

DISPLAY NETWORKS

# DOSGEN

## Purpose

Creates a boot image file (NET$DOS.SYS) in the SYS:LOGIN directory, enabling diskless workstations to boot from the server's hard disk.

## Syntax

```
DOSGEN source file
```

## Options

*source*   The drive in which DOSGEN can find the boot disk. If you omit this drive indicator, NetWare assumes that you want to use drive A.

*file*   The output file name. If you do not specify an output file name, NetWare uses the name NET$DOS.SYS.

# DOWN

## Purpose

Shuts down the NetWare operating system by writing all cache buffers to the disk, closing all open files, and updating all directory and file allocation tables.

## Syntax

```
DOWN
```

## See Also

MONITOR

# ENABLE LOGIN

## Purpose

Enables users to log in to the file server once more, after DISABLE LOGIN has been implemented.

## Syntax

```
ENABLE LOGIN
```

## See Also

DISABLE LOGIN

LOGIN

# ENDCAP

## Purpose

Terminates the capturing of one or more LPT ports at the workstation.

## Syntax

```
ENDCAP option
```

## Options

(ENDCAP ends capturing to LPT1, unless you enter one of the options in the following list.)

| | |
|---|---|
| Local *n* | Indicates the LPT port from which you want to end capturing. Replace *n* with the number of the desired parallel port, such as 1, 2, or 3. |
| ALL | Ends the capturing of all LPT ports. |
| Cancel | Ends the capturing of LPT1, and deletes the data without printing it. |

| | |
|---|---|
| Cancel Local *n* | Ends the capturing of the specified LPT port, and deletes data without printing it. Replace *n* with the number of the desired parallel port, such as 1, 2, or 3. |
| Cancel ALL | Ends the capturing of all LPT ports and deletes the data without printing it. |

### See Also

CAPTURE

# EXIT

### Purpose

Sends the file server console back into DOS after the DOWN command.

### Syntax

```
EXIT
```

### See Also

DOWN

REMOVE DOS

# FLAG

### Purpose

Displays or changes files' attributes.

### Syntax

```
FLAG path flag
```

### Options

| | |
|---|---|
| path | Designates directory path that leads to the name of the file you want to view or change. |

**353**

flag | Specifies one or more of the following attributes:

**Shareable** (Enables a file to be opened by more than one person at a time. Shareable is often used in conjunction with Read Only and also is used to mark application programs; that is, EXE or COM files.)

**Read Only** (Prevents you from writing to, deleting, or renaming a specified file. The Read Only flag often is used in conjunction with Shareable on application program files.)

**Read/Write** (Specifies the file as a data file, which means that data can be written to it. This default setting is for files.)

**Normal** (Specifies the NonShareable and Read/Write flags together. All files loaded on the network are set this way by default.)

**Indexed** (Forces NetWare to keep a special File Allocation Table to speed data access; used with data files using more than 64 cache blocks.)

**Hidden** (Prevents a file from displaying when a DOS DIR command is executed. The file appears, however, if you have the File Scan right in that directory, and you use the NDIR command. You cannot copy or erase Hidden files.)

**SYstem** (Flags a file as a system file and is used for the system function. A system file does not appear when you use the DOS DIR command, but it appears when you use the NetWare NDIR command if you have the File Scan right. You cannot copy or delete system files.)

**Archive** (Attaches automatically to all files that have been modified since the last backup was performed.)

**Execute Only** (Enables the program file to execute, but prevents it from being copied. This special flag is attached to COM and EXE files. Files with this flag set are not backed up, nor can this flag be removed. The file must be deleted and reinstalled to remove this attribute. This attribute can be set only by the supervisor in the FILER utility.)

**SUBdirectory** (Displays or changes file attributes in the specified directory and its subdirectories.)

## See Also

NDIR

# FLAGDIR

## Purpose

Shows or changes the attributes of directories and subdirectories.

## Syntax

```
FLAGDIR path flag
```

## Options

path      Specifies the path to the directory you want to view or change.

flag      Specifies one or more of the following attributes:

**Normal** (Cancels all other directory attributes. Normal is automatically overridden if you include any other option.)

**Hidden** (Prevents a directory from showing when the DOS DIR command is used. The directory will appear if you have the File Scan right and you use the NetWare NDIR command. With these privileges, you can access a Hidden directory, but you cannot copy or delete Hidden directories.)

**SYstem** (Flags a directory as a System directory, which stores the network's operational files. A directory flagged as System will not appear when you use the DOS DIR command. A System directory will appear if you use the NetWare NDIR command and if you have the File Scan right.)

**Delete** (Prevents users from erasing a directory Inhibit even if they have Erase rights for that directory.)

**Rename** (Prevents users from renaming director-Inhibities even if they have Modify rights for that directory.)

**Purge** (Marks files that you want to purge immediately after deletion. These files cannot be recovered by using SALVAGE.)

**Help** (Displays the FLAGDIR help text.)

# GRANT

## Purpose

Grants trustee rights to a user or a group.

## Syntax

```
GRANT rights FOR path TO USER\GROUP name
```

## Options

| | |
|---|---|
| *path* | Specifies the path for granting trustee rights. |
| *name* | The name of the valid user or group on the file server to whom you want to grant trustee rights. |
| *rights* | Represents one or more of the following options: |
| | **All** (Grants all rights except Supervisory rights.) |

**Create** (Enables users to create files but not to write to them.)

**Erase** (Enables users to delete or erase files.)

**Modify** (Enables users to modify file names or attributes.)

**Access Control** (Enables a user or a group to control access to the directory.)

**Read** (Enables users to read from a file in the directory.)

**File Scan** (Enables users to "see" file names during a DOS DIR command.)

**Write** (Enables users to write to files.)

**Supervisor** (Gives all available rights to user.)

**ALL BUT** or **ONLY** (Switches that you can use before the *rights* option.)

# LISTDIR

## Purpose

Lists subdirectories and subdirectory information.

## Syntax

```
LISTDIR path options
```

## Options

path      Specifies the directory path for which you want more information. The path can include the volume, directory, and subdirectory.

option      Specifies one or more of the following options:

**/Rights** (Shows the Inherited Rights Masks of all subdirectories in a specific directory.)

/**Effective rights** (Shows the Effective rights for all subdirectories of the specified directory.)

/**Date** or /**Time** (Shows the date or time or both that a subdirectory was created.)

/**Subdirectories** (Shows a directory's subdirectories.)

/**All** (Shows all subdirectories, their Inherited Rights Masks, effective rights, and their creation dates and times.)

# LOAD

## Purpose

Loads NetWare Loadable Modules (NLMs) at the file server console.

## Syntax

```
LOAD path NLM parameter
```

## Options

| | |
|---|---|
| *path* | Represents the full path to the directory that contains the loadable module. The path variable can begin with either a valid DOS drive letter or a valid NetWare volume name. If you do not specify a path and the SYS volume has not been mounted, the operating system (OS) assumes that the NLM is in the default DOS partition or directory. After the volume SYS has been mounted, the OS assumes the loadable module is in the SYS:SYSTEM directory. |
| *NLM* | Specifies the name of one of the following types of NLMs: |

|  | Disk drivers |
|  | LAN drivers |
|  | Name space |
|  | NLM utilities |
| *parameter* | Settings are specific to each NLM. Refer to the NLM's documentation for more information. |

# LOGIN

## Purpose

Establishes a connection with the named or default server.

## Syntax

```
LOGIN option fileserver/login_name scriptparameters
```

## Options

| *option* | May be one or more of the following: |
|  | /Script |
|  | /NoAttach |
|  | /Clearscreen |
| *fileserver* | Identifies the file server you want to log in to. |
| *login_name* | Specifies your user name or login name (account name, for example). |
| *scriptparameters* | Specifies the parameters set in your login script. |

## See Also

ATTACH

LOGOUT

# LOGOUT

## Purpose

Logs you out of file servers you are attached to.

## Syntax

```
LOGOUT fileserver
```

## See Also

ATTACH

LOGIN

# MAKEUSER

## Purpose

Creates and deletes user accounts.

## Syntax

```
MAKEUSER
```

Keywords used in a USR file to create and delete users in MAKEUSER are the following:

#ACCOUNT EXPIRATION month, day, year

#ACCOUNTING balance, lowlimit

#CLEAR or #RESET

#CONNECTIONS number

#CREATE user name [option ...]

#DELETE user name

#GROUPS group

#HOME_DIRECTORY path

#LOGIN_SCRIPT path

#MAX_DISK_SPACE vol, number

#PASSWORD_LENGTH length

#PASSWORD_PERIOD days

#PASSWORD_REQUIRED

#PURGE_USER_DIRECTORY

#REM or REM

#RESTRICTED_TIME day, start, end

#STATIONS network, station

#UNIQUE_PASSWORD

# MAP

## Purpose

Shows and changes logical drive mappings in NetWare.

## Syntax

```
MAP parameters drive:=path
```

## Options

*parameters* can be any of the following:

| | |
|---|---|
| INSert | Alters search drive mappings. |
| DELete | Deletes a drive mapping. |
| REMove | Deletes a drive mapping. |
| Next | Maps next available drive letter to the specified path. |
| ROOT | Maps the drive as fake root (useful for Windows applications). |
| *drive* | The drive letter mapped to the directory with which you want to work. |
| *path* | Directory path with which you intend to work. |

# MEMORY

## Purpose

Shows the total amount of memory the operating system can address in the file server.

## Syntax

MEMORY

## See Also

REGISTER MEMORY

# MENU

## Purpose

Invokes a custom menu that you have created.

## Syntax

MENU *filename*

# MODULES

## Purpose

Shows the modules currently loaded on the file server.

## Syntax

MODULES

## See Also

LOAD

# MONITOR

## Purpose

An all-purpose utility, it locks the console, turns on the screen saver, and monitors how efficiently the network is operating.

## Syntax

```
LOAD path MONITOR parameter
```

## Options

| | |
|---|---|
| *path* | Full path beginning with a DOS drive letter or NetWare volume name. If you do not specify a path, and volume SYS has been mounted, the operating system assumes the module is in SYS:SYSTEM unless other search paths have been added. |
| *parameter* | can be any of the following: |

| | | |
|---|---|---|
| | ns | (No screen saver.) Disables the screen saver option. If you do not use ns, a utilization snake appears on-screen after a few minutes of console keyboard inactivity. To redisplay the MONITOR screen, press any key. |
| | nh | (No help.) Prevents MONITOR HELP from loading. |
| | p | Displays information about the file server microprocessor. |

# MOUNT

## Purpose

Makes a volume available for users to access.

## Syntax

```
MOUNT volume or ALL
```

**363**

## Options

| | |
|---|---|
| *volume* | Specifies the volume name you want to put into service or mount. |
| ALL | Enables you to mount all volumes without specifying the names of each volume. |

## See Also

DISMOUNT

# NAME

## Purpose

Displays the name of the file server.

## Syntax

```
NAME
```

# NCOPY

## Purpose

Works like the COPY command in DOS except NCOPY performs the copy at the file server itself, rather than reading data from the file server and then writing it back to the file server over the network.

## Syntax

```
NCOPY path FILE to path FILE option
```

## Options

| | |
|---|---|
| /A | Copies only files that have the archive bit set. Will not reset the archive bit. |
| /COPY | Copies files without preserving the attributes or name space information. |
| /EMPTY | Copies empty subdirectories when you copy an entire directory with the /S option. |

| /FORCE | Forces the operating system to write sparse files. |
| /INFORM | Notifies you when attributes or name space information cannot be copied. |
| /M | Copies only files that have the archive bit set, and will reset the archive bit after copying. |
| /PRESERVE | Copies SYSTEM and HIDDEN files and preserves attributes. |
| /SUBDIRECTORIES | Copies all the files and subdirectories. |
| /VERIFY | Verifies that the original file and the copy are identical. |
| /Help /? | Displays usage guide. |

# NDIR

## Purpose

Shows information on files and subdirectories.

## Syntax

```
NDIR path option . . .
```

## Options

| path | Identifies the directory path leading to and including the directory and file you want to show. You can include a file chain of up to 16 file names. |
| option | Can be one of the following: |
| | Attribute options |
| | Format options |
| | Restriction options |
| | Sort options |

| RO | Shows files that have the Read-Only attribute set. |
| S | Shows files that have the Shareable attribute set. |
| A | Shows files that have their archive attribute set. Files are displayed in the backup format, which shows the last-modified and last-archived dates. The archive flag is set whenever a file is modified. |
| EX | Shows files that are flagged as Execute Only. |
| H | Shows files or directories that have the Hidden attribute set. |
| SY | Shows files or directories that have the System attribute set. |
| T | Shows files that have been flagged as Transactional. |
| I | Shows files that have been flagged as Index files. |
| P | Shows files or directories that have the Purge attribute set. |
| RA | Shows files flagged as Read Audit. |
| WA | Shows files flagged as Write Audit. |
| CI | Shows files flagged as Copy Inhibited. Restricts copyrights of users logged in to Macintosh workstations. Only valid for files. |
| DI | Shows files or directories flagged as Delete Inhibited. Prevents users from erasing directories or files, even if they have the Erase right. |

| | |
|---|---|
| RI | Shows file and directories flagged as Rename Inhibited. Prevents users from renaming directories and files even if they have the Modify right. |
| D | Shows time and date stamp information about files. Shows the date last modified, last archived, last accessed, and date created. |
| R | Shows your access rights on selected files; shows inherited and effective rights on files and subdirectories, and shows file flags. |
| MAC | Shows Macintosh subdirectories or files in a search area. When you list only Macintosh files or subdirectories, they appear with their full Macintosh names. |
| LONG | Shows all Macintosh, OS/2, and NFS long file names for the file under all loaded name spaces in a given search area. |
| HELP | Shows the NDIR command format and available command options. |
| OW | Shows files created by a specific user. |
| SI | Shows files by their sizes. |
| UP | Shows files by their last update date. |
| CR | Shows files by their creation date. |
| AC | Shows files by their last accessed date. |
| AR | Shows files by their archive date. |
| FO | Shows only files in a directory. |
| DO | Shows only subdirectories in a directory. |

|  |  |
|---|---|
| SUB | Applies the NDIR command to all subdirectories and subsequent subdirectories in a directory. |

### See Also

FLAG

# NPRINT

### Purpose

Like the PRINT command in DOS, it sends a file from a disk to a NetWare print queue.

### Syntax

```
NPRINT filespec options
```

### Options

| | |
|---|---|
| Banner=*banner name* | Determines whether a banner (a word or phrase up to 12 characters) is printed. Spaces are entered by using the underscore character (above the minus on most keyboards). The default is the name of the file you are printing. |
| Copies=*n* | Specifies the number of copies to print from 1 to 999. |
| Delete | Deletes a file immediately after it is printed. |
| Form=*frm* | Specifies the name or number of a previously defined form. The default is the form specified in your default print job configuration if it has been defined. |
| FormFeed | Sends a form-feed to the printer after the job has printed. The default is enabled. |

| | |
|---|---|
| Job=*job* | Specifies which print job configuration to use. Print job configurations can be created using PRINTCON. A single print job configuration can define the settings for all of the options for NPRINT with a single option. |
| NAMe=*user* | Specifies the name that appears on the top part of the banner page. The default is the user's login name. |
| NoBanner | Prints without the banner page. The default is for the banner page to print. |
| NoFormFeed | Does not send a form-feed to the printer after the job has printed. The default is to send a form-feed to the printer after a job has printed. |
| NoNOTIfy | Prevents the operating system from notifying you when a print job has finished printing. (This option is only necessary if NOTIfy is enabled in your print job configuration and you want to ignore it.) |
| NoTabs | Stops NetWare from altering your tabs before they are sent to the printer. |
| NOTIfy | Notifies you when the print job has been sent to the printer. |
| Queue=*queue* | Identifies which queue the job is sent to. Queues can be defined with PCONSOLE. |
| Server=*server* | Specifies which server the print job should be sent to for printing. The default is the current server. |

| Tabs=$n$ | Indicates the number of spaces between tabs, ranging from 0 to 18. The default is 8 spaces. |

# NVER

## Purpose

Shows the NetBIOS, IPX/SPX, LAN driver, workstation shell, workstation DOS, and file server operating system versions for the file server and workstation.

## Syntax

```
NVER
```

# PSC

## Purpose

A command-line version of PCONSOLE, it enables you to check the print server status and to control its operations.

## Syntax

```
PSC PS=printserver P=printernumber options
```

## Options

| AB (ABort) | Cancels the current print job and continues with the next print job in the queue. |
| CD (CancelDown) | Use this option to reverse the effects of the "Going down after current jobs" selection in PCONSOLE. |
| STAT (STATus) | Displays the status of the printer. |
| PAU (PAUse) | Pauses printing temporarily. |

| | |
|---|---|
| STO (STOp) | Stops the printer. Use STOP Keep to resubmit the current job. Without Keep, the current job is deleted. |
| STAR (STARt) | Starts the printer after it has been paused or stopped. |
| M (Mark) | Prints a line of asterisks on the current line. |
| FF (FormFeed) | Advances the printer to the top of the next page. The printer first must be paused or stopped. |
| MO F=$n$ (MOunt Form) | Replaces $n$ with the number of a form that has been defined in PRINTDEF. |
| PRI (PRIvate) | Changes a remote printer to a local printer so that network users cannot access it. |
| SH (SHared) | Changes a private printer back to shared status. |

# PURGE

## Purpose

Removes previously erased files from the disk and keeps them from being salvaged.

## Syntax

```
PURGE filepath /ALL
```

## Option

| | |
|---|---|
| /ALL | Deletes all recoverable files in the current directory and in all subdirectories. |

# REGISTER MEMORY

## Purpose

Enables NetWare to recognize more than 16 MB of system memory.

## Syntax

```
REGISTER MEMORY memstart memlen
```

# REMOVE

## Purpose

Deletes users and groups from file and directory trustee lists.

## Syntax

```
REMOVE GROUP\USER name FROM path option
```

## Options

/S        Removes the user or group from all subdirectories in the specified path.

/F        Removes the user or group from files in the specified path.

# REMOVE DOS

## Purpose

Removes DOS completely from a NetWare file server memory to eliminate access to DOS.

## Syntax

```
REMOVE DOS
```

# RENDIR

## Purpose

Changes a file server subdirectory name without affecting the trustee rights to it.

## Syntax

```
RENDIR dirpath newname
```

# REVOKE

## Purpose

Revokes individual trustee rights for files or directories from users and groups.

## Syntax

```
REVOKE rights path FROM USER/GROUP name /SUB or /FILE
```

## Options

| | |
|---|---|
| rights | The rights can consist of one or several of the following rights attributes. Each attribute must be separated by a space: |

Right (Description)
ALL (All)
A (Access Control)
C (Create)
E (Erase)
F (File Scan)
M (Modify)
R (Read)
S (Supervisor)
W (Write)

| | |
|---|---|
| /SUB | Affects subdirectories of the selected directory. |
| /FILE | Affects files of the selected directory. |

**373**

# RIGHTS

## Purpose

Displays your effective rights to a file or subdirectory.

## Syntax

```
RIGHTS
```

# SEARCH

## Purpose

Establishes a file server to be searched for NLMs and network configuration (.NCF) files.

## Syntax

```
SEARCH option
```

## Options

ADD *number searchpath*    Adds a new search path. The *number* variable is optional and refers to the desired position for inserting the new search path. The *searchpath* variable refers to the new search path.

DEL *number*    Deletes an existing search path. The *number* variable refers to an existing search path and must be included.

# SECURE CONSOLE

## Purpose

Removes DOS from the file server.

## Syntax

```
SECURE CONSOLE
```

## See Also

REMOVE DOS

# SECURITY

## Purpose

Shows a list of potential security problems.

## Syntax

```
SECURITY
```

## See Also

GRANT

REVOKE

SETPASS

# SEND

## Purpose

Sends a message from your workstation to any logged-in user or group, the file server console, a particular workstation, or a set of workstations.

## Syntax

```
SEND message TO destination
```

## Options

| | |
|---|---|
| *message* | Can be a maximum of 44 characters minus the length of the sending user's name. |
| *destination* | Specifies the user or group that will receive the message. Using any of the following formats, this variable can designate users, groups, the file server console, specific workstations, or all workstations. |

USER *user*

Enables you to send messages to one or several users. The USER specifier is optional. The *user* variable is an optional file server name followed by the name of a user. Multiple users are separated by commas.

GROUP *group*

Enables you to send messages to one or several groups. The GROUP specifier is optional. The *group* variable consists of an optional file server name followed by the name of a group. Separate multiple groups with commas.

*server* /CONSOLE

Enables you to send messages to the file server console. The optional *server* variable specifies a file server; CONSOLE specifies the file server console.

*server* /EVERYBODY

Enables you to send messages to all workstations. The optional *server* variable specifies a file server; EVERYBODY specifies all workstations.

STATION *server* /*station*

Enables you to send messages to specific workstations. The STATION specifier is optional. The following variables are optional:

*server* defaults to the current server; *station* consists of a station number. Additional station numbers are separated by commas.

# SET

## Purpose

Displays or changes values used to tune the NetWare operating system.

## Syntax

```
SET variable = value
```

# SET TIME

## Purpose

Sets the time, date, or both from the console on a NetWare file server.

## Syntax

```
SET TIME mo/dy/yr hh:mm:ss
```

# SETPASS

## Purpose

Used to change passwords from the command line.

## Syntax

```
SETPASS server
```

## Option

*server*  Optional variable that is set to the name of the file server that stores the password you want to change.

## See Also

SECURE CONSOLE

SECURITY

# SLIST

## Purpose

Shows file servers that are available for your workstation.

## Syntax

```
SLIST server
```

## Options

| | |
|---|---|
| *server* | Specifies a file server. If you enter **SLIST** with a file server name, the file server displays if it is available. |
| /C | Specifies that SLIST continuously scroll the screens rather than pause at the end of every screen page. |

## See Also

LOGIN

MAP

# SPEED

## Purpose

Shows an arbitrary number signifying the relative speed of a NetWare file server.

## Syntax

```
SPEED
```

# SYSTIME

## Purpose

Changes the date and time on the workstation to that of a file server.

**Syntax**

SYSTIME

**See Also**

SET TIME

TIME

# TIME

## Purpose

Displays the date and time at the file server console.

## Syntax

TIME

## See Also

SET TIME

SYSTIME

# TLIST

## Purpose

Displays a list of trustees for the specified file or directory.

## Syntax

TLIST *path option*

## Options

| | |
|---|---|
| *path* | A NetWare file or directory on the currently logged file server. |
| *option* | Shows group or user trustees or both, depending on the specified option. Leave *option* blank to see both group and user trustees. Specify GROUPS to see group trustees, or specify USERS to see user trustees. |

**379**

# UNBIND

## Purpose

Removes a communications protocol from a LAN driver for a network adapter card that was added to the LAN driver with BIND.

## Syntax

```
UNBIND protocol FROM landriver
```

## Options

*protocol*   The previously bound communications proto-col, usually IPX.

*landriver*   The name of the LAN driver from which to remove the communications protocol.

## See Also

BIND

# UNLOAD

## Purpose

Removes a NetWare Loadable Module (NLM) from file server memory.

## Syntax

```
UNLOAD nlmspec
```

## Option

*nlmspec*   The name of the NLM to unload from memory.

## See Also

LOAD

# UPS STATUS

## Purpose

Checks the status of the UPS attached to the file server.

## Syntax

```
UPS STATUS
```

# UPS TIME

## Purpose

Sets or changes the estimates for UPS battery discharge and recharge times.

## Syntax

```
UPS TIME dischargetime rechargetime
```

## Options

| | |
|---|---|
| *dischargetime* | The length of time the battery will keep the file server running after commercial power loss. |
| *rechargetime* | The length of time the UPS needs to recover after it has been used to run the file server after commercial power loss. |

# USERLIST

## Purpose

Shows the users currently logged in and some status information on them.

## Syntax

```
USERLIST userspec /C /Option
```

**381**

## Options

*userspec*   An optional file server specification followed by a user name for which you are requesting status.

/A   Displays network address information with the user list display.

/O   Displays object type information with the user list display.

/C   Displays a continuous list without pausing at the end of each screen page for long lists.

## See Also

SLIST

TLIST

WHOAMI

# VERSION

## Purpose

Shows the NetWare operating system version and copyright information.

## Syntax

```
VERSION
```

## See Also

NVER

# VOLUMES

## Purpose

Shows the available drive volumes.

## Syntax

VOLUMES

## See Also

DISMOUNT

MOUNT

# WHOAMI

## Purpose

Gives connection, identification, and security information.

## Syntax

WHOAMI *option*

## Options

/ALL      Displays group membership and security equivalence along with the basic WHOAMI information.

/G      Displays group information along with the basic WHOAMI information.

/O      Displays object supervisor information along with the basic WHOAMI information.

/R      Displays effective rights for each attached volume along with the basic WHOAMI information.

/S      Displays security equivalencies along with the basic WHOAMI information.

/SY      Displays general system information along with the basic WHOAMI information.

/W      Displays workgroup manager information along with the basic WHOAMI information.

# WSUPDATE

## Purpose

Updates NetWare shells on workstations with newer versions.

## Syntax

```
WSUPDATE source dest
```

# Glossary of Networking Terms

**abend:** An abnormal end to processing that stops the network—usually the result of a software or hardware problem.

**account:** A record of information used to permit and keep track of the users accessing a server. See individual account, group account.

**adapter:** Same as Network Interface Card.

**address:** A unique number assigned to every component on the network. The address allows each machine's messages (packets) to be identified as to sender and receiver.

**agent:** In the client/server model, the part of the system that performs information preparation and exchange on behalf of the client or server application. See NMS, DUA, MTA.

**ANSI (American National Standards Institute):** The U.S. standardization body. ANSI is a member of the International Organization for Standards (ISO).

**application layer:** The top-most layer in the OSI Reference Model, providing such communication services as electronic mail and file transfer.

**asynchronous:** Varying, uneven length transmissions wherein characters are separated from the message by means of start and stop bits.

**attenuation:** How much signal is lost over a distance.

**attribute:** The form of information items provided by the X.500 Directory Service. The directory information base consists of entries, each containing one or more attributes. Each attribute consists of a type identifier together with one or more values. Each directory Read operation can retrieve some or all attributes from a designated entry.

**backbone:** The cable connecting the main server, in the case of a dedicated network, to other components.

**bandwidth:** How many simultaneous transmissions a cable can carry.

**baseband:** Characteristic of any network technology that uses a single carrier frequency and requires all stations attached to the network to participate in every transmission. See broadband.

**batch processing:** A mode of computer operation in which the instructions in a computer program are executed one after another without user interaction. The process seen by the user is as follows: the job is submitted; the computer processes the information without any user interaction; the results are returned.

**bindery:** A database maintained by a NetWare network containing all users, their passwords, and associated information.

**bridge:** A device that connects two or more physical networks and forwards packets between them. Bridges usually can be made to filter packets; that is, to forward certain traffic. Related devices are repeaters that simply forward electrical signals from one cable to another, and full-fledged routers that make routing decisions based on several criteria. In OSI terminology, a bridge is a data link layer intermediate system. See repeater and router.

**broadband:** Characteristic of any network that multiplexes multiple, independent network carriers onto a single cable. This task usually is done using frequency division multiplexing. Broadband technology enables several networks to coexist on one single cable; traffic from one network does not interfere with traffic from another, because the "conversations" happen on different frequencies in the "ether"—rather like the commercial radio system.

**broadcast:** A packet or frame transmitted over the network that is copied by each computer on the network.

**buffer:** An area of memory used to temporarily store data—usually on the server.

**cache:** RAM used to temporarily store data for quicker access than reading from the drive. As a general rule, the more RAM contained in a PC/server, the quicker the data access time.

**card:** Same as Network Interface Card (NIC). One card is installed in each computer connected to the network, and it provides the gateway between the network cable and the PC itself.

**client:** A user on the network.

**client/server:** A method of networking wherein the processing of a given application is shared between a client's PC and a central server.

**coax:** Also known as coaxial cable, a solid wire surrounded by insulation and wrapped in conductive metal mesh. Due to its flexibility and adaptability, it is a favored cable for networking.

**collision:** A network disruption caused by two messages corrupting each other.

**D-Connector:** A multiple pin connector that has a D-shaped shell encompassing the pins. RS-232C serial connections commonly use a 25-pin D-Connector.

**daisy chain:** A physical topology for connecting workstations to a network.

**data:** Any information that is transmitted, stored, or processed.

**data link layer:** The data link layer defines the protocol that detects and corrects errors, which may occur when transmitting data through the network cable.

**database:** A collection of relevant information in a single file.

**digital:** The method of symbolically representing data in numeric format.

**DMA (Direct Memory Access):** One method by which NIC cards communicate between workstations and the network.

**directory:** The next level of division beneath a volume. Volumes are broken into directories, which in turn are then divided into subdirectories.

**DOS (Disk Operating System):** Usually implies Microsoft's Disk Operating System, currently in release 6.22.

**duplexing:** The action of storing the same information on separate disks, with a controller card for each. When the primary system fails, the secondary system comes into action without interrupting processing.

**dynamic memory:** RAM.

**Ethernet:** The original network standard from which the IEEE 802.3 protocol standard developed.

**fault:** An error in transmission.

**Fault Tolerance:** The ability to use redundancy to reduce the number of faults.

**FDDI (Fiber Distributed Data Interface):** An emerging high-speed networking standard. The underlying medium is fiber optics, and the topology is dual-attached, counter-rotating rings. FDDI networks can often be spotted by the orange fiber "cable."

**fiber-optic cable:** A cable that consists of a strand or strands of glass fiber that carry data transmitted in the form of light. Fiber-optic cable can transmit data over a relatively long distance and is not affected by electromagnetic radiation as is conventional cable.

**File Allocation Table:** Within DOS, an index to the disk areas where data is stored. Virtually every operating system uses some sort of index to the data, but there are different names for each.

**gateway:** A router devoted to a single task—very often the action of moving electronic mail from one network to another.

**group account:** An account used by several individuals. See account, individual account.

**hot fix:** A method by which NetWare performs Fault Tolerance. If NetWare fails to write the contents of memory to a block, it moves the memory contents to another storage area on the disk set aside for just such an occurrence. The operating system then remembers the address of the original block and marks it in memory as being bad.

**hub:** A centralized hardware component that repeats data signals sent on the network. A hub also can also used as a bridge and a router, and is also known as a repeater.

**impedance:** The amount of resistance, usually measured in ohms, that cable is providing to the transmission it is carrying.

**individual account:** An account that is assigned to a single person. See account, group account.

**IEEE (The Institute of Electrical and Electronics Engineers):** Authors of several networking standards, primarily those used in Token Ring networks.

**ISDN (Integrated Services Digital Network):** A standard for digital communications networks, whether they carry data, video, or any other digital messages.

**ISO (International Organization for Standardization):** The originators of the OSI network protocol model that is widely accepted today.

**internet:** A collection of networks interconnected by a set of routers that enable them to function as a single, large virtual network.

**IPX (Internetwork Packet eXchange):** A protocol that sends packets to requested destinations on the network.

**interrupt:** A signal to suspend a program temporarily while another job runs. When that jobs finishes, the first job continues processing from the point that it left off.

**leaf object:** In NetWare 4.x, the lowest level object in any structure. For example, a file in a tree of subdirectories. Other examples include a printer or a user.

**loadable module:** A program that can be loaded and unloaded, at will, into the server's memory while the server is up and running.

**LAN (local area network):** One or more servers and the workstations they are physically connected to. When multiple LANs are connected together, they form a wide area network (WAN).

**map object:** In NetWare, the search path that you use to locate an executable file in a directory other than the one you are currently in. Map object is particularly useful with login scripts that set default maps.

**MAU:** Multistation Access Unit.

**MTU (Maximum Transmission Unit):** The largest possible unit of data that can be sent on a given physical medium. Example: The MTU of Ethernet is 1,500 bytes.

**Media Access Control (MAC):** The rules that LANs utilize to avoid data collisions. These rules may be the type used in Token Ring or CMSA (Carrier Sense Multiple Access).

**Megabyte (MB):** One megabyte is equal to 1,048,576 bytes of storage space.

**MHS:** Message Handling Service (Novell).

**mirroring:** The action of storing the same information on the same controller (but separate disks). If the disk fails, then the secondary disk comes into action without interrupting processing. If the controller fails, however, then the system is completely down— thus duplexing is a superior fail-safe to mirroring.

**modem:** A derivative of MOdulator-DEModulator, it is a hardware component that converts digital signals to tones for transmission across telephone lines, or vice versa when receiving data.

**multi-homed host:** A computer connection to more than one physical data link. The data links might or might not be attached to the same network.

**MSO (Multiple Systems Operator):** A provider offering interactive access to the "Information Superhighway."

**multiprocessing:** Computers with multiple processors divide the requests into multiple parts. Each processor then performs its own task, then reassembles the answer when the other processors complete their own functions.

**multitasking:** The capability to switch from one application to another without interrupting the processing of the first application.

**multithreading:** A method of multitasking wherein each process acts as a stand-alone entity. If one process crashes, it does not affect the other processes running. Operating systems can be multitasking without being multithreading, and one collision will bring down the entire operating system.

**multiuser:** The ability for more than one user to access the software at a time without interfering with the actions of the other users.

**NLM (NetWare Loadable Modules):** Loadable utilities specific to NetWare.

**network:** A series of computers connected together for the purpose of sharing data or peripherals.

**NetBIOS (Network Basic Input Output System):** The standard interface of networks on IBM PC and compatible systems.

**NFS(R) (Network File System):** A distributed file system that enables a set of computers to cooperatively access each others' files in a transparent manner.

**NIC (Network Interface Card):** NICs provide the physical connection between each workstation and the network cable. All communications between the server and every workstation are carried across the cable and into every NIC. It is the responsibility of the card to determine whether the packet is intended for the workstation and to continue processing, or to ignore it.

**NOS (Network Operating System):** The shell that surrounds the COMMAND.COM file and receives network commands before they pass through to DOS, or another operating system. This is the actual network software utilized (that is, Novell, Banyan, Windows NT, and so forth).

**node address:** A unique number that identifies each network board on a network. Every station must contain at least one unique node number to distinguish it from the other workstations.

**OSI (Open Systems Interconnection):** An international standardization program that facilitates communications among computers from different manufacturers.

**ping:** Packet internet groper. A program used to test reachability of destinations by sending them an ICMP echo request and waiting for a reply. The term is used as a verb: "Ping host X to see if it is up!"

**presentation layer:** The OSI layer that determines how application information is represented (that is, encoded) while in transit between two end stations.

**repeater:** A device that propagates electrical signals from one cable to another without making routing decisions or providing packet filtering.

**router:** A system responsible for making decisions about which of several network paths traffic will follow. To make these decisions it uses a routing protocol to gain information about the network, and algorithms to determine the best route available, based on several routing criteria known as "routing metrics."

**Thicknet:** The thick coax cable used in the 10BASE5 implementation of Ethernet.

**Thinnet:** The thin coax cable used in the 10BASE2 implementation of Ethernet.

**transceiver:** Transmitter-receiver. The physical device that connects a host interface to a local area network, such as Ethernet. Ethernet transceivers contain electronics that apply signals to the cable and sense collisions.

**transport layer:** The OSI layer that is responsible for reliable end-to-end data transfer between end systems.

**unshielded twisted pair (UTP):** The cable used in the 10BASE-T implementation of Ethernet.

# INDEX

## Symbols

## A

**397**

# E

## G

## H

## I

# K–L

# N

# Q–R

**409**

## PLUG YOURSELF INTO...

# THE MACMILLAN INFORMATION SUPERLIBRARY™

### Free information and vast computer resources from the world's leading computer book publisher—online!

*FIND THE BOOKS THAT ARE RIGHT FOR YOU!*
A complete online catalog, plus sample chapters and tables of contents give you an in-depth look at *all* of our books, including hard-to-find titles. It's the best way to find the books you need!

- STAY INFORMED with the latest computer industry news through our online newsletter, press releases, and customized Information SuperLibrary Reports.

- GET FAST ANSWERS to your questions about MCP books and software.

- VISIT our online bookstore for the latest information and editions!

- COMMUNICATE with our expert authors through e-mail and conferences.

- DOWNLOAD SOFTWARE from the immense MCP library:
  - Source code and files from MCP books
  - The best shareware, freeware, and demos

- DISCOVER HOT SPOTS on other parts of the Internet.

- WIN BOOKS in ongoing contests and giveaways!

**TO PLUG INTO MCP:** ➞ WORLD WIDE WEB: **http://www.mcp.com**

GOPHER: gopher.mcp.com

FTP: ftp.mcp.com

# WANT MORE INFORMATION?

## CHECK OUT THESE RELATED TOPICS OR SEE YOUR LOCAL BOOKSTORE

**CAD and 3D Studio**

As the number one CAD publisher in the world, and as a Registered Publisher of Autodesk, New Riders Publishing provides unequaled content on this complex topic. Industry-leading products include AutoCAD and 3D Studio.

**Networking**

As the leading Novell NetWare publisher, New Riders Publishing delivers cutting-edge products for network professionals. We publish books for all levels of users, from those wanting to gain NetWare Certification, to those administering or installing a network. Leading books in this category include *Inside NetWare 3.12*, *CNE Training Guide: Managing NetWare Systems*, *Inside TCP/IP*, and *NetWare: The Professional Reference*.

**Graphics**

New Riders provides readers with the most comprehensive product tutorials and references available for the graphics market. Best-sellers include *Inside CorelDRAW! 5*, *Inside Photoshop 3*, and *Adobe Photoshop NOW!*

**Internet and Communications**

As one of the fastest growing publishers in the communications market, New Riders provides unparalleled information and detail on this ever-changing topic area. We publish international best-sellers such as *New Riders' Official Internet Yellow Pages, 2nd Edition*, a directory of over 10,000 listings of Internet sites and resources from around the world, and *Riding the Internet Highway, Deluxe Edition*.

**Operating Systems**

Expanding off our expertise in technical markets, and driven by the needs of the computing and business professional, New Riders offers comprehensive references for experienced and advanced users of today's most popular operating systems, including *Understanding Windows 95*, *Inside Unix*, *Inside Windows 3.11 Platinum Edition*, *Inside OS/2 Warp Version 3*, and *Inside MS-DOS 6.22*.

**Other Markets**

Professionals looking to increase productivity and maximize the potential of their software and hardware should spend time discovering our line of products for Word, Excel, and Lotus 1-2-3. These titles include *Inside Word 6 for Windows*, *Inside Excel 5 for Windows*, *Inside 1-2-3 Release 5*, and *Inside WordPerfect for Windows*.

Orders/Customer Service **1-800-653-6156**    Source Code **NRP95**

**New Riders Publishing**    201 West 103rd Street ◆ Indianapolis, Indiana 46290 USA

# REGISTRATION CARD

## Managing the NetWare 3.x Server

Name _____  Title _____

Company _____  Type of business _____

Address _____

City/State/ZIP _____

Have you used these types of books before?  ☐ yes  ☐ no

If yes, which ones? _____

_____

How many computer books do you purchase each year?  ☐ 1–5  ☐ 6 or more

How did you learn about this book? _____

Where did you purchase this book? _____

Which applications do you currently use? _____

_____

Which computer magazines do you subscribe to? _____

_____

What trade shows do you attend? _____

_____

Comments: _____

_____

_____

Would you like to be placed on our preferred mailing list?  ☐ yes  ☐ no

☐ **I would like to see my name in print!** You may use my name and quote me in future New Riders products and promotions. My daytime phone number is: _____

**New Riders Publishing**   201 West 103rd Street  ◆  Indianapolis, Indiana 46290  USA

Fax to  317-581-4670      Orders/Customer Service  1-800-653-6156      Source Code  NRP95

Fold Here

# BUSINESS REPLY MAIL

FIRST-CLASS MAIL PERMIT NO. 9918 INDIANAPOLIS IN

POSTAGE WILL BE PAID BY THE ADDRESSEE

**NEW RIDERS PUBLISHING**
**201 W 103RD ST**
**INDIANAPOLIS IN 46290-9058**

# Disk Install

The PRIMER.EXE program is used for all the Practice Exercises in this book. You can run it directly from the 3.5" disk, or you can install it on your hard drive. To run it from the disk, change to the drive of the disk, and follow the instructions given in the Practice Exercises.

To install the PRIMER.EXE program on your hard drive, change to the drive on which you want it to be placed, and copy all files from the disk. A total of six files—PRIMER.EXE and five .DAT files—are needed. Once you have copied the files over, you can run the Practice Exercises from the directory specified.